Taking the Lead without Jerking the Leash
The Art of Mindful Dog Training

Pat Blocker, CPDT-KA

Published by Barking Dog Publishing and Design
P.O. Box 201581
Denver, CO 80220

Illustrations by Pat Blocker
Author photo by Judy Hamilton
Title page photo by Jennifer Pearson
Cover art and design by Pat Blocker
Cover photo from L to R: Mr. MoJo, Bob (Barker) and Jude

The author and publisher have made every effort to provide complete and accurate information and to give credit where due, The author and publisher assume no responsibility for unintentional omissions, errors or changes to information after publication. No responsibility is assumed for third-party web sites and their content.

DEDICATION

This book is dedicated to my mother, Shirley M. Blocker

Table of Contents

Introduction

As flowing water smoothes and shapes rough stone, time and experience have softened my perspective and leveled my attitude about life and dog training. Now, I'd like to pass on the lessons that life with dogs has taught me. This book is part memoir, part laughable musings, and part practical edification. It's about dog training and canine behavior—exploring the intersections of experience and spirit, training mechanics, and mindfulness.

Paradoxically, much of what this book intends to teach cannot be taught. Mindfulness, acceptance, and a sense of humor can be explained and intellectualized, but not taught in a curriculum. I can only hope to point you, the reader, in the right direction and let you take your own unique journey.

Writing a book is a daunting prospect. Setting down the facts may seem easy, yet facts change as we learn more about the given subject matter. Life and learning is a constant flow. Statements will be taken by some to mean that a particular message is concrete, immutable. That is not the intent of this book. The intent is to create a foundation for learning; and I believe that learning involves curiosity, humor, and independent thinking. This means questioning the facts.

Some of the contents of this book involve step-by-step instructions. Yet, even these directives should be open to interpretation. Every case, every dog, every dog owner, every day, and each moment is new and different. Effective teachers and students are mindful of the present moment, open and able to make even the missteps a part of the dance. Dogs know how to do this. Listen to them, and let them teach you how.

It has been said that the word "water" does not get you wet. To get wet, water must be experienced. Use this book as a springboard to leap in and get drenched.

I will do my best to clearly convey the facts, my thoughts, and my opinions. However, the reality is that I can only be responsible for what I say and not how the reader interprets it. The printed word is arguably the best way to download the contents of my head into yours. But, without the nuance of vocal inflection, facial expressions, dialogue, and hand gestures, the print medium leaves something to be desired.

Writing a book is also an adventure in time travel. Because life and knowledge are in perpetual flux, some of the facts and theory herein may have changed by the time the ink hits the page or the files are uploaded. I wonder in what world readers will be living fifty or even five years from now. Maybe much of the content will be outdated. Surely, some of my opinions will change. Then again, maybe some concepts are timeless. Nonetheless, I boldly express with the printed word what is in my head and in my heart.

As you read this book, I hope you'll be open and present. I hope you will read it with a healthy dose of curiosity. I hope you will learn and laugh.

My desire is to make a positive difference in the lives of as many people and dogs as possible. I hope you will take this information and do the same. Run with these concepts. If you do, I've done my job.

Thank you for joining me. Thank you for enriching and improving the lives of dogs and the people who love them.

Foreword

Our modern lives are complicated. We juggle multiple balls without rest. We bury ourselves under mile-long to-do lists. We face a barrage of decisions from trivial to life-changing. We fight traffic, try to eat well and get a little exercise, plan a bit for the future, get a good night's sleep as often as possible. Why, in the middle of all this ongoing chaos, do we decide to get a dog?

Our ancestors most likely welcomed dogs into their lives for protection, and possibly mutually beneficial hunting. Most of us needn't worry these days about being stalked by large prey animals, and a quick stop at the grocery store has thankfully replaced the need for bows and arrows. So why are we still sharing our homes and lives with dogs?

Some of us have grown up with dogs and can't imagine home without one. Some of us succumb to the sad face of a shelter dog in a cage during an adoption drive at the local mall, or a moment's temptation at the site of wriggling puppies in a cardboard box outside the local grocery. Others see a movie or meet a particular dog and decide they must have one of those, and seek out a breeder.

However we've come to have a dog in our homes, we probably share one thing in common: We had a vision of a relationship. We imagined coming home to a wagging tail and the perfect couch companion after a long work day. Or perhaps long weekend walks through the neighborhood or on the trails outside of town. Like most early relationship expectations, we thought the companionship would be easy. And like most relationships, it was kind of exciting at the beginning. And then the honeymoon ended, as they do.

So now you have a dog and your relationship with her, like so many relationships, is a mix of committed love and bouts of frustration. You're looking for some help to get things back on track. A great trainer is just the thing, and this book you're holding is written by just such a person. Here's something you may not know about dog trainers: Good dog trainers know their learning theory science and have excellent training mechanical skills. Great dog trainers also understand that training is as much about the human end of the leash as it is the canine end.

I've met few trainers with as much mindfulness about both ends of the leash as the author of the book you're about to read. This book will teach you a lot about your dog, and about how to train her to do the things you want her to do (or to stop doing the things you don't!). But if you let it, you may also learn a bit about yourself—as a dog owner, a dog trainer, and as a person in this complicated world of relationships.

Oh, and you'll laugh a lot, too.

Happy training, and congratulations for choosing this book. You really couldn't have done better.

--Veronica Boutelle, dog*tec.org founder, author of *How to Run a Dog Business, The Business of Dog Walking,* and co-author of *Minding Your Dog Business*

May 2014

Acknowledgements

Every author has many people to thank for their support, encouragement, and patience while we create. I think I can speak for others when I say that unfortunately, we are all but brain dead upon completion of the book. We are so weary and worn that we can barely remember our own names let alone the names of those whom we wish to acknowledge. Apologies to anyone whose name has escaped the feeble grasp of my brain.

I'd like to thank my dear friend, Barrie Finger for reading this work for content and accuracy. You have lent your dog training expertise and life wisdom to this project. Your forthcoming honest and constructive criticism kept me on track and your support kept me motivated. You made me laugh at myself when I most needed to. You gave me your Mr. Coffee when mine was about to give up the ghost. This book would not exist without mass quantities of coffee.

My thanks to Veronica Boutelle of Dog*Tec. Your inspirational coaching and encouragement have seen me through a few disheartening times. You've helped me to put one foot in front of the other and one word after another. You told stories on yourself to lift the gloom at times when my confidence waned. You listened to (and laughed at) my stories. Thank you for writing the foreword to this book.

Authors thank their editors, and it's with good reason. They keep us from global embarrassment. My editor, Kelly Jo Eldredge, saved me from punctuation mortification by putting me on a 12-step program to kick my comma addiction. Kelly Jo, your dedication to this project is surpassed only by your eternal patience with me. I am grateful to have shared this experience with you and thanks for making me look good.

Several years ago, I mentioned to my friend and entrepreneurial mentor, Barbara Winter that I was writing a book. She asked me where I was in the process. My answer was that I'd not actually written anything yet and that the book was in my head. She asked me, "What the heck good is it doing in your head?" Thanks for the nudge that set my feet on this path and my hands on the keyboard. A journey of a thousand miles begins with a single step. Writing a book begins with writing a single word. Thanks for being on this path with me, Barbara.

I am grateful to the trainers, behaviorists, and other dog professionals whose work, research, and on-the-ground experience has been inspirational and educational. You have also been recognized in the resources and recommended reading list.

This book would never have been published if not for the prompting of friends to stop my eternal editing and reminding me of the difference between a writer and an author—the author ships.

I'd like to thank all of the amazing and wonderful canines that have come into my life. You showed up to teach me the lessons that I've needed to learn. You've taught me about loyalty, compassion, trust, and living in the moment. Your hearts have inspired me to follow my own heart. You have enriched my days. Because of you, I've dedicated myself to bettering your life and the lives of as many dogs as possible.

I'd like to thank all of my muses for leaning close and whispering your wisdom. You are the people and spirits who helped me to believe in myself enough to carry this project through. I have written 125,000 words on dog training, but I find that I have none to adequately express my gratitude to you.

A Note to Readers

You will notice the use of the pronoun "he" throughout this book when referring to our canine companions. The word is intended to be nonspecific and is not meant to show any gender bias. This author has equal fondness for both male and female dogs.

This book uses the word "owner" when referring to canine guardians or caretakers. I pondered at length about whether to use the word "owner," "guardian," or to call us "pet parents." The word "owner" is used strictly in the interest of simplicity. It is not used to imply that pets are dispensable property or to devalue them as companions, family, and friends.

Disclaimer

This book is intended for educational purposes and to provide accurate and pertinent information. While every precaution has been taken, the author assumes no responsibility for any errors or omissions. Application of the techniques described herein with regard to behavior modification should be done under the guidance of a reputable trainer or behaviorist. The reader understands that the author can in no way be held responsible for any loss, accident, injury or damages caused or allegedly caused by the information in this book. The reader understands that no degree of training is absolute and thereby the author assumes no liability in any related claims.

Taking the Lead without Jerking the Leash
The Art of Mindful Dog Training

1

Zen and the Art of Mindful Training

My mind is a neighborhood I try not to go into alone. — **Anne Lamott**

My dog training business is Peaceful Paws. The name comes from my hippie past as someone who's forever peaceful and Zen-like, a master of meditation and going with the flow. Well okay, the perpetual peace thing, not so much.

The name actually refers to the canine end of the leash, because I happen to be hopelessly human, a recovering perfectionist. My critical, overactive mind assaults me with thoughts like, "Hurry up and meditate! According to your schedule, you have until 1:30 p.m. to achieve inner peace!" Dogs know that hurrying is reserved for mealtime and chasing the trash truck.

In this chapter, we'll explore happy training, what it is, and why it's worth achieving. With regard to canine behavioral problems, some people cannot see the forest for the trees. Furthermore, many aren't even aware that there is a forest. That forest is the place where happy training occurs. It's a positive, centered place where both dog and human are listening and learning.

The art of happy training entails opening the lines of communication between humans and dogs in order to learn from each other. It means to remain calm and compassionate. The art of happy training allows for victimless dog training, which is accomplished without harming or creating feelings of helplessness in the dog. Sorting out emotions and expectations, training without judgment or blame, and learning to accept what is makes for a happy training experience. In regard to these points, the human end of the leash needs the most work.

I enjoy reading about Buddhist philosophy, as I think it embraces some pretty cool notions. I'm especially fond of the Buddhist ideas of hungry ghosts and the monkey mind. The concept of hungry ghosts describes beings that are driven by intense emotional needs. Monkey mind refers to the state of being unsettled, capricious, confused, and uncontrollable. By definition then, I have a hungry ghost's monkey mind.

My hungry ghost's monkey mind (her name is Marcia) is officious and discontent. When Marcia makes her bid for a mental takeover, I tell her to either sit down and shut up or move out and get a job. If dogs have monkey minds, I'll bet they tell theirs to stop barking and learn to work the can opener.

As a dog trainer and imperfect perfectionist, I see that dogs and humans are not so much *different as we are the same. Dogs are probably more at peace than humans, because they are better at living in the moment and never worry about the stock market crashing. Furthermore, I believe that German shepherds invented yoga.*

What brings me to this conviction is the behavior of two of my German shepherds, Jude and Penny Lane. A couple of years ago, I began practicing Qigong, an exercise discipline similar to Tai Chi. Since the routine included some yoga postures, I unearthed my yoga mat from storage where it had been since before Jude moved in. As I unfurled it, Jude came running across the room, planted his feet dead center on the mat, and assumed the downward dog yoga posture. He did this each day, unfailingly when he heard the mat hit the floor (and I have video to prove it).

Since Jude's passing, Penny has filled his indelible paw prints on my yoga mat, by leading me in the downward dog posture daily.

The art of happy training is about finding the place that gives both dog and human peace. That place is in the center between hungry ghosts and poo-flinging monkey mind. Humans are the ones who need to seek that center. Dogs are already there, and they can show us the way if we are willing see.

The Art of Happy Training

Dog trainers cope with the unique and monumental task of training two species simultaneously. Successful dog trainers possess the essential traits of mindfulness and compassion, demonstrated in the instruction of both species. Mastery of these traits paves the way to happy training for all. Whether you are reading this book as a dog owner or a professional dog trainer, the concepts will apply equally. After all, whether you are training your own dog or someone else's, you *are* the trainer.

An effective dog trainer achieves happy training through mindfulness. A mindful trainer works in the moment. We strive to be nonjudgmental and to keep compassion at the heart of our methodology. A skillful instructor is a good listener, a perceptive observer, and has the ability to think on his or her feet. I have observed these qualities in top authorities on canine behavior. Many of these authorities are human, and many of them have four legs and fur. If we are willing to be students as well as instructors, we will learn more than we will teach.

This chapter will explore the intersections of experience and spirit, training mechanics and mindfulness. We'll investigate the attributes that are vital to the art of happy training.

I've had a lot of worries in my life, most of which never happened.
—Mark Twain

The Art of Staying Present

It's human nature to dwell on the past and worry about the future. We get stuck when focusing on the past and are equally stuck when fretting about the future. While it is useful to understand the past and have a forthcoming training plan, the most effective training happens in the moment.

As a former member of the 4:00 a.m. Club, I understand the anxiety surrounding a would-be simple walk in the park. Members of the 4:00 a.m. Club have aggressive or reactive dogs and walk them at oh-dark-thirty. If we didn't walk at this lonely hour, we'd find ourselves in canine congested parks, bumping into other dog walkers. Parks have become, in our minds, arcades where we're inside a real-life pinball machine. However, our goal in the game is *not* to hit any targets but quietly, surreptitiously go down the drain. And we're woefully aware that we're not pinball wizards.

Back then, when I'd see someone approach with a dog, I'd immediately tense up, grit my teeth, and grumble, "Oh, no! Why are these people walking their dogs in *our* park? Who invited them?" Next, I'd formulate an easy, expeditious flight plan, only to see that the interlopers had turned in the opposite direction, oblivious to my anxiety.

Getting back on my feet (because I had to sit down and put my head between my knees), I realized that I'd interrupted our happy walk with worry over a non-event. Finally, I'd judge the walk as a terrible experience, and the thought of walking my dogs became clouded with negativity and anxiety.

Staying present means that we don't jump anxiously into the future to live an event that may never happen. Yes, we need to be prepared and to implement a training program for the dog's behavior but, in the meantime, remember that if it isn't happening right now, it isn't happening.

Dogs are experts at staying present. I should take a page from their book next time I'm worried about the stock market forecast. This is not to say that dogs can't remember or think ahead. They just don't doggedly dwell on the past and future, as we humans do. With the right motivation and environment for success, most dogs can readily focus on the present task.

By staying in the moment and with proper training, we can transform the presence of another dog into a positive event and withdraw our membership from the 4:00 a.m. Club. Staying present is an important brushstroke applied in the art of happy training.

It's so wonderful to watch an animal, because an animal has no opinion about itself. **—Eckhart Tolle**

The Art of Non-Judgment

It is easy to be hypercritical of our own dogs. We want to hold them to a higher standard and place them in the "perfect dog" mold of expectation. We want our dogs to be as "good" as the neighbor's dog or the faultless pet dog of our youth. However, to achieve happy training, the temptations of judgment need yield to acceptance of the dogs we have at present, complete with their shortcomings. Only from here, can we move forward on a training path.

Judging people can come ashamedly easy. Yet, doing so causes great unhappiness. When I'm caught in the throes of judgment, I find it helpful to reframe my critical thought by changing it from a statement to a question. For instance, I recently saw a jogger wearing the oddest footgear. He was running in high, black boots fitted with bowed slats for soles that put a lofty spring in his step. The ridiculous footwear made me think, "That guy is really weird, and he's going to scare my dog!" Catching myself in a moment of judgment, I thought again. I asked myself if that guy really *was* weird. My conclusion: maybe not. Perhaps he had a disability, and those bionic feet enabled him to run. On the other hand, maybe he worked for a research and development company as a test pilot for weird running gear! By changing how I looked at things, I did not pass judgment by mistaking perception for fact.

Note: Reframing my attitude worked for me. However, my dog did bark her opinion of the man's outlandish footwear. Being a German shepherd, she thinks she's the K9 unit of the fashion police. We'd recently and successfully worked through her disapproval of people wearing hoodies, so I guess next on the agenda is changing her opinion about bionic boots!

Dogs are experts at being nonjudgmental and non-prejudiced. They certainly can differentiate between genders, colors, sizes, and shapes of both human and canine species. However, unless influenced by an unpleasant experience or lack of socialization, dogs usually choose the path of equality. Equanimity is perhaps their secret to happiness.

For after all, the best thing one can do when it is raining is let it rain.
—Henry Wadsworth Longfellow

The Art of Acceptance

Flexibility and a willingness to adjust expectations save undue anguish. Wishing that Scooby had a penchant to play fetch or to run agility courses when he clearly does not makes everyone unhappy. This is like wishing one's child would have a passion for neurosurgery, when she really aspires to do stand-up comedy. With a certain level of acceptance, we can reach a more contented relationship with our dogs. We must meet them where they are, accept them, love them, and forgive their foibles. They will be the first to do the same for us.

We'd do well to broaden the view of our relationships with our dogs—to paint a landscape view in order to see them for who they are and not a caricature of breed or circumstance. The art of happy training comes from a space of acceptance, and from this space we will set our training goals.

Whatever gets you through the night. —John Lennon

The Art of Letting Go

The story of Cleo and Buddy illustrates the art of letting go. In our initial consultation, Cleo demonstrated her dog's stellar and militaristic style obedience. She had been taught by her previous trainer to expect and achieve perfection from Buddy through total dominance and control. Sadly, this training method had Cleo administering harsh leash corrections and barking out incessant commands. Cleo was told that she should never speak to her dog other than to give him commands.

During one of our training sessions, I shared that my dog once had similar issues as Buddy's. I told Cleo what success (not perfection) looked like for us specifically. With a sigh of relief she asked, "Your dog has issues, too? He's not perfect? Does this mean that my dog doesn't have to be perfect?" Cleo was so focused on having a faultless dog, that they were missing out on a mutually loving relationship. With that, Cleo let go of the glorified picture of Buddy's perfection, and both are much happier for it.

As human beings, we tend to focus on the negative and see only our dogs' *wrongdoing*. We expect our dogs to automatically know how to live in the human world. Furthermore, we expect them to know how to live in *our* world (in my world it's okay to sleep on the bed, but it's not okay at Grandma's house).

Dogs are skillful opportunists with a matchless ability to cohabitate with us. They behave in ways that get them what they want. I suggest we make the most of this canine approach by reinforcing the *good* behaviors offered. Dogs will repeat behaviors that have been reinforced, so let's catch them doing it right and reward them. This is so much easier and more fun than fixing the undesirable behaviors.

Allowing desired behaviors that dogs offer brings out their creativity and personality. To avoid chaos at mealtime, a dog could be trained to sit and wait before being given permission to eat. This is one outcome, but we need not fixate on it or be attached to someone else's idea of how mealtime should look. My dog sits and waves bye-bye before I put his bowl down. This was his idea, because the trick had been reinforced in the past. I enjoy his performance of this cute, polite behavior, so it became part of his mealtime ritual.

It is easier to resist at the beginning than at the end.

–Leonardo da Vinci

The Art of Overcoming Resistance

Resistance magnifies the negative. Resistance is wily, taking on many forms. We don't have to look very hard to find it in ourselves, but we must look closely to find it in dogs—even the ones we deem *stubborn*. Yet, the act of labeling is, in itself, a form of resistance.

For humans, resistance often comes in the form of excuses. We say, "It's going to be difficult" or "I don't have the time or the right outfit." Resistance can present itself as distractions such as, "I'll get to training the dog as soon as I answer the 652 emails in my inbox." Perfectionism can be a form of resistance, as well. "I'll never get Sparky to do a perfect recall, so I won't bother."

Happy training happens when we prioritize our goals, adjust our expectations, and set our minds on the positive. If we catch resistance lurking, we won't sell Sparky short.

If I don't have red, I use blue.   **–Pablo Picasso**

The Art of Thinking on Your Feet

Happy training involves the ability to be flexible. Dogs are expert problem solvers, and nature programmed them to expend the least amount of effort in achieving their objectives. This can cause frustration if we are not constantly reading the dog (as he is reading us). If we can find the dog's motivation and set him up for success, we have the ability to intercept instead of react. We draw from our pallet of experience, stay present, and adapt.

Be kind whenever possible. It's always possible.   **–Dalai Lama**

The Art of Compassion

Mindful trainers have compassion not only for the dog but also for the people involved, including themselves.

I take full responsibility for what my dog learns, but I try to do this with compassion and not blame. Like children, dogs are constantly learning by watching us. Because reinforced behaviors are repeated, I'm vigilant about which ones I've supported, whether right or wrong, intentional or accidental. If training setbacks occur, I look at my culpability with compassion, because I know that blame only brings frustration and confusion. Instead, I try to look objectively at the undesirable results, then look for a better way.

It saddens me to know how often we create disagreeable behaviors in dogs and then hold them accountable for it. I recently saw a woman walking her small dog off-leash at the park. The dog gave chase to a passing jogger, which resulted in the woman screaming, grabbing the dog's collar, rolling him on his back, and holding him there until he submitted. Alas, the dog was punished for acting naturally (albeit inappropriately). The woman may never realize her accountability in the creation of her dog's manners. Therefore, he may never be leashed or taught an acceptable behavior.

Compassion and mindfulness are important design elements in the art of happy training.

Water flows because it's willing. **–Marty Rubin**

The Art of Going with the Flow

I am a hot air balloon pilot. The wonders of balloon flight have taught me many valuable life lessons. There is no steering mechanism in a balloon, so you must ascend or descend through the air currents to find one that will take you where you want to go. Talk about going with the flow!

Each time I launch, my landing site is unknown. In flight, I need to stay present, taking whatever winds I can find. If I can't find a wind to take me where I *want* to go, I accept the fact that I have found the wind to take me where I *will* go, maybe even where I *need* to go.

Strong winds can be frightening, but it has always been the strongest winds that take me the farthest on my journey. This is quite a metaphor for the art of happiness in life and dog training. The biggest challenges always teach the greatest lessons. To learn them, one must remain present, be accepting and open. One must let go and go with the flow.

A true leader is not someone who feels fully informed but someone who continuously receives insight and guidance. **–Martha Beck**

The Art of Maintaining Curiosity and Openness

Curiosity goes hand-in-hand with letting go of expectations. Be willing to be a student. Happy training comes from being inquisitive and open to the possibility that the outcome might look different than imagined. If we allow the dog's ingenuity and personality to shine through, he will teach us great lessons. This philosophy may not apply to dog sports and obedience trials, but it certainly makes pet dog training a lot more fun.

Ray and Nancy called me to help them with their dog Bentley's potty training issues. We decided to teach Bentley to ring a bell at the back door, giving a clear signal that he needed to go out. As a side note, I'll add that

Bentley was extremely attached to Nancy, following her everywhere around the house—except the basement. He was afraid to go down the stairs.

Bentley was making good progress with bell ringing, but he had not yet taken the initiative to ring it without prompting. Then one laundry day, while Nancy was in the basement loading the washer, she heard the bell ring. She rushed upstairs to let Bentley out. But when she opened the door, Bentley just stood there smiling. With that, Nancy realized her dog had just trained her to come when he rang the bell! That outcome looked a bit different than what we'd expected, but in the process, Bentley showed us his resourceful individuality in communicating his needs. By the way, Bentley did learn to ring the bell to signal that he needed to go outside.

Curiosity and openness are useful attributes for the trainer. They help us find creative solutions to even the most critical issues. Without them we might dwell on expectations, failing to see the progress made and the power of our innovation.

Humor is the affectionate communication of insight. –**Leo Rosten**

The Art of Maintaining Humor

Sometimes dogs are hilarious. I don't know what I'd do if I didn't have my dogs to laugh at and to be the butt of my jokes. I'm sure I'm the butt of theirs when they tell stories with their friends.

I have one client who says that her Border collie is so smart that she'd give him a chore list if only he had opposable thumbs. We worked with this dog on his aggressive behavior toward other dogs. While he had some intense issues, his mom was able to see the lighter side of her loveable companion. This illustrates that a sense of humor diminishes the drama and helps us to accept all of our dogs' quirks and our training quandaries.

I'm not saying that aggression or other serious behavioral issues are laughing matters. I'm saying that we can lighten up a bit and see the humorous side of our dogs in order to have a happier training experience.

More importantly, we need to be able to laugh at ourselves. My most embarrassing and humiliating moment as a trainer was falling into a client's swimming pool. Afterward, I borrowed some dry clothes and gave my cell phone and myself some time to air out. I then laughed! The best thing to do was to accept my fall as part of the dance—part of the art of happy training.

Life is pure adventure, and the sooner we realize that, the sooner we will be able to treat life as art. **—Maya Angelou**

The Art of Enjoying the Journey

The path of dog training success does not go directly from point A to point B. It is a circuitous and sometimes an uncertain and adventurous course. If we focus too sharply on the outcome, the negatives, the big things, we'll miss out on the little things. In hindsight, we often realize that the little things actually *are* the big things.

Sometimes we make mistakes and feel that we've strayed off the path. However, if we never walk off the road, we'll never find new ground. I suggest that we take it all in stride and enjoy the journey to happy training with those wacky, wonderful canines.

2

That's the Spirit:
Building Relationships and Loosening the Lead

People think that, because I'm a dog trainer, I have perfectly mannered dogs and a perfect relationship with them. To these folks I say you are overestimating the concept of perfect. Every relationship is different and uniquely ideal.

For nine years, I lived with three large, hairy, male dogs. It was like living in a frat house. Life was loud and smelly. All furniture was in some state of disrepair and there was a lot of public urination. It was a perfect relationship…for us.

I currently live with Mr. MoJo, the last remaining frat boy, and a three-year-old German Shepherd named Penny Lane. I must say that it's refreshing to have a bit of female energy back in the household. Even though my three males were neutered, the testosterone level was at critical mass, confirming my belief: testosterone should be a controlled substance.

Penny does, however, bring her own charm and challenges to the table. I'm not certain what I've done to offend her canine sensibilities, but I suspect that she is plotting to murder me and make it look like an accident. She diabolically leaves select dog toys in doorways where I am sure to trip over them. If you notice my prolonged absence from Facebook or hear raucous canine merrymaking at my house, please call the authorities. Otherwise, consider that we are living out our own unique and happy relationship.

I do practice what I preach when it comes to training my dogs. I'm a big supporter of training that fits into one's lifestyle and the personalities of all humans and dogs therein. This is to say that whether one is into obedience trials or potty training, learning can be a fun and bonding experience.

I believe in setting dogs up for success and in teaching them that polite behavior gets them what they want. I believe in compassionate leadership and proper motivation. (My dogs will do the laundry for a piece of dried lamb lung—eew!) I believe in loosening the lead enough to let dogs be dogs within the limits of leash laws and safety.

Living with dogs is not, in my mind, about dominance and control. It's about the give and take of a peaceable coexistence and acceptance. It's about what works, whatever that may look like for me, for you, and for our dogs.

In a perfect world, we'd bring home our new puppy, do everything right from day one, and live happily ever after with our well-socialized, well-trained companion. Of course, this is fantasy. The reality is something called life, which can derail the greatest of ambitions.

Occasionally, we find ourselves at odds with our dogs. Building sound, enjoyable relationships sometimes requires deconstructing them first. In this chapter, we'll investigate some thoughtful tools that we can use to construct, deconstruct, and rebuild canine/human relationships.

The Quiet Leader is the Quiet Learner

It is human nature to want control. Too often, the human/canine relationship is about humans seeking complete control, making the dog do our bidding. This is the message set forth in the dominance-based training philosophy popularized by television, books, and the self-proclaimed dog behavior experts at the dog park.

We often assume we will gain control of our dogs if we just tense up enough, worry sufficiently, and repeat commands often (and loudly). This training philosophy is a direct path to unhappiness for both dog and trainer. I suggest we use communication instead of control, thus building a two-way street.

Why not let training be an exchange of mutual communication and positive reinforcement? I propose we listen to the dog and respond to what he or she is telling us. If the dog is not learning through our methods, we need to adjust our teaching to the way the dog learns. Let's create an atmosphere in which the dog is a willing and happy participant.

Positive reinforcement works with both species. When trainer is effectively communicating, the trainer is reinforced; when the dog presents the desired behavior, the dog is reinforced. Everybody's happy!

Knowledge speaks, but wisdom listens. –Jimi Hendrix

Even after decades of teaching group classes, I'm amazed at the level of verbosity in my human students. Whenever the room sounds like a beehive, I intercede with a moment of training silence. I ask my students to say nothing to their dogs and to use hand signals only, or simply capture a desired behavior. I'm often told that this is the hardest task I ever ask them to do.

Most people can read a book or watch a video on dog training, follow the instructions, and have some level of success teaching dogs a new behavior. The lesson that is missing here is one of effective communication; a lesson that is difficult to teach egocentric humans. The superficially self-proclaimed knowledgeable trainer speaks to the dog and "makes" him do what he is told. The wise trainer listens to the dog and opens the lines of communication, which makes training a mutual activity.

Whenever we teach, we must be open to learning. It follows that if we are open to learning from the dog, he will learn more from us.

Mutual Respect

The unbridled human ego is a dangerous thing. I sometimes imagine that given a nice tiara and brass bracelets, I could be the Wonder Woman of dog training. Inevitably, at this point in my unrestrained fantasy, dogs will befuddle me with some new challenge. I am thankful to them for humbling the heroine in me.

Successful relationships require mutual respect. I don't live with dogs because I want to dominate and control them. I value life, and I won't be bogged down in the egotistical quagmire of dominance and power over another. Dogs are incredible, intelligent creatures. I respect them.

When I'm walking with my dogs, it's easy to forget that we have different agendas. I might be interested in burning calories or thinking about the monthly budget. My dogs are interested in sending and receiving pee mail. If I get impatient with them for sniffing every blade of grass, I remember that they might in turn be impatient when I pause to greet a friend. Relationships are about give and take. They are about reciprocal respect.

Communication and Clarity

In order to live in the human world, dogs must be bilingual. A dog's first language is body language, which they use to communicate with their own species and with humans. Dogs are experts at reading human facial expressions, even micro-expressions. In fact, many canine facial expressions are similar to ours. Patricia McConnell, Ph.D. has written an excellent book on the subject of human and canine emotion entitled *For the Love of a Dog— Understanding Emotion in You and Your Best Friend.* There is a fascinating photo spread in this book showing the similarities between human and canine facial expressions.

Dogs are highly attuned to our emotional energy. If you question this, ask any dog owner about their dog's response to moments of sadness in their lives. They will likely recount stories of tears being licked from their cheeks or the dog's muzzle placed gently on their lap. During times of sorrow or physical illness, my dogs have simply helped me to be with the sadness and to be in the moment in order to move past it.

Dogs are highly perceptive to our emotions and able to understand our body language so well it seems they can read our minds. Now we must learn their language to better understand their emotions.

Successful relationships require clear communication. Since a dog's second language is English (or any human language) and their vocabulary is limited, we need to be clear with our words. We also need to be clear with our own body language and hand signals. We readily refrain from using cue words that sound alike. For example, when I taught my dog to do a play bow on cue, I decided not to use the word *bow* because it sounds too similar to *down*, which is his cue to lie down. Likewise, our hand signals need to be clear and distinct.

Repeating cues is a human foible in dog training. Somehow, we think that if we say it again, this time louder, the dog will suddenly understand. Think about it. If someone speaking Swahili (assuming you don't speak the language) asked you to do something, and you didn't understand, do you think that you would comprehend the request if it was repeated at increased volume?

Clear communication and mutual respect are pillars of any successful relationship. It doesn't matter whether the bond is between humans or between humans and canines. These pillars are the main support system for a happy relationship.

It's Just a Dog, Right?

It's probably safe to assume that anyone reading this book wouldn't ask this question. I'm asking it here to have us think a little deeper about why we would want to build a better relationship with our dogs. As a trainer, people employ my services to help them with canine challenges ranging from potty training to severe cases of aggression. That's what I'm hired to do. But finding solutions to behavioral problems goes beyond "making" the puppy stop peeing on the rug.

When in the throes of behavioral issues, it's difficult to see the dynamics at work. It's tough to rise above conflict when in the heat of emotional battle. You can't build a successful relationship in the midst of conflict any more than you can build a plane during flight.

Start where you are. Use what you have. Do what you can.

—Arthur Ashe

The following story of Maggie and Sheryl illustrates how sometimes a relationship needs to be deconstructed and then rebuilt in order to repair it. Sheryl knew that there could be a much stronger, loving connection between her and Maggie. She just needed to take a step back, breathe, and make a blueprint for rebuilding the relationship.

Maggie's Story

Maggie came to live with her new family at eleven weeks old. She was a delightful, energetic pup, sparkling with personality. Maggie's mom, Sheryl, wanted a puppy for companionship and to help ease stressful challenges in her life. Maggie fulfilled her mom's expectations in every way, with one critical exception. Maggie had a penchant for stealing her mom's personal items, and she guarded those items vehemently if Sheryl tried to take them back. In fact, one guarding incident resulted in Maggie biting Sheryl's hand, an injury that required several stitches.

Maggie's resource guarding behavior was not global. She only stole Sheryl's belongings. Consequently, Sheryl was the only person in occasional conflict with Maggie.

Sheryl desperately wanted to mend the relationship, so she was forthcoming about challenges in her life that created high levels of stress for everyone, including Maggie. It was apparent that the tense environment was a contributing factor to Maggie's behavior. This is where we needed to begin. We would meet Maggie and Sheryl where they were on their path and map out a course to a healthier relationship.

Sheryl and I discussed setting boundaries for Maggie and how to manage or eliminate specific stressors. I also outlined how Sheryl could teach Maggie a few simple behaviors: sit, down, and stay for starters. This would help them to bond and change their contentious interactions to interactions of fun, learning, and accomplishment. We needed to deconstruct the relationship between Sheryl and Maggie in order to give it a makeover.

Sheryl's commitment and compliance were instrumental in this process, and Maggie happily learned new behaviors in a calmer environment. Next we were ready to begin a course of treatment for the resource guarding behavior.

The progression was sometimes slow and not without setbacks. In the end, Maggie and Sheryl overcame the conflict and chaos and moved toward a relationship of mutual understanding and communication. All relationships take work to maintain—human and canine. Moreover, all good relationships are worth the effort.

Loosening the Lead

When I was young, we had dogs on the farm where we lived. I don't remember having so many choices in training methods, worrying about exercising them, or even owning a leash. Our dogs weren't fenced or crated, yet they hardly ever left the property. Our dogs weren't trained to do their business in a specific area of human choice. My brother says that he was ten years old before he realized that dogs pooped, because he'd never stepped in any. Our dogs naturally chose to eliminate far from where they ate, played, and slept.

Our farm dogs, like all our family members, had assigned chores. They worked the livestock and protected our family and property. In their spare time, they roamed the fields hunting and exploring. Left to their own devices, they became well-rounded, trustworthy companions. The truth is dogs are better at teaching themselves to be dogs than we are. When we choose to bring them into our lives, we are obliged to teach dogs how to live harmoniously in the human world.

Urban life comes with different challenges for dogs and their people than life in the country. These challenges have city dog owners asking valid questions in regard to management, exercise, leadership, and training methods. How does one amuse an adolescent Border Collie when keeping a flock of sheep is against HOA covenants?

City dogs require management, necessitating the likes of fences, crates, and leashes. It requires intentional exercise. Management is essential. However, it needn't be overdone or used as a substitute for training. The caveat here is that micromanagement, as well as the lack of exercise and mental stimulation, can lead to a host of canine behavioral problems. Those problems include over-attachment issues, aggression, obsessive-compulsive behaviors, leash frustration, and generalized fear. Overprotection interferes with a dog's inherent need to explore and socialize. It seems that dogs allowed to make their own decisions (with our gentle guidance) tend to be a more intelligent and well balanced.

Owners often ask about leadership and whether the use of force is an appropriate training method. In dog training, as with human interaction, the use of force produces a counterforce, resulting in conflict. I do not want to make an enemy of my dog, nor do I wish to create a timid robot. Intimidation as a leadership style is ineffective. If I use intimidation to get a dog to behave in a certain way, then he'll only behave that way as long as I have the power to threaten him.

Years ago when I first studied to become a dog trainer, the choice of methodology was limited. Back then, I learned to train dogs using compulsory tactics. We employed prong collars and choke chains to correct the dogs when they were disobedient. Corrections consisted of yanking on the leash of a noncompliant dog. These techniques often worked (a subjective term), but the problem was that fear and intimidation were at the core of the approach. The dogs timidly offered a behavior in hopes that it was the right one, for if it were wrong, they would get their necks jerked.

We used this technique for all behavior modification, including fear-based issues. I will never forget the class in which my dog reacted fearfully to another dog by barking and snapping at him. It still pains me to think of what happened next. I witnessed the instructor "hang" my dog as punishment for her behavior. Using the leash and choke chain, she lifted my dog's front paws off the ground, holding her there until she "submitted." At that very moment, I knew in my heart there was a better way to train dogs!

When you know better you do better. –Maya Angelou

I now use gentle, positive reinforcement training methods. With these methods, dogs enthusiastically offer behaviors, seek out opportunities for reinforcement, and have fun.

Some argue that positive reinforcement methods equal lenience. Some say that liberalism means lack of leadership. I'm not against leadership. However, I establish myself as a benevolent leader by teaching my dog that polite behavior will get him what he wants. I depend more on my relationship with my dog than on the leash and give him space to think for himself.

The words listen and silent are anagrammatic. The greatest leader is the one who says the least and listens the most. This is true of leaders of dogs or humans. Think of authority figures that bellow commands constantly in order to gain control. Ultimately, their subordinates learn to ignore and avoid them. Now, think of a soft-spoken authority figure. If on the rare occasion he or she raises their voice, they are more likely to be met with compliance and respect.

Effective trainers open the lines of communication by becoming astute observers. Therefore, it is essential to become fluent in dog body language, the subtle form of canine communication. Let's begin to hear what dogs are saying. Instead of merely correcting dogs for undesirable behavior, we must hear them, and then show them what is acceptable instead. If we don't, we leave our dogs out of the loop, failing to give them feedback and acknowledgment.

The best leaders don't actually lead anyone; they guide them. Furthermore, followers retain their dignity and feel respected. There is a sense of participation as opposed to domination. I believe this concept to be valid in our relationships with dogs as well is humans.

Make dog training a two-way street. Replace ownership mentality with an attitude of cooperation. Doing this diffuses many frustrations that come with expectations of complete control. Trust yourself and your dog. When you do not trust your dog, he will not trust you.

Set your dog up for success. Effective and fun training means setting dogs up for success and helping them to act responsibly. For example, if jumping on guests is the dog's issue, show him that the behavior does not get him the attention he seeks. Have him on leash when greeting guests at the door. If he jumps, have visitors move away from him, then ask him to sit instead. When he sits, give him attention. With consistency and repetition, he will learn that sitting gets him what he really wants. I call this the "magic butt syndrome." MBS has dogs believing that their butts are magic, because putting them on the ground makes good things happen.

There is a time for restraint and a time for letting go. But letting go comes with accountability. We send a powerful message when we take our dogs off leash, implying that they are under full voice command. If the goal is to have a responsible dog off leash, we must have a well-established foundation of training and communication with the dog beforehand.

It is possible to afford dogs freedom within the margins of safety and the law. We can manage and train them so they remain safe, happy, and active. We will be gentle compasses to guide our dogs while loosening the lead enough to let them be dogs.

3

Is My Dog Winning?
Exploring Pack Leadership

Leadership by Example

I believe in being the leader of my household, the queen of my canine castle. However, I do not advocate the tactics of despots or Victorian-age, knuckle-rapping schoolteachers. Neither am I the alpha trainer who emulates wolves as advocated in certain popular dog training culture.

I admit that occasionally I find myself at the top of the hierarchy quite by accident. And I fear my dogs are secretly learning by example. After all, what else do they have to do but constantly watch me, like miniature quadrupedal spies?

I reached the zenith of accidental, exemplar leadership in a recent nocturnal recycling episode. After placing the bin of recyclables curbside for collection, I settled in for a bit of R & R. Some time later, my repose was disrupted by a mysterious commotion outside. Not wanting to alarm the three ferocious guard dogs fast asleep at my feet, I surreptitiously peered out the front window. To my dismay, I spied a carload of young men rifling through the bins. How dare they ravage my recyclables?

I stormed out into the night, a formidable figure in my bathrobe and fuzzy slippers with the cow faces. I demanded the intruders leave the premises immediately. My maniacal discourse, enough to panic any self-respecting dumpster diver, sent those trash hunters scuttling.

I woke up the dogs to boast of my triumph. They sat in disbelief cocking their heads, intent on my narrative. Then, suddenly I experienced a moment of clarity. I asked myself how I could be so frustrated with them for chasing the trash truck when I had just set such a perfect example. From that night forward, I pause and smile before asking them to stop barking at the trash truck. I think they might be saying, "Stop stealing our trash, or we'll sic Mom on you!"

My behavior surrounding garbage events isn't the only demonstration of consummate leadership. Another sterling model is the chronicle of the iPod delivery.

I found myself in need of a new iPod when, sadly, my MP3 player was destroyed in a bizarre household laundry accident. I was listening to it while removing a blanket from the dryer, when a static discharge administered violent and unexpected electroshock therapy directly through the ear buds to my brain. It blew out the MP3 player in the process.

Living without the MP3 player was like living without air, so I decided to purchase a shiny new iPod. I anxiously awaited the gadget's arrival and tracked its path on the *delivery company's web site. On the estimated day of arrival, I cleared my schedule and waited breathlessly for the doorbell to ring.*

Wouldn't you know, I was on the phone when the long-awaited delivery occurred? I hung up and burst through the door to find a "Sorry We Missed You" note and the sight of the brown delivery truck disappearing over the hill.

Screaming and wildly waving my "Sorry We Missed You" note, I chased that driver for two blocks before catching him.

Perhaps it was the accidental electroshock therapy, or my addiction to portable tunes, that caused my extreme behavior. Once again, I had become an unwitting model of leadership, showing my dogs that delivery people must certainly be barked at and chased.

That'll show 'em!

My father always used to say, "Don't raise your voice. Improve your argument."

–Archbishop Desmond Tutu

Clients sometimes ask, "If I don't dominate my dog, aren't I letting him win?" I always respond to that question with another, "Win what?" It seems that somewhere along the line dog training has become a perceived battle of wills, a conflict over who is dominant.

Don't worry. The dog and cat are not plotting to overthrow your kingdom to become evil overlords. (Well, I'm not so sure about the cat.) We do want to establish ourselves as leaders, but not because the dog will seize the throne if we don't. We want to be good leaders for the same reasons we want to be good parents—to set limits, teach good manners, maintain peace in the household, and educate our charges on how to get along in the world.

If we don't set boundaries and teach manners, dogs will be out of control. They will "run the house" the same way children do who have not been taught these things. Dogs don't misbehave because they want to be dominant. They misbehave because they don't know how not to.

Alpha and *dominance* are trendy words used in dominance-based dog training methods—methods that attempt to emulate the pack behavior of wolves in a dominance hierarchy. *Alpha* and *dominance* describe leadership status, but they infer that a struggle has taken place in which the leader fought his way to the top position. Dominance-based training methods espouse controlling dogs through the use of force and intimidation—methods that include physical punishment like scruff shakes and alpha rolls*.

This approach suggests that dogs see humans as their pack members, and that we structure our relationship with them accordingly. This doesn't make much sense because, while dogs may have descended from wolves, they are *not* wolves.

There exists a great disparity between domestic dogs and wild wolves. These differences are so vast as to kindle discussion about whether dogs should be considered a separate species or subspecies of wolves. This makes the paradigm of wolf pack behavior as applied to domestic dog training even more questionable.

Much of the information used in dominance-based dog training comes from the observation of captive wolves. Wolves in captivity live in forced packs within a relatively small area and do not behave the same as wild wolves. Unrelated wolves put together by humans will form a dominance hierarchy in order to live together in relative peace. However, wild wolves do not live in forced packs but in family units. The parents become the natural leaders by mating and producing offspring, not through vicious battle.

We need not throw the baby out with the bathwater by dismissing pack theory altogether. Nor should we say that social status in the canine/human relationship is irrelevant. It is an important factor in understanding social behavior in both species. Both humans and dogs are communal animals. Both use social hierarchy to resolve and avoid conflict within structures that allow greater social freedom to the higher-ranking individual.

Instead of modeling dog training strictly on wolf dominance hierarchies, I suggest we take a broader look at our mutual history—the history of man's association with wolves and how it evolved into our relationship with domestic dogs. With a broader brush, we can paint the landscape of training and social structure in our relationship with dogs—the art of happy training.

A scruff shake means to grab the dog by the back of the neck and stare him down until he submits. An alpha roll means to roll the dog on his back, stare at him, and hold him there until he shows submission. These techniques are considered dangerous and ineffective. The response described as submission is actually the dog giving up. The danger lies in the fact that the dog may decide to fight back. This is no way to build a trusting relationship.

Defining Dominance, Status, Submission, and Aggression

The misunderstanding and misuse of terms does much damage and disservice to our relationship with dogs. Confusion about the ideas of dominance, status, and aggression has compromised dog training theory and practice. To establish proper leadership and social order with dogs, we must define the concepts correctly.

By definition, status is the relative standing within the social order. High-status individuals influence social interaction among individuals within the ranks and enjoy a higher level of social freedom.

Dominance is a relationship among individuals describing one's influence over another and is contextual. Dominance means to exercise the most control in a social interaction, and it is asserted to control not to destroy.

Submission means to yield willingly to the authority of another in social relations.

Aggression is a violent action with intent to do harm. It is the launching of attacks and initiation of sometimes-unprovoked hostilities. Aggression does occur within social hierarchies, but it is not the best answer to conflict because it is dangerous, distracting, requires a lot of energy, and is often unproductive.

If humans used aggression liberally and fisticuffs broke out with every interoffice disagreement, the workplace social structure would be in complete shambles. On the other hand, we could form a hockey team.

Social hierarchies are complex and subject to change, but keeping these simple definitions in mind will help to maintain perspective.

Packs

We believe that dogs form packs because their wolf-like ancestors formed packs. We've transferred that paradigm to life with domestic dogs, because it's handy. It gives us structure and, for some, an excuse to control or even bully dogs.

The dominance theory is a convenient dumping ground to explain away canine behavior. The absence of solid research on hierarchies in domestic dogs allows anecdotal evidence and social memes to dictate theory. We just can't seem to let it go. And, we are a narcissistic bunch. What if dog behavior is not actually about us? What if the dog wanting to go through the door first is not about domination but simply about a strong desire to go outside?

We tend to link the domestic dog with his wolf ancestry through glimpses of wildness in him. However, domestication leaves a wide division in behavior of the two animals. Socialized wolves raised by humans might show signs of domestication, but they do not turn into dogs. Stray dogs may form a loose social order organized by age, but they do not revert to being wolves by forming packs with a single breeding pair. They are sociable but do not create an organized hierarchy or hunt cooperatively, as wild wolves do.

Environment also plays a part in social structure. In the wild, they can be fluid and flexible to accommodate environmental changes. Many species, coyotes for instance, will live in packs during times when food is concentrated; but at other times when food is sparse, they live and hunt small animals on their own. In early interaction with man, scavenging wolves or those fed by humans would not have had to depend on the social group for cooperative hunting. Pet dogs living inside where high quality food is readily available will act differently than dogs living in kennels or as scavenging strays.

Basing the human/dog relationship on wild wolf pack behavior alone can make for some interesting deductions. Wolf packs consist of one breeding pair and their offspring—one or several generations, with pack members assisting in raising pups. Hunting may be done individually and the food shared, or several individuals may hunt together to bring down larger prey. If I base my relationship with my dogs strictly on wild wolf pack behavior, then I would expect my dogs to help raise the children and accompany me to the store to bring down that 50lb bag of kibble.

We tend to form our *domestic pack* with a rigid chain of command, but wolves do not live by such strict linear hierarchy. Wolves in packs depend on the social mechanism to live in peace. Pack rank is more about age than dominance, with young wolves learning their status by observing the social behavior of other pack members. Younger wolves acknowledge older wolves' seniority with body language. Rank can be and is occasionally reinforced through aggressive interactions, but pups learn their rank more by observing pack mates than by being punished and forcefully put in their place.

Dogs also learn by observation and use body language to communicate. As wolf pups observe their elders' response to their behavior, dogs can observe our positive reaction to their desired behaviors and learn how to live peacefully within our social structure.

Domestication

Using wolf pack behavior to explain the behavior of domestic dogs overlooks tens of thousands of years of evolution and domestication. Accepted theory of wolf domestication speculates that interactions between wolves and man became more frequent as humans became less nomadic. When humans settled into villages, opportunistic wolves scavenged human trash. Natural selection began with the most intrepid wolves (probably juveniles that had not yet developed the adult wariness of new things) and humans habituating to each other.

It makes no sense that one of the first animals man chose to domesticate was a predator. However, the wolf's social adaptability and ability to form new social groups (subordinate wolves separate from their original pack to form new ones) made this possible. The advantages of forming an association with man are obvious for the wolf scavengers. But what's in it for humans? Well, for one thing, companionship, the main reason we choose to live with dogs today.

Theory has it that less fearful wolves would have scavenged from, and perhaps been fed by, humans. This relationship may have further developed into one of wolves guarding humans and helping them to hunt. Natural selection would have given the *tamer* wolves a reproductive advantage, because food was plentiful. Humans would have also had reproductive advantage because of the wolf's protection and assistance in hunting.

If we look to our common history for a model in dog training, we should not ignore the fact that dogs became dogs because of a mutual benefit in the relationship, not because one species wanted to dominate the other. I can't imagine that the first interactions between humans and wolves involved domination. I don't picture a human alpha rolling a wolf because the wolf failed to retrieve the morning paper.

Some theorize that man domesticated the wolf by taming him. This conjures up images of Timmy the cave boy luring a wolf pup from the den, taking it home, and saying, "Look what followed me home, Mom! Can we keep him?"

The story of Timmy the cave boy and the wolf pup is not a likely one, because domestication and taming are two different things. Domestication is the process whereby a population of animals or plants is changed at the genetic level through a process of selection. Taming is simply the process by which animals become accustomed to human presence.

Domestic dogs are much more like juvenile wolves than adult wolves. Dogs, like young wolves, tend to be less shy of new things. Maybe our ancestors selected them, or maybe the "tamer" wolves—those acting more like juveniles—hung around humans. The result of these interactions is that two species, similar in that we both retain our playful nature into adulthood, bonded and chose to travel into the future together.

Juvenile wolves are less interested in hierarchy than adult wolves. Domestication of dogs involves a process called pedomorphosis or neoteny, the retention of juvenile features in the adult animal. This means that puppies stop developing earlier than wolf cubs do. We've "designed" many dogs to look more like puppies, with shorter noses and floppy ears. We've "designed" breeds that perpetually act more like puppies. If dogs are more like wolves that never grow up, and juvenile wolves are not as interested in hierarchy, then it follows that dogs are not either. It's yet another reason to look at our early relationship with wolves and put less emphasis on hierarchy in the dog training paradigm.

If you are patient in one moment of anger, you will escape a hundred days of sorrow. **–Chinese Proverb**

Dominance vs. Leadership and Force vs. Power

We may have gotten the idea that dogs form dominance hierarchies because we do see many animals, including insects, form them in nature and in captivity. Adult animals that live together, such as wild horses, form dominance hierarchies, as do captive animals put together by humans.

The question of whether dogs see us as pack members is one that has yet to be clearly answered. It would seem that two species with similar social structures could live in harmony based on the similarities of those social structures. Instead of modeling our relationship with dogs strictly on the organization of wild wolf packs, stray dog social constructs, or human families, we can draw parallels to bring us into accord.

One similarity between wolf packs and human families is that they are both usually small. Typically, we live with one or two dogs. If we lived with a larger number, say ten or twenty dogs that are unrelated and made to live together, there may very well be a need for a strong, dominant pack leader (and a good scoop service). That leader would preferably be human.

Another likeness in our species' social structures is that rank is important. Control of resources gives one higher rank and greater social freedom. Therefore, top rank belongs to those having *priority access to limited, critical resources*. Two species living in the same household full of resources need a social structure to live peacefully.

Some training methods use the nothing-in-life-is-free program. This is a benevolent, effective training technique, but we need not take the word *nothing* too literally. Establishing leadership in part means to control valuable resources. In other words, "I have the cookies, that's why!" However, your dog needn't be a hangdog Oliver Twist pleading, "Please, sir, I want some more." A dog need not dwell in a militaristic existence, where every word of praise, every dog biscuit, and every pat on the head is earned.

A good leader graciously manages the resources—the good stuff that dogs want. These things are food, playtime, attention, preferred resting places, and personal space. Many believe that the alpha dog always eats first or goes through doors first. I don't believe that I have to eat first to be the leader. I believe that until my dog grows opposable thumbs and can work the can opener, I'm in charge. I'm the one who provides the critical resource (food) in exchange for polite behavior (sitting quietly).

Benevolent leadership is not only about controlling resources; it is also about initiating activities and being the provider. Leaders know what direction they want to go. They set the pace and tone, and they are convincing without being aggressive. Dominance is not synonymous with leadership, and aggression is not a necessary factor of dominance. In fact, social hierarchies are designed to decrease or avoid aggression.

Problems arise in dog training when we equate dominance and aggression. This mistake often leads to force as the chosen tool of the trade. In this case, we've also confused the concepts of power and force. High social status means having the power to control without force. If an individual has enough power, there is no need to use force and no need to prove oneself. This leader is one whom others want to follow.

We often label dogs as dominant. Dominance means to exercise the most control in a social interaction. Dominance is better described as a state, not a trait. It is a relationship between individuals, and it's contextual. In a human paradigm, the company president may prevail over her employees at work, but those same employees make the rules with their children at home. In both human families and wolf packs, the parents are always the parents, and their rank is not normally challenged.

Good leaders are in charge of keeping the peace. Instead of using force or intimidation to establish status, they use their heads. In wolf packs, the alpha wannabes are the troublemakers jockeying for position. The same goes for humans. Middle management with its dramatic office politics is commonly where the most discord exists.

Sound leadership is important for successful behavior modification and effective training. All dogs, whether fearful or overconfident, will respond positively to firm, fair leadership over ambiguity. A dog must have confidence and trust in his teacher. A leader that is above conflict and controls resources will instill a sense of self-assurance and order for her followers.

Dominance vs. Leadership in Training

To brand a dog as dominant filters our perception of his behavior. It translates actions like pushiness or willfulness into the dog's desire for power and control. Many behaviors viewed as dominant are less about struggling for rank than they are about maintaining the social unit. Good leadership that manages resources and sets fair, consistent rules and limits will hold the social structure peacefully in place.

One problem with the dominance-based training theory is that so many of the behaviors we are trying to modify, such as excessive barking or failure to come when called, have nothing to do with critical resources. These behaviors occur because the dog is getting reinforced for them in some manner. Positive training methods look objectively at the facts of the behavior. Knowing that dogs do what works for them, we ask what the payoff for the behavior is, stop the payoff (the reinforcement), and then train a preferred behavior. No conflict. Problem solved.

Dog training seen through the filter of the dominance theory can result in some ridiculous ideas. I've even heard some say that a dog's obsession with chasing a laser light can be attributed to the fact that the dog wants to dominate the light!

In training, the dominance label limits creativity by setting a tone of conflict. Remember that dominance applies only to relationships between individuals. Dogs and humans have complex relationships, where experience and context determine what behaviors are reinforced for the dog.

For example, if harsh, painful training methods have been used with the dog to train him not to get on the furniture, he may display aggressive behavior when forced to get off the couch. If his first responses of appeasement or avoidance were overlooked, he may resort to aggression. If aggression works, even for a moment, then the aggressive behavior is reinforced. In this case, the aggression originates as a defensive behavior but turns into an offensive one. Here, if we brand the dog as dominant, we limit training to the confines of conflict and anxiety.

What is often interpreted as dominance toward the owner might actually be attributed to the dog's confusion and anxiety due to lack of direction. He challenges his owner, because he doesn't know where he fits into the hierarchy. Confusion can cause anxiety, where some dogs will defer and some will react with aggression.

In addition to explaining away undesirable behavior, the dominance theory is often a justification for physical punishment. Aggression begets aggression. Therefore, I don't use aggression with my dog, because I don't want him to use it with me.

A benevolent leader is not a tyrant, but simply the one who gets to make the rules—the one who leads. A benevolent leader has the ability to elicit the desired behavior from a dog and maintain it with proper reinforcement. Others wait for undesirable behaviors to occur and then punish the dog. Both methods will get the behavior. However, the positive leader augments the dog/owner relationship; the leader using punishment can destroy it.

Training dogs with positive methods does not translate to permissiveness. With positive methods, a dog learns that polite behavior gets him what he wants (e.g. sitting before he receives his food or greeting people at the door with a polite sit/stay garners the attention of incoming guests).

A dog that is trained using positive methods will enthusiastically offer behaviors to discover which ones work for him. A dog that has been continually punished in his quest may become afraid of the trainer and shut down. Shutting down is often mistaken for submission. In reality, the dog has given up. A worst-case scenario for punishing a dog is that the dog will decide to fight back.

Our leadership position is not a one-way street. We need to communicate with our dogs and listen to what they are telling us. No one wants to live in an atmosphere of tyranny, confrontation, and unyielding obedience. A caring environment engenders learning.

Being the pack leader is not about conflict. Leadership is about the ability to influence the pack to behave in a desirable manner. Let's not wait for our dogs to make a "mistake" and then correct them. Let's teach them acceptable, polite behavior and reward them for it. Life is so much happier that way, and *everyone* wins.

4

Great Expectations

Being realistic about what a dog can and cannot do is an act of love.

–Suzanne Clothier

I don't believe that we fail. I believe that we simply achieve a result. I give an endeavor my best shot; then at the end of the day, I see the outcome. I have not failed or succeeded but merely produced a result. To say that one has failed is a negative judgment based on how well the consequences fit the expectations. In dog training as in life, we need to be open to unexpected results.

My dog Mr. MoJo has been training me for the past thirteen years. However, he lets me think that I am training him. So when we're faced with a new challenge, I must be prepared for whatever his creative, opportunistic mind derives.

Recently, I was faced with the question of how to prevent my dogs from eating goose droppings while on our daily walks in the park. They have been trained to "leave it" on cue, but to them, goose manure is the Holy Grail of edible, found treasure. The "leave it" cue is not always effective.

I pondered the problem and devised what I thought was a brilliant solution. My dogs know how to change pace on cue, so if I could ask them to "hustle," we could break into a trot and literally run the goose poop gauntlet. I was certain that this idea would prevent them from grazing on goose goo.

It worked for maybe the first three tries. After that, Mr. MoJo became adept at eating on the run. Now, we were into the realm of fast food, with Mr. MoJo dipping his head quickly and scooping up the tasty morsels.

But wait, it gets worse. That savvy, too-smart-for-his-own-good dog of mine began to take the word "hustle" as his cue to start scooping—a most unexpected result!

Did I fail? If success is defined by whether the results fit the expectations, then the answer is yes. But, I prefer to withhold judgment and look objectively and optimistically at the outcome. Thus far, I've simply discovered something that did not work. Mr. MoJo and I will keep trying until we get a result that satisfies us both.

Perhaps I need to adjust my expectations and my perspective. Maybe I'll train Mr. MoJo to be a wildlife scat detection dog and invent goose poop flavored treats. He'll make me a millionaire!

A wonderful gift may not be wrapped as you expect.

—Jonathan Lockwood Huie

A great disparity exists between our expectations of dogs and their canine reality. Expectations can lead to disappointment and resentment, but if we open our minds and the lines of communication—if we're willing to be flexible and accepting—we can find equal ground on the path to happy training. It's helpful to pause for a moment on our journey to adjust or ease our expectations and to define individual success. Instead of relying strictly on management or corrections when problems arise, we can get out in front of the behavior, see around the corner, in order to anticipate and plan. We can expect to be patient and flexible, and we can expect the unexpected.

Training vs. Management

We expect dogs to fit effortlessly into our lives. But effortlessly for whom? This question might have us wondering about when to train dogs, when to use good management, or when to use a combination of both.

For example, I met a dog owner browsing the muzzle section of a pet supply store. Striking up a friendly conversation, I asked why she was considering a muzzle. The shopper explained that each day when the mail carrier made a delivery through the letter slot, the dog chewed up the mail. She thought that muzzling the dog during the day would solve the problem.

It's true. This management technique would have solved the problem, but it would have caused another. I explained the dangers of the dog wearing a muzzle for extended lengths of time* and suggested another option. The trouble is we often try to modify the dog's behavior without thinking about the consequences for the dog or alternative solutions.

Let's have a look at some options for solving the problem of the mail-eating dog:

Training only: The dog could be trained to "leave it" when the mail is delivered, but that will only work if someone is there to issue the cue.

Management only: One could install a mailbox outside of the house, which would disallow the dog access to the mail.

A combination of training and management: In this case, management alone (moving the mailbox) is the best solution. However, if the letter-eating dog had also threatened the mail carrier, then training and behavior modification would be in order, along with strict management.

Common canine predicaments—such as house training, destructive chewing, leash walking, chaos at the front door, and escaping the yard— have many a bewildered dog owner wondering whether training or management is the best solution.

Management can be the easy way out, but the most important consideration is that of the dog's safety and wellbeing. It's not safe or kind to muzzle or crate dogs all day to solve house training or destructive chewing issues. Here, a combination of training and management are in order. Leash walking can be trained as well as managed with the use of humane equipment. Training dogs to do a sit stay while guests enter will solve chaos at the front door. Escaping the yard must be managed with secure fencing or a dog run.

If we give thought to lifestyle and personal preferences—if we're not afraid to change our expectations or think outside the box—we'll find solutions to problems encountered in everyday life with dogs. This allows us to focus on the joys of life with them, which far outweigh the problems.

The muzzle the woman was considering was a sleeve muzzle, which does not allow a dog to eat, drink, or breathe properly. Its use is intended for short periods of time only.

Do not worry about the results, but be concerned with the process.
—Masao Nemoto

The Meaning of Success

If success is based on the judgment of how well results fit expectations, then it's helpful to define success. We tend to focus on the negative, the *problems* our dogs have, such as potty training, pulling on the leash, aggressive behavior, and more. Instead of simply naming trouble, let's also define success. Doing so takes into consideration the individual and unique circumstances of different dogs and their people.

It's part of the human condition to compare. We grade ourselves in school;

we compete in the workplace and on the playing field; we even compare our dogs' behavior with that of our friends' and peers' dogs. We want him to do what the neighbor's dog does—a down stay in the front yard while other dogs and their people pass by. But let's not compare apples to oranges; Airedales to Old English Sheepdogs, if you will.

The grass always seems greener on the other side of the fence. Perhaps, if we pay attention to what's on our side and tend to it, the grass will be just as green—maybe a different shade, but just as healthy.

It's important not to let others define our success. Individual success takes into consideration numerous elements, such as environment, breed, age, history, health, trainability, and lifestyle. Success is not about changing dogs to fit our ideals or the ideals of others. For instance, training success would not look the same for a hand-picked, working Border collie as it would for a rescued Beagle.

Success involves having realistic goals. If we expect the aforementioned Beagle to win herding competitions, it isn't going to happen. This is an extreme example to make a point that achievable goals are an important component in the definition of success.

Consider the following elements that characterize success:

Trainability: Trainability is not about intelligence. It's about the dog's individuality and what he's been bred to do. At first glance, a scent hound may appear less intelligent or stubborn and unwilling to please. Response time to cues might be longer than, say, a Border collie. But remember that Border collies are bred to work flocks of sheep, taking cues far afield from their master. Scent hounds are bred to find a scent and stay on it, no matter what is happening around them. We can modify behaviors only within the window that genetics has set for a particular breed or individual.

Lifestyle/Environment: Consider what training success would look like for a young Australian Cattle Dog living in a caring, busy family with four children under the age of ten. Now, consider a young Australian Cattle Dog living in a downtown loft apartment with loving people who are gone twelve hours a day. Each situation has its own challenges to overcome, which means that individual success would look very different. The obvious lifestyle difference here is the amount of daily exercise the dog is getting naturally with the children, as opposed to the intentional exercise that must be provided for the downtown dog. Adequate exercise and proper training provide physical activity and mental stimulation. Although the two situations require different paths, the results are calmer, well-behaved, healthy dogs: AKA, success.

Age/Health: The behavior differences between a two-year-old and a ten-year-old Labrador retriever are obvious, but let's also look at physical issues that affect behavior. Take common allergies for example. Imagine a dog that is not comfortable in his own skin. His learning would be compromised by his discomfort and possibly by prescribed medication. Healthy bodies and healthy minds are essential in the formula for success.

History: A dog's background can certainly influence the definition of training success. For instance, pet-store puppies may be challenging to potty train. This is because puppies confined in cages early in life have no choice but to eliminate where they eat and sleep, which is unnatural behavior. We don't typically know a rescued dog's history, which can sometimes pose a challenge to training. However, we can do our best detective work to discover the root cause of a behavior and begin our training there.

Training success is best measured in baby steps. We tend to look at the final goal and gauge how far away it seems. We're inclined to think that we'll travel a straight line from Point A to Point B, and then live happily ever after. Instead of overwhelming ourselves or focusing on the negative, we can view training success as a journey that we take together with our dogs.

The path to happy training includes acceptance of where we need to begin and recognizing that there will be challenges. But if we stop comparing and see training as a journey, complete with unexpected turns, we will define our individual success, and the path will be easier to walk.

Blessed is he who expects nothing, for he shall never be disappointed.
–Alexander Pope

It Depends

We expect definitive answers. A well-known dog trainer and author says that she's going to write a book entitled *It Depends*. This is because so many dog-training questions have answers that begin with "it depends." This fact illustrates how dog training is a moment-by-moment, think-on-your-feet endeavor.

It is human nature to have linear expectations. We expect to follow a recipe, moving from start to finish easily and quickly. Occasionally a client will request precise directions for training their dog, like instructions for assembling a newly purchased piece of IKEA furniture. They want instructions that read "insert tab A into slot B."

That's not exactly how dog training works. It tends to take a circuitous path, especially when doing behavior modification. Often, we must first deconstruct a behavior to learn its origin, and then construct a plan using basic tools of learning theory. Training requires the ability to be flexible, read the situation minute by minute, and think on one's feet.

Training is fluid. At any given moment, we must be able to read the dog and adjust to immediate conditions. Different dogs have different needs and personalities. However, even when working with the same dog, the mood and circumstances are in constant flux. Successful training means knowing how to remain in the moment and be flexible in one's approach.

Successful training sessions mean constantly observing what the dog is telling us and what the dog is asking us. From there, we make adjustments in technique to accommodate the moment and to facilitate continued learning.

A good trainer has a toolbox of training techniques. Like a mechanic, she assesses the problem and then chooses the right tool for the job. However, unlike a mechanic who knows that she needs a 3/8" wrench, the dog training toolbox is not so black and white. Ten minutes ago, the 3/8" wrench was needed; now a Phillips-head screwdriver is in order. But keep that wrench handy, because it may be needed again any minute. (This is a metaphor. Don't worry, I would never use a hand tool for training a dog.)

Success is about understanding which tool to use and when—even recognizing when to stop a session. Success involves knowing when to adjust expectations, what to accept, and when to accept it.

Success is about working with what the dog is offering. Success recognizes the fact that sometimes moving forward means taking steps back. If something is not working, we need to back up, break the behavior into small steps, and proceed from there. Paradoxically, success can come faster by moving slower.

Training is contextual. We need to know the milieu, the back-story, and the timeline for what's happened today, yesterday, an hour ago. We operate within the framework of these events in order for optimum learning to take place.

If we remember to relax, stay in the moment, and breathe, we will reach our training goals. How quickly?

It depends.

Infinite patience produces immediate results.   *—A Course In Miracles*

Are We There Yet?

We expect instant gratification NOW! We live in a downloadable, microwaveable, instant messaging world. However, when it comes to training a dog, I favor the dictum of slower is faster.

There is no remote control in dog training, so we must get up and change the behavior ourselves. We must decide whether training or management is the solution and remember not to complain about the results we didn't get if we didn't do the work.

Canine behavior does not happen in a vacuum. Consciously or unconsciously, we might create our dog's undesirable behavior and then hold him accountable for it. If we are living in a chaotic environment, stressed, or distracted ourselves, it makes sense that our dogs will tune in to our tension and perhaps become stressed and distracted, as well. Dogs have an amazing ability to connect with human emotions. The leash can act as a telegraph wire to communicate our tension. However, even off leash dogs can sense the slightest anxiety, read the micro expressions on our faces with pinpoint accuracy, and detect minute changes in voice inflection.

Dog training is not an exorcism but an exercise in communication and understanding. For successful relationships, we must navigate the emotional landscape with compassion and the ability to listen—to hear what dogs are saying to us. Both canine and human species have moods and emotions. Humans can emotionally crash and burn over a bad hair day or a downward turn in the economy. Fido's moods may not encompass the wide scope that ours do, but they are nonetheless worthy of our attention and appreciation.

Patience itself is a form of action; inaction can be as effective as doing something. At times, it's best to simply take pause. One doesn't need to be a Zen master to train a dog. However, it's helpful to assess our own emotions, understand how connected our dogs are to them, and breathe. If we check in with our emotions, we can take the moments of highest frustration and turn them into training opportunities. For instance, if my dog is pulling me down the street, I refrain from giving a leash correction or scolding. Instead, I stop, breathe, and remember that my dog's agenda on a walk is different from mine. I ask myself, "How can I turn this into a training opportunity?"

As mentioned, a dog's agenda on a walk is different from ours. Bear in mind that dogs live in an intense olfactory world that is inaccessible and unfathomable to humans. We cannot imagine the level of distraction that our dogs experience through their noses. If we simply remember how very different their world is from ours, it will help us to blend the two.

Patience is also a deeper form of acceptance. If you always want more, faster, you'll never have enough soon enough.

Expectation and Exception

We expect to find patterns and absolute answers even where none exist. We expect dogs to seek dominance, except when they don't. We expect dogs to come when called, except when they don't. We expect dogs to pay attention, except when they don't. The words expect and except contain the same letters. Let this remind us to *expect* the *except* part of life with dogs.

There is a fine line between hope and expectation. Expectation is looking toward outcome with attachment and judgment. Expectation is premeditated resentment. Hope is looking toward outcome without attachment. Hope is compassionate. If we recognize the difference between hope and expectation, we can detach from the outcome. We can stop judging success by how the results fit our expectations. We can expect success no matter what it looks like. There is hope. Communication, understanding, and realistic expectations allow both dogs and humans to participate in the training experience. As such, we do not suppress the uncontainable spirit of dogs, but join them.

5

Living at Peace in the Pack

All marriages are happy. It's the living together afterward that causes all the trouble. –Raymond Hull

For nine years, I lived with three large, hairy, male dogs. It was like living in a frat house. Life was loud and smelly. What little remaining useable furniture we had was stained and in disrepair. And there was a lot of public urination. I regularly felt as though I lived in a kennel, outnumbered and outmaneuvered, and most certainly outwitted by the Border Collie of the pack.

Living with Mr. MoJo, Jude, and Bob (Barker) was challenging, yet a deep, abiding learning experience. Talk about the school of hard knocks. Professional wrestling had nothing over those boy dogs when it came to showing off their athletic and theatrical aptitude. Their indoor agility course (the domestic accoutrements formerly known as furniture) was the focus of envious conversation around the dog park water bowl.

During frequent tag-team wrestling matches, my cries of, "Use your inside voices!" and, "Don't stand on your brother's head!" fell on deaf, furry ears.

When living in a multi-dog home, one finds oneself doing and saying things one would never imagine saying or doing. Challenges occur at an exponentially higher rate than in a single-dog household. Without training and management, life is a regular canine Cirque du Melee. Trust me. I know whereof I speak:

Mealtimes are never interrupted just once to accommodate dogs' requests to be let in or out. Dogs never want to be let in or out at the same time. Thus, I haven't had an undisturbed meal in eleven years.

One might find a dead bird in the living room, which could happen in a single-dog home, but the ensuing fight over it only happens when living with multiples.

One's chances of stepping in poop or puke in the middle of the night are exponentially higher. I've learned never to walk around barefoot in the dark.

One must conduct a nose-count roll call at bedtime or before leaving the house. I originally learned this when my family moved and forgot to bring my little brother. The lesson was

further reinforced the time my German shepherd inadvertently spent half the night sleeping outside in the yard.

One might find oneself taking a squooshy dead rabbit out of one dog's mouth, while the other dog is freaking out about the surprise jogger just rounding the corner. I kindly thanked the jogger for her offer to help and for not laughing at the insane spectacle.

One might find oneself driving poop to the vet's office. This can occur in a single-dog home, but a multi-dog household requires detective work to determine which dog passed the worms, stolen sock, or whatever fecal anomaly transpired. I'm not only my dog's chauffeur, but I'm also their poop taxi.

One might find oneself making separate consecutive trips to the vet's office, because all of my dogs don't fit into a Ford Focus (which in my world is less like a car than it is a crate on wheels). Thus, I'm ineligible for the veterinarian fleet discount.

One might find oneself having to determine which dog's dietary indiscretion caused the offensive odiferous stain on the carpet. This is why I have Oriental style rugs—they are handy for hiding biological based blemishes. Furthermore, you can't even see where I dropped the pizza.

One might find oneself having to determine which dog's lapse of reason caused the mass of shredded window treatments. What can I say? I wanted new curtains anyway.

One will find oneself learning the leash dance, which is the dog walk waltz of untangling leashes. I can do the tangled tango and the leash limbo, as well.

The secret to surviving nine years with the three amigos was to recognize the lessons that they came to teach me. I learned to teach my boys that polite behavior would get them what they wanted. It was also helpful to know when to sit back, fasten my seatbelt, and enjoy the ride.

Bob Barker taught me about barking. Jude taught me about loose leash walking. Mr. MoJo taught me the secret to training is to have the student think that performing a given behavior is his idea. (In Mr. MoJo's case, it was a matter of him training me by having me think the task was my idea.) All three of these boys taught me about benevolent leadership, patience, unconditional love, and which brand of vacuum cleaner gives the most dog-hair-sucking bang for the buck.

For nine years, I lived in a cozy 1,000 sq. ft. home with about 650 sq. ft. of dog!

I'm sure that what I learned from Bob, Jude, Mr. MoJo, their predecessors, and successors has made me a better dog trainer. I'm reasonably sure it's made me a better person, as well.

We all have to live together, so we might as well live together happily.
— Dalai Lama

The more the merrier? It can be done, but beware! Living with two dogs is not just double the work and cost; it's much more. Living with three or more dogs is off the management, expense, and worry charts. On the other hand, multiple dog households are off the fun and the love charts, as well.

Dogs are pack animals. Therefore, we expect they should live effortlessly in perfect accord within a group. Many dogs can. Our function as leaders is to create a harmonious home. This can be achieved through a commitment to management, training, and attention to the needs of all family members, both canine and human.

When contemplating the practicality of multiple dogs, we first think of the obvious: the cost, time, and work involved. However, there are other less-evident factors to consider:

Walking a whole pack of dogs together is a challenge. It doesn't come naturally to any of the participants. Therefore, each dog must be trained separately to walk nicely on leash. This requires time, patience, a good pair of footwear, the ability to juggle leashes, and resisting the urge to text while driving the team.

Perhaps cleanliness is next to Godliness, but I say that with multiple dogs it's next to impossible! I could vacuum every four hours and still be witness to hairballs the size of house cats tumbling across the floor on route to a permanent home under some immovable piece of furniture.

Preserving the landscape is another challenge of living with the pack. Visible areas of my property are kept respectable in appearance, but the section relegated to the dogs looks like a government missile testing site. My neighbors and I are thankful for privacy fences.

Training Multiple Dogs: The Real Life Facts

Living with and training multiple dogs would seem a Sisyphean task. With a bit of planning, thought, and radical patience it's not. Nonetheless, it's not exactly a walk in the park. Well, it can be, but we'll get to that later.

Train Each Dog to be Comfortable Alone

In a multi-dog household, we need one-on-one time with each dog for training. Consequently, we must be able to separate them and make sure those dogs not being trained are comfortable with some alone time. It's difficult to train one dog with the distraction of another scratching at the door or whining woefully.

Peaceful individual training can be achieved by putting the dog not being trained in a crate, another room, or outside. Dogs can be confined individually in different locations or together if they are more comfortable.

Additionally, training dogs to be comfortable apart from each other prevents codependence. Dogs that are together 24/7 may become so bonded that they can experience extreme anxiety in the absence of their canine housemates. Implement separate training time, walks, and going for rides into your multi-dog household. Make sure the dog left behind gets to enjoy a stuffed ® or other interactive toy. My dog Penny knows that when the Kong® Wobbler™ toy comes out, she's going with me. MoJo is happy to see its appearance, because he gets to stay home and work it to get the treats inside. Conversely, MoJo gets excited to see Penny go to her crate for a Kong® toy, which means that he's the one who gets to go along with me.

Teach the Basics

Each dog in a multi-dog household must be well trained. Otherwise, the situation is ungovernable. The key to success is to teach each dog individually. When he's reliable with the new behavior on his own, it's safe to ask him to perform in a group. If a dog can't do it when it's easy (alone), he can't do it when it's difficult (in a group). Each dog needs to *master*, not just *know*, the basic skills. At the bare minimum, every dog needs to know sit, down, stay, and recall.

Training in a multi-dog household presents challenges that require a measure of both discipline and tolerance. Even the world's best dog trainer would find it extremely challenging to teach a new behavior to more than one dog at once. Neither of you can concentrate on the business of teaching and learning in the presence of another dog.

Once each dog is reliable on the basics, start training in the presence of one other dog. If you have three or more dogs, begin by having Fido work in the presence of only Spot, then in the presence of only Rex, then in the presence of only Rover. Next, have Fido work in the presence of Spot and Rex, then Spot and Rover, then Rover and Rex. Finally, have Fido work in the presence of all of the other dogs. When the other dogs are introduced on to the scene, have them gated, tethered, or on a down stay if they are capable. When the trainee dog is able to perform in the presence of another (quiet) dog, you can gradually increase the activity level.

Never dial up more than one criterion at a time. In other words, if Fido can do a 30-second stay in the kitchen alone with you, it would be unreasonable to ask him to do a 45-second stay in the yard while Spot, Rover, and Rex are having a rousing game of chase. When introducing a mild distraction, ask Fido to do a shorter stay. When you take him to the yard, ask for a 15-second stay. Work up to a 30-second stay there before you ask him to do it in Spot's presence.

Individuality

In relationships, often the space given to each other brings us closer. To continually treat dogs as a pack instead of the individuals they are is a detriment to training and our relationships with them. It's like treating human triplets as a unit instead of recognizing their uniqueness. Spending one-on-one time with each dog builds a bond and opens the lines of communication. It's reinforcing to the dog. If we don't establish individual relationships, then dogs will naturally relate to and bond more strongly with each other than with us. This makes establishing our leadership position a challenge.

Individual dogs have different needs, which must be attended to specifically. Forever treating each dog equally in the interest of fairness does not teach him frustration tolerance or patience—things needed to live peacefully together.

Training as a Group

We often need dogs to do things, such as waiting at the door, simultaneously. In order to perform cues in a group, each dog must first be a master of the behavior.

Dogs need to know their own names. Additionally, they need to know common verbal markers, such as "no" (which means to stop what they are doing) and "yes" (which says they are doing the right thing).

Teaching a collective name, such as "dogs" or "kids" is quite helpful in having dogs perform simultaneously. This is done the same way we teach a puppy his name. Say it, mark the behavior of looking at you, and treat each dog that does it.

Competition

Dogs often compete for attention and resources in the presence of other dogs. We can mitigate canine contests by training each dog to stay while the others get attention. With each dog having learned a solid stay, you are ready to teach them how advantageous it can be to hold a stay while others get attention.

Put one dog in a stay beside or behind you. Give the other dog some pets and attention for one or two seconds, then turn to the dog in the stay, treat and release him. Repeat this exercise a few times until the dog in the stay learns that good things happen to those who stay. Now, switch roles by having the dog that got the attention do the stay.

You can strengthen the stay even more by asking the dog to stay, giving the other dog attention, and treating the dog in the stay, but not releasing him. Next, give the other dog some more attention, and then return to the dog in the stay, treat, and release.

Train dogs to take treats individually while sitting side by side. Do this by asking both dogs for a sit stay. Say one dog's name and give him a treat. To help the dog not getting the treat, you can use your hand signal for stay (usually a flat palm held toward the dog) as you treat the other dog. Repeat the exercise alternating which dog gets the treat first. Saying the dogs' names as they get their treat helps them to know that they are the receiver. It also helps the other dog to know that his patience will be rewarded.

Playtime

Who needs TV when you can watch your dogs play? Bob, Jude, and MoJo engaged in endless wrestling matches for my enjoyment. I did not need to participate. All I had to do was go outside and stand on the patio for them to show off their stuff. Living with three large, hairy boy dogs was like being a referee in the World Wrestling Federation.

For safety's sake, we must know what is appropriate play and how to intervene when necessary. Knowing the signs of stress and fear (see *Conversations with Dogs*, the chapter on canine body language) helps us to determine whether all dogs are willing participants and when it's time to mediate.

Dogs have different play styles. Some use paws and body checks more often; others are more vocal. Both appropriate and inappropriate dog play involves teeth. Canine playtime is similar to a human wrestling match. Human wrestling involves pinning one's opponent to the ground; dog play involves copious amounts of play biting. Play bites are inhibited bites delivered to the legs and feet where teeth are not connected for more than a second.

Canine play involves a great deal of inefficient motion. In addition to play bites, there is often a lot of batting each other with paws and body checks—maneuvers delivered without enough force to hurt each other.

Dogs exhibit a few common predominant play styles. It's important to know your dogs' play styles if you take them to dog parks or daycare, where they will be playing with lots of different dogs. Typical play styles include rough and tumble with lots of body slams and forceful body contact, chase-and-be-chased play style, and lots of mouth wrestling. Some dogs like to run in, freeze, poke, and retreat.

Most play styles blend well together, with the exception of the rough and tumble. These dogs can play well together, but when they attempt to engage dogs of a less physical play style, trouble can ensue. The inherent danger is that rough-and-tumble dogs can scare those with more relaxed play styles. This hard-hitting style may be perceived as aggression by the dog with the less physical approach to play. If he becomes scared or hurt by a body slam, he might feel that he must defend himself. If he does so, the rough-and-tumble dog might then fight back. Each dog feels the other dog has unpredictably started a fight. If this happens repeatedly, dogs may feel threatened by all unfamiliar dogs and thus greet them with offensive aggression.

Even appropriate play can escalate into an inappropriate fracas. Ever been to a hockey game? Canine play is all fun and games until somebody ends up in a cone!

Because dog play is play fighting, it can be difficult to know whether the game is tipping into a real fight. Even if it doesn't turn into a backyard brawl, we want to observe whether both dogs are having fun. Following are some pointers on determining whether or not play is appropriate:

Is one dog always on top? In appropriate play, the dogs will switch positions voluntarily. One dog is not constantly pinning the underdog to the ground.

Is one dog always doing the chasing? Dogs love to chase and dogs love to be chased. However, if the chaser and the chased roles are never reversed, the dog being hounded may not be having fun. Some dogs love to be chased more than they like to pursue, so observe whether the dog being chased is inviting it. He may approach the chaser, do a play bow, bark, and then run away in a happy enticement to a game of chase.

Is there any yelping going on? If one dog is not aptly inhibiting his bites, there is a problem. If a yelp is due to the likes of an accidental collision, the dogs should stop shortly, then resume appropriate play.

Excessive placement of paws over shoulders, mounting, pouncing, or play on hind legs can indicate that one dog is trying to intimidate the other. Dog play fighting involves open, smiling mouths and copious inefficient motion. A real dogfight is intentional, fast, and furious. It looks and sounds like dogs in a blender.

Play fighting can be loud. Mouthing and biting during appropriate play is normal, as is growling. However, if growling escalates and/or deepens, if mouths are not open and smiling, it is wise to intervene. Simple overstimulation can lead to play tipping into aggression.

If we allow our dog to engage in constant rambunctious play, we run the risk of him becoming a bully or playmate that is simply overwhelming for other dogs. There is also the risk of a dog developing leash aggression, because he wants to interact with all dogs he sees. This may cause the dog to bark and lunge on the leash when he sees another dog. Extreme frustration could possibly even turn to aggression.

As mentioned earlier, to watch dogs play is highly entertaining, but it is advantageous for us to participate as well. As with training, playing with dogs both individually and in a group helps to keep us in the loop. Housemates that only play among themselves and their friends can bond more with each other than us. I want my dogs to have fun interacting with me, so that I'm not just mean old mom or the hall monitor, always breaking up the party.

Intervention

If rough-and-tumble play becomes questionable, do a "bully test." Separate the dogs for a moment to let them chill, and then observe their behavior. If a dog walks away and does not want to continue, then he's had enough. If all dogs willingly return to the game, let them carry on.

Teach dogs a solid recall that is strong enough to call them out of play (see emergency recall in *The How-To of Training*). Rehearse these recalls during playtime. First, practice at the beginning of play before the dogs have had time to get in the "zone" and before they develop playtime-induced deafness. Strengthen the recall by gradually increasing the time the dogs are allowed to play before calling them.

Status (Social Rank and Social Standing)

Multi-dog households require clearly defined, benevolent leadership, as conflict can arise when there is confusion regarding status. However, we want to be mindful that *every* conflict is not a dominance issue (see the chapter *Is My Dog Winning?* on the alpha theory and dominance). Still, conflicts do occur, and a way to handle them peacefully is to establish an unambiguous social order. Do this by setting boundaries and teaching manners, so that dogs learn that polite, patient behavior gets them what they want.

Group Wait and Individual Release

A group wait is handy to control chaos at the door or in the car. A pack of dogs jockeying for position and crashing through the door all at once is not a demonstration of polite behavior. It could even cause a fight. You may hear that in order for you to be alpha, you must always go through the door first (a disproved theory.) I don't really care who goes through first; I believe that until my dogs grow opposable thumbs and can open the door themselves, I'm in charge. Besides, the theory doesn't work for car rides, as I don't find it feasible to get into the car before my dogs.

Learning to wait at the door prevents dogs from seeing every open door or gate as an opportunity to escape—a chance to bolt. Training a group wait and individual release teaches patience, polite behavior, and prevents doorway mêlées. Dogfights often occur in doorways, so group waits are helpful in their prevention. (If serious aggression is an issue, owners should seek help from a reputable professional.)

First, work with each dog individually, teaching him to wait at the door (see *The How-To of Training*). Once each dog can do a reliable wait, you are ready to teach the group.

Even if you have three or more dogs, start with just two. Using your group name in a calm, steady tone say, "Kids, wait." Be prepared to use a body block or to close the door quickly if one or both of the dogs break. Even though they can do a solid wait individually, the presence of another dog is a distraction. Excitement is high, and there is the possibility of a competition to get out the door first.

As soon as both dogs are waiting politely, say one dog's name in your release word tone, and allow her to go through the door. Body block any forward motion from the other dog. When he is holding his wait, then say his name in your release word tone, and allow him to go through the door. Repeat the exercise in reverse order.

If you are training more than two dogs to do a group wait, practice with every combination of two dogs. If you have Fido, Spot, Rover, and Tippy, work with Fido and Spot, Fido and Rover, Fido and Tippy, Spot and Rover, Spot and Tippy….you get the picture. Once you've worked with every combination of pairs, do the same with each combination of three. Finally, add in the fourth dog.

Engender patience by varying the order in which you release the dogs, so that the same dog is not always going first.

Teach a Group to Wait for Food
Teaching a dog "wait" means that he must wait for permission to take food.

Teach this to individual dogs, and be sure that they are reliable alone before teaching it as a group (see *The How-To of Training*).

If you have three or more dogs, start with just two. Put the dogs in a sit. Say, "Kids, wait," and drop a piece of food on the floor. Be prepared to use a body block if one or both of the dogs break. Even though each dog is capable of doing a solid wait, having another dog present is a whole new ball game. It is a huge distraction, and there is the possibility that the dogs will compete for the food.

As soon as both dogs pause, say one dog's name in your release word tone, and allow him to take the food. Use a body block to prevent any forward motion from the other dog. Repeat the exercise in reverse order.

If you are training more than two dogs to do a group wait, practice with every combination of two dogs as you did with waiting at the door. Once you've worked with every combination of pairs, do the same with each combination of three. Finally, add in the fourth dog.

Vary the order in which you release the dogs, so that it's not always the same dog getting the food first. This engenders patience in each of the dogs and can prevent fights over found or dropped food.

Do not teach a group wait for food if any dog has an issue with resource guarding food. Resolve the resource guarding behavior before teaching the group wait.

Walking Multiple Dogs

Picking up leashes usually elicits a high level of enthusiasm. It's akin to an audience member hearing their name called on *The Price Is Right*.

Anything that a dog wants is a reinforcer. Dogs want walks. Learning follows a pattern or formula, which is A-B-C (A=antecedent, B=behavior, C=consequence), and behavior is driven by consequence. Picking up the leashes is the antecedent. Jumping around, barking, and doing back flips is the behavior. Going for a walk is the consequence.

By taking those maniacal mutts for a walk, we reinforce the wild behavior. To avoid the pre-walk chaos, we must change the B in the formula. Teach dogs to be polite while leashing them up instead of acting like game show contestants.

All dogs should know how to sit and wait in a group (see above). Next, teach each dog individually to sit and wait while you put the leash on. Cue the dog to wait, and then pick up the leash. If the dog goes crazy, simply sit and do nothing. Wait for the dog to calm down and to disassociate from the crazy behavior (at least 20 seconds), then start again. Repeat this until the dog can wait patiently while he's leashed up. You can desensitize dogs to the antecedent (picking up the leash) by picking up the leash and then putting it back without going anywhere.

Once you've incorporated all dogs into the group wait, you can put leashes on individually. Have each dog hold his stay until you are ready to walk out the door.

By the way, you've already taught dogs to walk nicely on leash and integrated them to walking as a group. Enjoy your walk!

Fights

Into each life some rain and rivalry must fall. Notwithstanding serious aggression between dogs, occasional small scuffles are to be expected, and we must be prepared to handle them. Knowing how to manage and intervene means, we can stop most fights before they start.

There are different reasons that dogs living in the same household fight (see the chapter *Aggressive Dogs*). Many intramural fights are about status and possession, but not necessarily in the most obvious or direct way. Frequently fights take place in the presence of the owner. This illustrates how fights about rank are commonly about the status of a dog's relationship to the owner and not their status among the other dogs. Fights over possessions are frequently about resources, and the most valuable resource in the house is the owner.

Rank among resident dogs is dynamic and not always clear-cut. However, there is usually one dog that holds the highest rank in most circumstances. Conflicts can arise when status among the dogs is ambiguous and if the dogs are nearly equal in standing.

Many owners question whether they should support the high-ranking dog. We can exacerbate fights simply by the influence that we have over our dogs. For example, if one dog growls at another, it is natural for us to correct the growling dog by telling (or yelling at them) to stop. This communicates to the growler that we are siding with the dog being growled at. We're also sending a message to the dog being growled at that, with our support, he has the power in this situation. This can confuse the dogs as to their standing in the hierarchy. Growling is a warning and is most often used appropriately. If there is otherwise, no serious aggression or excessive growling going on, the issue will most likely be sorted out peacefully.

That being said, even with supervision and management in place, sometimes intervention is necessary. Intervention begins at the show of teeth, first growl, or hard stare. Although counterintuitive, we must refrain from shouting which only makes matters worse. As stated above, we need to be mindful of whether we are supporting one dog over the other and how our actions can be confusing them. Our involvement must be neutral and unemotional. Interrupt with a firm "no" and diffuse the situation by calling dogs or putting them in a down stay at the first sign of trouble. (Fight intervention is another reason that dogs must be trained to reliably perform basic obedience.)

If an all-out fight does occur, know how to break it up safely (see the chapter *Aggressive Dogs*).

Helpful points in the prevention and management of aggression between dogs living in the same household:

- Train all dogs in basic obedience

- Establish firm, fair rules through benevolent leadership

- Manage resources (food, toys, treats, chews, etc.)

- Prevent further altercations, so that fighting doesn't become habit

- Identify all triggers to aggression, and enforce management

- Provide adequate exercise and mental stimulation

- Know canine body language to predict and prevent fighting

- Manage household stress levels

• Maintain good health, as medical conditions can contribute to behavioral issues

• Do not interfere with the dogs' established hierarchy

Mealtime – Food – Multiple Dogs

In a multi-dog household, mealtime can be chaotic, with numerous dogs doing the happy mealtime dance and singing for their supper. If mealtime is too chaotic or unsafe (i.e. one or more dogs resource guard), then feeding them in separate rooms or in their crates is a must.

If the dogs can safely dine in the same room, but one likes to finish his meal quickly and then go shopping in the other dogs' bowls, teaching an alternative behavior can divert the situation. This alternative behavior would be to wait by their bowl or to go to another location to get a special treat—something better than what is in the other dogs' bowls—dessert, if you will.

Do this by waiting beside the first finisher. Immediately after the last bite of kibble is down, lure him to another location. Use body blocks if necessary to prevent him from making his shopping rounds. Once at the new location, deliver the special treat. You've just made going to the "dessert bar" better than procuring another's kibble.

If you prefer to have the dog wait by his bowl when he's finished his meal instead of going to another location, you can train him to do so. As soon as the last piece of kibble is eaten, drop a yummy treat into the bowl. Gradually increase the time between the last bite of kibble and delivery of the treat, so that the dog learns to wait by his bowl.

If you have more than one shopper and more than one person in the household, assign one person per dog to do the training. If it's only you against multiple shoppers, you can use gates and barriers while they are learning to wait for dessert.

In a dog's life, some plaster would fall, some cushions would open, some rugs would shred. Like any relationship, this one had its costs. They were costs we came to accept and balance against the joy and amusement and protection and companionship he gave us.

> — **John Grogan,** *Marley and Me:*
> — *Life and Love with the World's Worst Dog*

Keys to a Peaceful Pack

Management: Multi-dog households require the use of tethers, gates, barriers, and crates during training.

Training: All dogs in the household need to be well trained. Training must take place individually before training as a group. The more dogs in the household, the better trained they must be individually. Bad manners within the group can be a precursor to aggression, and it should be noted that good manners are much easier to train than aggression is to treat.

Calm in the face of chaos: Calm, benevolent leadership is paramount to an ordered pack. The more dogs in the household, the more clear the rules and leadership must be.

Well-trained, well-exercised, and well-managed dogs are calm dogs that make for a peaceful pack.

Exercise: Excess energy can cause tension. Tension can lead to aggression. Providing adequate breed- and age-appropriate exercise and mental stimulation is a must for a quieter, more harmonious pack.

Health: A healthy pack tends to be a more peaceful pack. Medical conditions that cause pain or discomfort produce stress, which can sometimes lead to aggression. Extra management will be needed for fragile members of the pack. Any pack member whose physical abilities are compromised by infirmity or age will need extra supervision and separation when necessary.

6
Get Along Little Doggies
Socialization

I consider social skills a bit like learning a language. I've been practicing it for so long over so many years I've almost lost my accent.

–Daniel Tammet

Does the mention of canine socialization evoke visions of Canine Cotillions where doggie debutantes are presented to society? Perchance, the notion elicits visions of poker-playing dogs wagering for liver snacks. What does it all mean? Do we set up doggie play dates or enroll our dogs in canine charm school? And, what does one wear to the Canine Cotillion anyway?

We've all observed, perhaps with a bit of jealousy, dogs that seem to have a certain, perfect social veneer. My dogs are not those dogs.

Both of my dogs are rescues. One has been rehabilitated from severe fear aggression toward people; the other has a history of aggression toward other dogs. In each, a bit of a dark side remains, but for the most part, they now live mostly on the dork side.

Socializing and re-socializing is essential to integrate dogs into their own social structure as well as the human one. New social experiences must be pleasant and not overwhelming. For example, taking a shy dog or new puppy to the dog park is akin to forcing your wallflower friend to attend a frat house kegger! Left to his own devices, a dog with a propensity for roughhousing will not enjoy the accolades of Mutt of the Month at doggie daycare. We must provide dogs a little guidance in proper social conduct. It's not just a matter of sink or swim, or throwing them in to learn the ropes.

Because their behavior has been modified through careful training, my dogs are socially acceptable. However, they are not the dogs they might have been had proper socialization been provided early on before they came to me. They remain somewhat unvarnished and will probably never be canine charm school valedictorians.

Socialization is Vital

Behavioral problems are the main reason dogs are relinquished to shelters thus, the number one cause of death for dogs less than three years of age. Adequate and appropriate socialization can prevent many behavioral issues therefore; socialization is life saving as well as life enhancing.

In the past, standard advice was to keep puppies at home until they had completed their full series of vaccinations, which is at 16 weeks of age. The late Dr. R.K. Anderson, DVM, Diplomat, American College of Veterinary Preventive Medicine and Diplomat of American College of Veterinary Behaviorists stated: *"The risk of a dog dying because of infection with distemper or parvo disease is far less than the much higher risk of a dog dying (euthanasia) because of behavior problems."*

The American Veterinary Society of Animal Behavior's statement on puppy socialization affirms: *The primary and most important time for puppy socialization is the first three months of life. During this time puppies should be exposed to as many new people, animals, stimuli and environments as can be achieved safely and without causing over- stimulation manifested as excessive fear, withdrawal or avoidance behavior. For this reason, the American Veterinary Society of Animal Behavior believes that it should be the standard of care for puppies to receive such socialization before they are fully vaccinated.*

The dictionary defines socialization as: to teach (someone) to behave in a way that is acceptable in society; to take part in social activities; make (someone) behave in a way that is acceptable to their society. Uniquely, our job with dogs involves socializing them in two worlds. We must teach them not only to behave in a way that is acceptable within their social order, but in ours as well.

Socialization makes for a mutually contented existence with dogs. We are happier living with them and they are happier living in the human world. Most dog professionals will tell you that lack of socialization is the primary reason dogs become fearful, particularly of strangers, novel environments, and unfamiliar dogs.

Socialization is an active process, not a passive one. Because it has a permanent emotional and cognitive effect, it must be a positive and well-planned experience. Indiscriminate attempts at socialization could be detrimental to the cause. Successful socialization includes controlled introduction to various situations, novel things, and activities in a manner that builds confidence and trust. It should be accomplished gradually and positively, never forced, allowing the dog to investigate new situations and things voluntarily.

Every Dog Must Be Socialized

Deficient early socialization puts dogs at risk for developing behavioral issues such as fearfulness. These entrenched behavioral disabilities are extremely difficult to deal with later in adolescence and adulthood. A puppy learns as much in his first 16 weeks as he does in a lifetime, so ideally, socialization begins early–before we acquire the pup. This makes for a more stable and resilient dog.

Reputable and responsible breeders understand the importance of early socialization and begin its implementation before the puppy goes to his new home. Puppies that are not exposed to mild environmental stressors early on can be emotionally reactive and lacking in social skills when they reach adulthood.

The optimum critical window for socialization closes by three months of age–the crucial developmental stage when puppies learn to accept people and other dogs. Furthermore, to ensure a puppy remains well socialized, he needs to continue meeting unfamiliar people and dogs, to be exposed to new environments and situations throughout his lifetime.

Can You Teach An Old Dog New Tricks?

Because we adopt dogs at various ages with diverse, often unknown backgrounds, we miss the chance for early socialization. Although the optimum age for socialization may have passed, it doesn't mean there is no hope for older dogs. Behavior issues for the unsocialized or under-socialized dog can still be positively impacted. However, these dogs will have more unlearning to do, which will require a higher level of dedication to their training. Furthermore, we may need to adjust expectations with the older dog, as socialization is limited and behavior modification may be necessary. Dogs that missed the window of opportunity may not reach their full potential, as he would have if adequate socialization had happened early on.

Does Size Matter?

In a word, no. All dogs, regardless of age and size, should be socialized. Often a small dog's anti-social behavior is overlooked or viewed as cute! Even biting is sometimes laughed off because no serious danger is perceived. Any act unacceptable in a 100-lb. dog should be unacceptable in a 10-lb. dog.

Some small dogs are under socialized in the name of protecting them. Owners are afraid their small dog will be pulverized in a playgroup of mixed sized dogs. A well-run playgroup minimizes the danger and most dog parks have a separate area for small or low-energy dogs. We don't want to throw Fifi, the teacup poodle to the dogs, but the bottom line is that there are all sorts of dogs in the real world and it's best if small dogs can cope. Careful and intentional socialization can give Fifi those coping skills.

Making Up for Lost Time

Lack of early socialization can be offset with training and behavior modification to varying degrees of success, depending on the level of the maladaptive behaviors presented. Treatment can include habituation, counter conditioning, and desensitization.

Adolescent or adult dogs with mild fear issues may respond to habituation. Habituation is defined as: decrease in responsiveness; the diminishing of a physiological or emotional response to a frequently repeated stimulus. Habituation is used in socialization by repeatedly exposing the dog to stimuli and novel experiences until they become commonplace—until he is comfortable, and not frightened by them.

Desensitization is defined as: to make somebody less responsive to an overwhelming fear by repeated exposure to the feared situation or object, either in natural or artificial circumstances.

Desensitization and habituation are very similar in definition. The difference lies in their use. Both are used to modify reflexive behaviors (those involving basic biological functions or instincts.) Habituation is a preventative measure, whereas desensitization is used to modify preexisting behavioral issues. Desensitization is used in modifying behaviors such as those associated with fear, over stimulation, and aggression.

The How-To of Socialization

Successful socialization is proactive, not reactive. Whether working with a puppy, adolescent, or adult dog, it's hands-on and happy. The following exercises are a few things to do which will set your dog of on the right paw. Couple them with pleasant things such as food, praise, and/or toys for to help the dog to make a positive association with the event. For example, gently handle the dog's ears, as you give him a treat. As he voluntarily explores a novel item, praise and encourage him. After he allows you go take hold of his collar, play with his favorite toy. Think up new and interesting exercises of your own. Get creative, but be safe.

Gentle Handling

Gently handle your dog's head, ears, mouth, tail, paws, and belly
Lightly groom him with a soft brush.
Take hold of the collar
Gentle restraint

Objects To Play With Other Than Toys (supervised)

Cardboard box
Bucket
Empty plastic bottle

Smells

Kitchen/household
Cats
Baby
Other dogs
Veterinarian's office
Groom shop
Boarding kennel

Sounds (played from audio file)

Thunder
Fireworks
Sirens
Doorbell
Baby crying
Loud conversation
Children playing

Types of people seen
Male and female
Infants and toddlers
Young adults
Middle-aged and elderly adults
People in wheelchairs, with canes and walkers
Loud, confident people and shy, timid ones
People wearing hats, helmets and glasses, big coats
Men with beards/facial hair
People in uniform
People of various races

Surfaces
Clean grass
Linoleum, tile, cement, and wood floors
Carpet
Slippery surfaces
Gravel and dirt
Open stairways
Enclosed stairways
Open back and closed back stairs

Experiences
Watching passing traffic
Car ride
Walk in the park
Watch bicycles, motorbikes, and buses pass by
See skateboards, roller blades and scooters pass by
Countryside
Crowds
A just-for-fun visit to the vet's office

Playing With Toys and People
Ball
Tug toys
Squeaky toys
Frisbee
Food-stuffed toys
Puzzle toys

Way to Go
Field trips are great opportunities for socialization. Following are some ideas on where to go to socialize your dog. For a positive, first-time experience, visit at times when the destinations are not busy. Chaos can easily over stimulate or frighten dogs.

Pet Supply Store
Leashed dogs are welcome at most pet stores. Here dogs will see a variety of people, shopping carts and maybe even forklifts. Dogs are exposed to a multitude of sounds, scents, and other pets.

Parks
It's a walk in the park! Dogs experience an assortment of people and activities at the park. He will see people on bicycles and roller blades. He'll see them pushing strollers, playing games, and walking their dogs. Here, dogs may see an abundance of waterfowl, wildlife and those great tormentors of dogs…squirrels.

Doggie Daycare
Most dogs love the company of other dogs. What better place to meet them than at doggie daycare? If the dog is a candidate for daycare, he can meet all types and personalities of dogs there. If you are not sure daycare is right for your dog, find a reputable facility and set up a trial day.

Dog Park
Dog parks can be a wonderful experience for dogs, but not all. Just because we have dog parks, does not mean we are obligated to take our dogs there. To determine whether your dog is a candidate for the dog park and training dog park manners, see the section on dog park etiquette in *Mannerly Mutts in the Real World, Beyond the Basics*.

Playgroups
Check with your dog care service providers, community newsletters, the Internet, or your local homeowners' association. See if anyone is offering a regularly scheduled playgroup, or put one together yourself. A well-run playgroup is organized and safe, not simply a free-for-all. Learn dog body language so that you know whether all participants are having fun–that no one is a bully, being bullied, or frightened. See the chapter *Conversations with Dogs*.

A Visit To The Vet

Schedule a just-for-fun visit to your vet's office. Your dog can meet the staff and experience all the sounds, sights, and smells without the stress of the not-so-fun stuff.

A Visit To The Groomer

Schedule a casual visit to your groom shop. It is a strictly a friendly visit. No nail trimmers, tubs, clippers, or blow dryers on the first visit–just a fun, get-to-know-each-other experience.

Handling

It is important for dogs and puppies to learn gentle restraint so that they can cope with vet visits, grooming, and hugging. In general, dogs do not particularly like direct eye contact or hugging. These things are going to happen living in the human world, therefore dogs must be prepared to handle being handled. It's not fair to ask a social animal to exist in a world where he will be touched, handled, examined, and groomed without teaching him to accept these eventualities. Furthermore, we want to teach dogs not to merely tolerate, but to enjoy handling. We can teach dogs that direct eye contact isn't always a threat. To teach puppies and dogs to make direct eye contact, see *Watch* in *The How-To of Training.*

Teach Puppies About Hugging, Relaxation, and Restraint

If puppies are handled frequently early in life by the breeder, they should be completely relaxed when picked up. If they did not have the benefit of early handling, we still have the opportunity to teach them to enjoy it. But, do not wait! Teaching an adolescent dog to accept gentle restraint and handling is much more challenging than teaching it to a puppy.

Puppies must learn to relax during handling. They need to learn about hugging and restraint first from familiar people in order to cope with the experiences from new people.

Dominance based training methods recommend putting the puppy on his back and waiting for him to submit in a show of dominance. Gentle restraint and forcing a dog into submission are two different things. Manhandling and forcible restraint engenders distrust and resistance from your dog and it's not an enjoyable experience for either of you.

To teach puppies to relax while being handled, start with the puppy in your lap, stroking him gently on the back and head. Massage his chest and/or the base of the ears. Massaging motions should be slow and rhythmic using gentle pressure and a soothing voice. Once he settles down, put the pup gently on his back and proceed to rub his belly. As the puppy continues to relax, pick him up and gently hug him. Gradually increase the length of the hugs. Everyone in the family should practice this exercise so that the puppy is comfortable with relaxing and being handled by all family members.

If the puppy struggles excessively or has a fit of temper, do not let go or he will not learn to calm down. Instead, he will learn that throwing a fit gets him what he wants–his freedom. This is not going to work at the vet's office or with the groomer.

To teach your puppy to accept gentle restraint, place him in your lap. Hold the puppy firmly, but gently so that he's sitting with his back against your abdomen and legs pointing away from you. Massage his chest with one hand and the ears with the other. The puppy will eventually calm down. When he does, wait for a few seconds and then casually release him. Repeat the procedure and your puppy will learn that struggling does not get him what he wants, but that calm behavior does.

Once the pup learns to calm himself, alternate short play sessions with calming sessions. See how quickly you can have the puppy relaxing after his play period. You will also want to practice the exercise with the dog on the floor instead of your lap, especially for medium or large breeds. No one wants to calm a 90-lb. German shepherd on his or her lap!

If these calming exercises are not working, you will want the assistance of a reputable trainer. No one wants to live with a dog that cannot be handled, because a dog that can't be handled is no fun to live with.

Handling for Examination and Grooming

Teaching an 8-week-old puppy to be handled is much easier than teaching an adult dog. Even if the dog was taught as a puppy to accept handling, he may become less tolerant if handling does not continue. If he never has his teeth or bum examined, he'll lose his tolerance for it. This is of paramount importance, so that your dog, the veterinary staff, the groomer, and you will be safe for exams, bathing, and coifing.

Dogs must be able to accept having their tails, mouths, ears, and feet (front and back) handled. They must allow people to taking hold of their collar. Such handling must be done regularly during happy times. If the ears are handled only when the dog has an ear infection, he will learn to associate ear handling with pain.

Desensitizing a puppy to being handled is quite simple and pleasant for both of you. It's also a bonding experience. Using your puppy's daily allotment of kibble is a good way to do this exercise, so that you don't fill his belly with treats and add extra calories.

- Take hold of the puppy's collar. Give him a treat (piece of kibble.)

- Look into the puppy's eyes. Give him a treat.

- Open the puppy's mouth. Give him a treat.

- Look into the puppy's ears. Give him a treat.

- Look into the puppy's other ear. Give him a treat.

- Take the puppy's paw. Give him a treat. Repeat with each paw.

- Handle the puppy's tail, backside, and private areas. Give him a treat.

- Repeat all of the steps above.

- Gradually and progressively, handle each area longer and more thoroughly.

- Have every member of the family practice the exercise.

Teaching Adolescent or Adult Dogs about Hugging, Relaxation, and Restraint

The above exercises are for puppies. Teaching puppies to be handled is easier than with the adolescent or adult dog. The dog may never be as accepting of handling as if he had learned it as a pup, but we can at least help him to feel more comfortable about it.

Do the exercises as described above for small dogs. Obviously, you will not be restraining and teaching an adult Great Dane to relax in your lap. For dogs that are not lap dogs, gently restrain them by placing one arm over the dog's back at the shoulders and the other across his chest. Do not restrain him by the collar as this may make him feel too vulnerable.

Gently massage the chest and ears while the dog is standing or lying down. Be sure the dog is comfortable with having your arm over his back. If he is not, desensitize him by placing your hand on the side of his shoulder and reward him with a treat for accepting your touch. Gradually and progressively, work to placing your hand on his back at the shoulders, then placing your arm over the shoulders. Be sure that the dog is completely comfortable before moving to the next step.

NOTE: If your dog is showing any aggression when handled or restrained, seek the help of a reputable trainer or behaviorist.

Adolescent Socialization: Beyond Puppy Kindergarten

We know the importance of socializing puppies before the age of 5 months. But, we don't want to stop there. It's important to continue a dog's education and social experience beyond puppy kindergarten and throughout his life.

We frequently see aggressive behavior "crop up" between the ages of 9 months and 2 years as dogs reach their social maturity. Aggression may seem to appear suddenly, without notice, but the behavior rarely comes without caveat. Warning signs may be so subtle that they go unnoticed.

Too often aggressive or fearful behavior is dismissed during puppyhood as cute or harmless. Frequently owners believe the dog will outgrow it or that the undesirable behavior will work itself out. When neither happens, the behavior becomes a major issue with the onset of adolescence. Add in the fact that adolescence is the time when some dogs become more territorial or protective, and you have a recipe for trouble.

We know that socialization means more than simply introducing dogs to other dogs and new people. It means to introduce them to new experiences as well. A puppy that has never been exposed to stairs, the sounds of traffic or the sight of children playing may become fearful of these events. This is also true of the adolescent dog whose socialization ceased at puppyhood.

Often, we avoid the problem instead of finding a solution. Take for instance, a dog that has become aggressive when unfamiliar people approach the front door. He will likely become more aggressive and frustrated if always dragged away and isolated when people arrive. Likewise, under socialized dogs can become aggravated when greeting other dogs if guidance in proper canine introductions is not provided.

It's even more important that socialization be done gently and systematically if the dog is showing signs of aggression or fear. Left alone, aggression and fearfulness do not usually improve. In fact, the behaviors typically escalate. The more dogs have the opportunity to rehearse a behavior, the more difficult it becomes for us to change it. Seek the help of a reputable trainer or behaviorist for dogs showing aggression or those that are overly fearful.

Prevent Developmental De-socialization

Adolescence is a particularly stressful time for young dogs, especially males, who may be repeatedly harassed by older dogs. The ritualized harassment is both normal and necessary, allowing older dogs to put developing youngsters "in their place" before they are strong enough to compete on the social scene. Harassment is triggered by rude adolescent behavior and by extremely elevated testosterone levels in five to eighteen-month-old male adolescents.

Additionally, adolescent dogs require many positive social interactions to maintain self-confidence and offset the stress of adult-doggy discipline. Regular play sessions and repeated friendly encounters are vital. For many dogs, socialization with other dogs is abruptly curtailed at between six to eight months, usually following the first couple of scraps. This is true for small dogs and large dogs. Worrying that a little dog may get hurt, the owner is more likely to pick him up and less likely to let him play. Similarly, worries about the large dog hurting others, will have owners keeping him restrained on a tight leash. Thus, at a crucial developmental stage, many dogs are seldom allowed to interact with unfamiliar dogs. A vicious circle develops—the dog de-socializes and his bite inhibition may begin to drift, whereupon fights and potential damage become more likely. It's now even more difficult to socialize the dog.

To prevent puppies from becoming asocial or antisocial during adolescence, he must continue to meet unfamiliar dogs on a regular basis. We should never take friendly behavior for granted. Throughout adolescence and adulthood, we will continue to praise and reward our dogs after every friendly encounter with another dog. See *Meeting and Greeting People* and *Proper Dog-to-Dog-On-Leash Greetings* in the chapter *The How-To of Training*.

Dogs and humans are naturally social. Just as we humans need a bit of guidance to negotiate society graciously, so do our canine friends that must learn the etiquette of *both* worlds.

7

Conversations With Dogs
Understanding Dog Body Language

Raise your words, not your voice. It is rain that grows flowers, not thunder. –Rumi

I'm one of those women who forgot to have children. My friends who did remember, tell me how their offspring have turned them into people who closely resemble their own parents. They are aghast as they find themselves echoing familiar parental adages from their youth. These are the very phrases they swore they'd never discourse to their own brood.

My friends point out the similarities of raising children with the experience of raising "kids" of the canine persuasion. We parallel our own upbringing with a propensity for barking unachievable orders. We embark on psychiatrically disordered tangents. All this, knowing full well that heaping on guilt and lecturing do not work with dogs.

Voices of reason do not always rise to the top. Yet, I carry on with, "This is why we can't have nice things! You're going to fool around and fool around 'til somebody gets hurt! Fight nice!" and "It's all fun and games until somebody pokes an eye out or ends up in a cone!" When a session of living room agility breaks out, I threaten, "Don't make me come in there!" And, for vehicular roughhousing, the word is, "Don't make me stop this car!"

I must resist the urge to bark out, "Don't give me that look!" or, "No back talk!" followed by the eternal parental rhetorical question, "How many times do I have to tell you?" Here's where my dogs should be glad they can't talk. If they could, they would learn early on, as I did; never ever answer a rhetorical question. Never.

I'm accomplished at stating the obvious, with lines like "You guys live like animals" and asking silly questions like, "Were you born in a barn?" Since most of my dogs are of undisclosed backgrounds, the latter question might truthfully be answered, "Yes!"

This is all about me talking to my dogs. I'm fully aware that my diatribes are futile. And, I speak dog quite well, albeit with a pronounced accent. Sometimes I wish that my dogs could talk. Then with return of reason, I realize that I'm glad that they don't. However, I am quite aware that dogs do, in fact, speak and it is they who are often the voices of reason.

It is quite possible that an animal has spoken to me and that I didn't catch the remark because I wasn't paying attention.

–E.B. White, *Charlotte's Web*

Canine Communication

Social animals like humans and dogs have highly evolved ways of communicating. There is a wide array of varying components to canine body language. Dogs use facial expressions, tail carriage, vocalization, and overall demeanor to communicate with each other and with us. It is helpful to break these signals down into individual components, in order to understand the often-subtle language. We will have a look at the individual signals as well as the big picture, because dogs use these signs in concert and in context.

Dogs primarily use communication to signal intent. This is by and large through body language, with vocalization being only a small part of their communication.

These signals may appear random to us. They are not. They serve to relay the dog's internal state or they are a purposeful attempt to tell us something. Many of these signals are used to negotiate disputes, navigate potentially conflictive situations and to avoid conflict altogether.

Canine body language is a window into the minds and feelings of dogs. In understanding the language, we'll build a stronger relationship because our dogs feel understood. Understanding builds trust.

Tongue Flick

This signal can be very subtle and quick. Sometimes the tongue is barely visible outside the mouth and other times it is extended to lick the nose. Black dogs and dogs with hairy or less expressive faces tend to use this signal more often.

Dogs may lick their lips after eating, but in the absence of food, dogs use licking the lips to signal intention. He could be saying that he means no harm as he approaches.

It may be used to tell us or another dog that he is feeling nervous and wants us to calm down.

When it is a displaced behavior (i.e. in the absence of food) tongue flicks indicate that the dog is experiencing anxiety. The behavior may be seen in dogs that are nervous when visiting the vet's office or the groomer.

Sniffing the Ground

Sniffing the ground can be a quick, sweeping, downward motion or a prolonged activity lasting until the situation is resolved. Dogs use this signal often when in groups.

Dogs are programmed to use their noses and it is enjoyable to them, so often sniffing means they are merely gathering information from the environment. Additionally dogs use sniffing the ground as a calming or intention signal in order to calm other dogs or humans.

The cause for sniffing depends on the situation. For instance if a dog suddenly stops playing with another dog and then suddenly ignores him and sniffs the ground, he may be telling the other dog to calm down.

Turning Away or Turning the Head

Turning away is a universal signal among dogs. They will turn their heads or whole body away from a perceived threat. The intensity of this signal can range from holding the head to the side for a long time, a quick turn of the head and back, or simply averting the eyes.

Some examples of when dogs use the turning away signal are; other dogs or people approach too quickly or head on, someone seems angry, or the dog is taken by surprise. The use of this signal is a wonderful way for dogs to avert conflict.

Play Bow

This signal is used as an invitation to another dog to play and as an intention signal. If the play bow is bouncy with the dog moving his front feet from side to side, it is most likely an invitation to play.

Most often, the head of the dog doing a play bow is lower than the head of the dog being invited to play.

Sometimes the play bow is intended to calm another dog. A dog that is fearful of another dog may demonstrate this, as the play bow would serve to diffuse a tense situation.

A play bow can be an active display of inefficient motion or it can be still and prolonged. If the dog is standing still, the play bow may be intended to calm the other dog.

Walking Slowly or Freezing

Chaos and speed can cause anxiety for many dogs. A dog that feels insecure will move slowly and deliberately, often freezing when approached too quickly or feeling threatened.

Often dogs will use these two signals together. They might walk slowly, freeze, and then walk slowly again.

A dog will use walking slowly or freezing as a calming signal with other dogs as well as with us. If your dog always walks slowly when you call him, check the sound of your voice. He may be feeling threatened if your voice sounds angry. He may also use this calming signal if he thinks he'll be punished or asked to do something he doesn't want to do when he comes to you.

Walking in a Curve

Dogs naturally do not approach each other head on. In a friendly meeting, the body is loose. They walk in a curve, do not make direct eye contact, and then proceed to sniff each other's behind.

We never want to force dogs to meet each other head on, especially when they are on leash. This can cause great anxiety, which could lead to a confrontation. Allow the dogs to curve toward each other at their own discretion. The more anxious a dog is, the wider circle he should be given.

Dogs have better peripheral vision than we do, so they are well aware of another dog that is not approaching straight on.

Butt sniff

A butt sniff is what we call a doggie handshake. Sniffing is how dogs get information about each other. Done politely, it does not invade the other dog's personal space by keeping the nose at a respectful distance and the sniffing is kept brief.

Pass by

A polite pass by is not a head-on encounter. The dog does not block the oncoming dog or display an aggressive posture (leaning forward, stiff, and/or on tiptoe.) A civil pass by does not invade the space of the oncoming dog, as it gives him a wide enough berth. Appeasement signals are given such as paw lifts and the dogs show a neutral, relaxed posture. Dogs passing by are alert, yet calm.

Humans on the other end of the leash can compromise pass bys. If we get nervous, we communicate our anxiety directly through the leash. A tight leash can also cause frustration.

If we allow our dog to strain on the leash, he presents a more aggressive posture to the approaching dog (leaning forward). In a perfect world, all dogs would meet off leash because they naturally do it better than we do. Keep leashes loose for successful pass bys.

Sitting or Lying Down

Dogs may try to calm humans or other dogs by sitting when approached. An even stronger signal is the dog sitting with his back to us when we advance too quickly or sound angry.

Additionally, a dog may lie down and turn his head away from the perceived threat. Humans tend to anthropomorphize this behavior and interpret it to mean the dog is ignoring us when actually he is trying to calm us.

Splitting

When a dog feels tension between other dogs or dogs and humans, he may physically place himself between them. This separates them, which helps to avoid escalating tension or conflict. We may see dogs use this when two people hug or when children roughhouse.

Herding dogs tend to use this signal a great deal, but it is seen in other breeds as well.

Chin Over

Dogs will often put their chin over another dog's shoulders or back as a signal of intent. It is frequently a status-seeking behavior to determine who is the higher-ranking dog, but it is sometimes seen during play.

Paw lift

A paw lift can mean curiosity, uncertainty, insecurity, submission, stalking, or anticipation (i.e. waiting for the ball to be thrown.)

The paw lift is a signal often used in conjunction with freezing when it is used to display caution. Frequently dogs use this when meeting for the first time to indicate that they pose no threat to the unfamiliar dog. Dogs may use their paws as a signal of appeasement or deference in greeting. The paws can be used to threaten another if he pins them using straight, stiff front legs.

Paw Over

As with a chin-over, dogs will often put their paw over another dog's back or shoulders as a signal of intent. This signal can be a status-seeking behavior to determine rank and is sometimes seen during play.

There is no one as deaf as he who will not listen. **–Yiddish Proverb**

Facial Expressions

The face is an honest expression of feelings in both humans and dogs. Human words can be false, but faces don't lie, and neither do dogs. A dog's facial expressions combine ears, eyes, eyebrows, and mouth. Wolf and dog facial expressions are identical but the differences in features among breeds can make a dog's facial expressions more difficult to read.

Eyes and Eyebrows

Expression of the eyebrows underlines what the dog's eyes are saying. A dog displaying a dominant posture will have a well-defined brow. A furrowed brow can be a sign of stress.

Eyes

Dogs' eyes vary in shape and size with some being very round while others are more almond-shaped. Within the limits of these shapes, all dogs can widen or narrow their eyes and change the intensity of their gaze. Eyes that are wide, showing the whites or the sclera (often called whale eye) and dilated pupils indicate that the dog is stressed.

The muscles around a calm, happy dog's eyes are relaxed and the face has an open, full appearance. A hard, fixated stare signals a threat, which is most often used toward other dogs. However, many dogs learn that looking directly at people can be okay, even pleasant. This is done with a relaxed, friendly expression. Conversely, an intense, hard stare and a rigid facial expression is a threat.

An unhappy dog will have a furrowed brow. The inside corners of the eyebrows are pulled together and downward. A furrowed brow on a worried dog will have the inside corners of the eyebrows raised.

A forward commissure (the corners of the mouth) with inside corners of the eyebrows pulled together and downward indicates a dog that is on the offensive and angry, as when guarding a resource. If the dog is simply on the offensive, as in barking at an intruder, the eyebrows will be relaxed.

Staring

Staring is used to show dominance and to show threat. The stare is very focused, intense, and the body is stiff.

Blinking

Blinking can be an appeasement behavior used to show submission. Dogs will use blinking with humans if he's feeling stressed, confused, or when being scolded.

The Ears

The vast diversity in ear types among dog breeds makes reading them a challenge. The size and shape dictate how effective their use in communication is. Add in ear cropping and the language of the ears becomes even more difficult to decipher.

No matter what the ear type, a relaxed dog holds his ears relaxed and natural. On alert, the dog will hold the ears higher and directs them toward the point of interest. A dog in an aggressive display will hold the ears forward. Friendliness displays a relaxed, slightly laid back ear carriage. Flattened ears are a signal of fear or submission.

The Mouth

A dog's mouth speaks volumes, but with more than sound. The position of the lips and the commissure (the corners of the mouth) are important cues to watch.

A dog that is relaxed will often have his mouth closed and relaxed or slightly open, tongue lolling out, and panting. The lower jaw is relaxed and there are no ridges around the lips.

A short commissure, which exposes the teeth and displays a wrinkled nose, is an agonistic pucker, which is a warning signal. It is often accompanied with a growl, furrowed brow, and flattened ears. However, the agonistic pucker can have other meanings, depending on the context. It may also be used as a defensive, territorial, or submissive/aggressive display. It can be used when a dog is feeling uncertain, warning another dog to go away or calm down or when guarding a resource.

A display of submission usually displays a closed mouth and the lips may be slightly pulled back. He might display tongue flicks. Occasionally, dogs display a submissive grin, which, as the name indicates, shows submission. The lips are vertically retracted showing the front teeth–the canines and incisors. Laid-back ears, squinty eyes, and a generally submissive body posture often accompany the grin. Submissive grins are easily mistaken for aggression because the teeth are bared.

A dog with intent to aggress will also retract the lips vertically to expose the teeth. The nose will be wrinkled.

Commissure showing the lips drawn back horizontally showing both the front and back teeth is often indicative of fear. A dog about to bite will open the mouth pulling the lips up and back with the teeth exposed.

The Tongue

The tongue of a dog panting because he is under duress is held tighter and flatter at the end (even curled upward) than a dog that is panting because he's happy or merely hot. The stressed tongue is often called a spatulate tongue and is held, not simply left to fall out of the mouth as in the relaxed dog.

Licking

Biologically, mother dogs communicate with their puppies by licking them. Licking stimulates her pups to start breathing and it's how she cleans them. In the wild, puppies will lick adult dogs' mouths to encourage them to regurgitate food after the hunt. Licking is essential to survival.

Licking in adult dogs is most often used to show friendly submission. They use it with us and with other dogs. In the wild, subordinate pack members may lick the more dominant members, which is important in maintaining pack harmony. In domestic dogs, it is most often a sign of affection.

Many dogs lick themselves (often their paws or legs) to relieve stress. Sometimes they will lick objects or the floor. Licking has a calming effect because it releases endorphins thus, relieving stress. Chronic licking can mean the dog is bored or anxious. It can also be indicative of skin problems such as allergies or that the dog is in pain.

Drooling

Profuse drooling in the absence of food is an indication that the dog is stressed. A dog may not appear to be stressed, showing few other signs, but if he is drooling excessively, he's anxious.

The Tail

Reading tails is difficult in that the natural carriage differs greatly between breeds. Greyhounds are one of a few breeds whose tail set is naturally down, tucked slightly between the hind legs. The saber tail of a German shepherd is much easier to read than the corkscrew tail of a pug. The sickle tail of a husky or the flagpole tail of a beagle is easier to interpret than the docked tail of a Rottweiler or the bobtail of a Welsh corgi. But, none are as easy to read as the tail carried most like that of the wolf.

The idea that a wagging tail is that of a happy, friendly dog is a dangerous conviction. Dogs wag their tails for a multitude of reasons, which include happiness, and alertness. Surprisingly to some, a wagging tail can be that of an aggressive dog. His tail can be wagging while barking and lunging at a perceived threat.

A dog feeling affable and relaxed will hold his tail in its natural position. A happy dog will wag the tail gently. A very happy dog will wag exuberantly, even doing a whole-body wag with lots of curves to the body's motion. Happy tails can even wag in a circular motion.

Nervous dogs will tuck the tail between the legs and can include a wag, but the wag is often more rapid than when the dog is relaxed. If the dog is extremely nervous, the tail may be tucked so high as to touch the belly. A rapid vibration at the tip of the tail held perpendicularly is a signal that the dog is anxious and stressed.

A dog on alert will hold the tail high, rigid, and still. A tail held high and stiff with slow, intentional, back-and-forth movement signals a threat. The whole body is tense, the weight is on the front legs, and the feet are positioned squarely--ready for fight or flight. Slow, large amplitude, catlike tail swishing is warning signal.

The Hair

Increased sudden shedding, and or excessive dander are a reflexive stress signals. Of course, these signals are not intentional or consciously controlled.

The hair is used in communication by raising it at the withers (the base of the neck above the shoulders) or it is sometimes raised in a ridge all along the spine. Some dogs raise the hair only at the base of the neck and the root of the tail. Raising the hair is called "piloerection" or more commonly termed "raising the hackles." Often, we interpret this action as an aggressive gesture, which it can be. However, dogs may raise their hackles anytime they are in a state of arousal. Raised hackles can mean that a dog is fearful, anxious, angry, unsure, surprised, or very excited about something; the human equivalent is goose bumps.

Stretching

Dogs often stretch as a greeting. Dogs do greeting stretches only with people and dogs they like and are comfortable with. It is similar to a play bow, but more relaxed and protracted. It is not an invitation to play followed by pouncing or an incitement to be chased. Some dogs will do a forward stretch, where they stretch their back legs out behind them. Some dogs will do the two stretches in sequence; first the front stretch (like the play bow) then the rear stretch (legs stretched out behind.)

Posture

Having looked at individual body parts to tell what a dog is feeling and saying, let's have a look at the bigger picture. This is the carriage of the entire body where the individual signals come together into one scene.

Neutral

A neutral body posture shows relaxed muscles with the weight evenly distributed on all four feet. The head and tail carriage are in their normal, relaxed position.

Anxious

A frightened dog will be hunched, as though attempting to look smaller. The head will likely be lowered, and he will possibly cower on the ground. The tail may be tucked slightly or held up tight to the belly.

Cautious

A cautious dog may hold his body low, approaching tentatively. His weight may be on his back legs in order to make a hasty retreat if deemed necessary.

Submissive

A submissive dog will lower his body or cower on the ground. He will display a cautious body posture on approach.

Alert or Aroused

A dog on alert will hold his head and tail high to appear larger. The muscles are tensed, ready for action. He's standing squarely on all four feet, usually with the weight centered more on the front feet, ready to move forward.

Aggressive

The aggressive dog looks similar to the alert or aroused dog, but will be showing other signs of aggressive intent, such as bared teeth, wrinkled nose, and growling.

Vocal Communication

Barking

Dogs bark as an alert to perceived dangers and warn of intruders. Dogs bark to get our attention and dogs bark when they're bored. During conflict, a more varied tone of the bark indicates submissiveness. A bark that invites play will be higher pitched and repetitive.

Howling

Dogs inherently howl as their wolf-like ancestors did. It's in their genes. Wolves howl to give information about territorial boundaries and to bond with pack members. Howling is the wolf's version of GPS, used to locate and communicate with individuals. Howling is more effective for long distance communication because it is sustained and protracted. The loud, sustained sound can travel for several miles.

Dogs howl because they're lonely. They do not howl to announce their territory and seldom howl to strengthen the pack bond. Howling is contagious among dogs. If they are howling to communicate, then the more howlers, the more volume, therefore the sound carries farther.

Human prompting and sirens can trigger canine howling episodes. This is possibly due to the fact that sirens sound like howling and some dogs will naturally mimic the sound in response.

Whining

Whining is typically associated with submission, fear, insecurity, and loneliness. It can also convey distress of pain and anguish and anxiety due to stress. Yet, some dogs will whine when they are excited, such as during greetings.

Whining may be used as an appeasement behavior when interacting with people and other dogs. In this context, other submissive body language may be displayed such as cowering, tucked tail, lowered head, and averted eyes.

Some dogs whine for attention from their owners or to solicit rewards, food, or other desired objects.

Snarling

Snarling is a signal of aggression. The lips are drawn back to expose the teeth and is often accompanied by a deep, guttural growl. A snarl with a forward commissure is an offensive or dominant signal. A snarl with a retracted commissure is a defensive or submissive signal.

Other Behavioral Communication

Marking

Urination and defecation are used to mark territory or objects by leaving one's scent on it. Marking communicates to other dogs that the territory is inhabited. In the wild, this is necessary because of competition for resources and mates. Many dogs mark visually by scratching the ground, often after urinating or defecating. Dominant and more confident dogs exhibit marking behavior more frequently.

Licking

Licking has its roots in the neonatal behavior of suckling. It can be re-oriented into a pacifying behavior of a submissive dog toward other dogs. Licking can be a self-pacifying and calming behavior.

Body Contact

A gentle bump with the muzzle to another dog or to the human hand or leg is a friendly gesture showing acceptance. It is an appeasement behavior, which also shows submission.

A soft push with the hip also indicates friendliness. It's often used in greetings, demonstrating trust and friendliness where the dog intends no harm. Lying together with bodies touching can strengthen the bond between individual dogs and help them to feel secure. A dog may snuggle up to you for security or for the company, but it can also be a status seeking space invader move.

Muzzle Grab, Muzzle to Throat

A puppy's early education includes being grasped around the muzzle or head by his mother. The puppy learns submission from this behavior. It can be seen in play and social interactions between adult dogs. Muzzle grabs can be a display of dominance with the higher status dog doing it to the submissive or lower ranking dog. A nudge to the throat with the muzzle is a pacifying behavior of a submissive dog to a higher-ranking dog. It shows acceptance of the dominant dog's rank.

Pawing

Pawing is the act of a dog touching or striking another dog, someone, or something with his paw. A dog may also paw the air. This is a gesture made with the intent to pacify, as in a paw lift. It's often used when the dog is confused or frustrated.

Shake Off

A shake off communicates non-threatening intent. The gesture means the dog is literally shaking off tension, energy--adrenaline. A shake off moves the dog from a reflexive state to a cognitive one. This says to us and to other dogs that he is thinking, communicating, and is more predictable than he was in the reflexive state.

Displacement Behavior

Displaced behaviors are behaviors in which a dog engages when he needs comfort or to escape. They are indicative that the dog feels conflicted or stressed. They are normal, familiar behaviors done out of context, which help achieve a sense of security in uncomfortable situations. Displacement behaviors are used when a dog is suppressing what he really wants to do. Displacement behaviors are contextual, as dogs do them for other reasons. For example, a dog will scratch when he has an itch. However, if he suddenly begins scratching during a training session, it might be an indication that he's confused, frustrated, or feeling pressured.

Yawning

Dogs yawn when they are tired, of course. Additionally, it's an appeasement behavior often used by a dominant dog to show friendliness to a submissive dog and vice versa. Yawning can be a displaced behavior done when the dog is feeling nervous, confused, or frustrated.

Scratching

Dogs might use scratching as a displaced behavior to calm themselves when feeling confused or frightened. They may also use it as an appeasement signal when feeling threatened.

Rolling

Rolling is often simply done as self-massage. Rolling in something stinky can communicate a scent from its location to another dog. It's the canine equivalent of human texting or passing notes. However, rolling can be a displaced behavior used to shed stress. This is why a dog rolls immediately after a bath in which he was not a happy participant.

Ambiguous Behavior

As mentioned, dog body language, actions, and vocalizations can have an assortment of meanings. His actions do not necessarily mirror his intentions. Therefore, we must rely on the whole picture of the dog and the context wherein the behavior occurs.

For example, a dog that growls at another with the vocalization followed by a play bow, a relaxed mouth with lolling tongue, and a paw lift is an invitation to play. A growl during a game of tug is part of the game. Conversely, a growl with a stiff, forward posture, and a hard stare is a warning, which if unheeded could lead to a bite.

To muddy the waters further, dogs can feel conflicted and give mixed messages. We must then make our best guess as to what the dog is feeling, but simply knowing that he is feeling conflicted is a big step toward helping him through the uncomfortable situation.

Learning to communicate with canines builds strong, trusting relationships. It engenders patience and relieves frustration on both ends of the leash. It develops confidence.

8

Choosing a Dog

Be Careful What You Wish For

Years ago, reason having temporarily deserted me, I adopted a four-month-old Border Collie mix from the local shelter. I thought that being a dog trainer qualified me for the challenges of life with an energetic, wickedly smart Border Collie. Painfully, I recognized the error of my thinking.

I was amazed by Mr. MoJo's unbridled abandon in the deconstruction of upholstery. In his younger days, MoJo could reverse engineer a sofa in under seven minutes. Perhaps in a former life he was an interior designer. While other artists labor in oil or clay, MoJo's preferred medium was stuffing. He was a contemporary master! In addition to de-upholstering furniture, MoJo had a penchant for window treatments. He once effortlessly plucked the living room drapes from their rods and shredded them into minuscule lacey bits.

I lay the blame for MoJo's wake of destruction squarely on myself. I was working three jobs and somewhat unprepared for life with a rambunctious pup of the herding breed persuasion. Having barely enough time to devote to MoJo's proper rearing, we both paid a price. Ironically, he has redeemed himself and now stands as the established voice of reason in a multi-dog household.

Personally and against all good sense, I like big, fluffy, exceedingly goofy dogs. However, with each passing year, I recognize that I'm twelve months closer to having a little sweater dog. I envision my twilight years with an attitude of entitlement. I will live life blissfully with my diminutive dog, Cargo, named so because I carry him everywhere.

I'm thinking ahead here. While I currently prefer to live with big, fluffy, exceedingly goofy dogs, I have to be realistic. I must consider my future capabilities and lifestyle. It's only fair.

Each year that I complete another trip around the sun, another year older, I wish for only one thing: I wish that my dogs would help around the house more. I've concluded that I must either train my dogs to do yard work and automotive maintenance or move into an assisted living facility.

I suppose all "parents" lament and wish for do-overs on certain parenting decisions. I wouldn't expect to raise children without the occasional Crayola mural or random object flushed down the toilet. Neither do I expect to raise a puppy without the accidental puddle, drinking from the toilet, or chewed shoe…within reason, of course.

Think carefully about your lifestyle, breed temperament, and how many couches you're willing to replace before choosing your new dog. It's easy to let sentiment override logic in this emotionally dangerous decision-making territory. For instance, a woman once told me that she wanted a Jack Russell Terrier. She wanted one, because on her daily commute she drove by an outdoor advertisement depicting a cute Jack Russell terrier puppy with his nose buried in a dog food bag. Anyone who has spent time with a hyper-drive Jack Russell Terrier understands why this is so amusing. The rest of us truly don't know Jacks!

Whoever declared that love at first sight doesn't exist has never witnessed the purity of a puppy or looked deep into a puppy's eyes. If they did, their lives would change considerably.

—Elizabeth Parker, *Paw Prints in the Sand*

Assess your Lifestyle

Adding a dog to your life can mean a minimum ten-year commitment. Before embarking on this life-changing decision, there are many questions to be answered. First, start with the general lifestyle assessment:

- Will a dog be compatible with all household members?

- Are there young children in the home, or do you plan on starting a family in the future? (See the chapter *Kids and Dogs*.)

- Do young children visit your home often?

- How big is your home?

- What other pets are already in the home?

- How much exercise are you able to provide for the dog?

- How long is your workday?

- How long will your dog be left alone?

- Do you have a fenced yard?

Dogs are our companions. They are social, and they want our company as much as we want theirs. A single dog doesn't go out in the yard and exercise himself.

If you do not have a fenced yard:

- Is there an off-leash park, trail, or greenbelt nearby?

- Is there a reliable dog walker available?

- Is there a reliable daycare in the vicinity of your home or workplace?

- Do you have a trusted neighbor or friend with a dog to arrange dog play dates with?

Where to Start

You've decided that a dog is a life-enhancing choice. Now it's time to choose where you'll find your new best friend. First, choose whether you prefer to purchase a dog from a breeder or adopt one from a shelter, taking into consideration the practical and moral implications.

Buying a Puppy

We might think that buying a puppy increases the probability of finding a healthy, good-tempered dog that is our perfect match. This can happen, but success hinges on locating a reputable breeder. Reputable breeders do their level best to produce healthy puppies with solid temperaments. However, there are no assurances when it comes to living, breathing beings; no 100 percent guarantee in predicting health problems. However, if you are working with a reputable breeder, you stand a good chance of getting a vigorous puppy with an agreeable disposition.

Adopting a Dog or Puppy

Adopting a dog from a shelter or rescue group is often less expensive and easier. There is no shortage of dogs needing homes.

Expect to find little or no history on the adopted dog. Know that there is a risk of possible temperament and health issues in puppies. Many adolescent dogs are given up due to behavioral problems, but the person surrendering may not give the whole story in a well-meaning attempt to give the dog a better chance of being adopted. Therefore, these behavioral issues may come as a surprise down the road.

There are varied reasons as to why a multitude of wonderful, loving dogs are up for adoption. Many were just not the right matches for their previous owners. Successful adoption depends on finding the right dog from the right shelter or rescue group. Ultimately the choice of whether to adopt or purchase a dog is a personal one. The thoughtful, informed decision will be the right one.

Saving one dog will not change the world, but surely for that one dog, the world will change forever. –**Karen Davison**

The Adoption Option

Shelters
Shelters are typically run by the Humane Society, the SPCA, or similar organizations. There are also private shelters, animal control facilities, and no-kill or low-kill shelters. Shelters usually have reasonable adoption fees with spaying/neutering and vaccinations included. Many have assessed the dog's behavior with other animals and people to measure their adoptability.

Private Shelters
Private shelters are usually operated by non-profit organizations. Many have contracts with local governments and operate similarly to city or county operated animal control facilities. Many accept all the homeless pets that they can, while others only accept owner-surrendered pets.

Animal Control Facilities
Animal control facilities, formerly known as dog pounds (now considered a pejorative term), employ animal control officers responsible for picking up stray animals in the city or county. Most facilities will also accept pets surrendered by owners. Each city and state has its own established holding period for animals to give their owners time to find and claim them.

Open Admission or Limited Admission Shelters
Open admission shelters accept any animals that come to the facility, whether they are adoptable or not. Limited admission shelters only accept animals that they deem adoptable.

No-Kill Shelters
The term no-kill is not clearly defined, because it can mean different things to different people and different facilities. Generally, no-kill shelters will not euthanize except in cases of extreme physical suffering. Adoptable dogs remain at the shelter for as long as it takes to find an adopter. Unadoptable dogs live out their natural lives at the facility. Some no-kill shelters euthanize aggressive or otherwise unadoptable dogs, but still call themselves

no-kill shelters to indicate their guiding principle of finding homes for their adoptable animals regardless of how long that takes.

Low-Kill Shelters

Low-kill shelters are limited admission shelters that will euthanize when necessary as the humane solution to illness, suffering, and severe aggression.

Once you've decided on a shelter, there are additional considerations. Know that animals in shelters may not show their true colors due to the environment, which can be loud, overcrowded, and have less-than-ideal comfort levels. Some animals are in shock, frightened, and overwhelmed. Spend time with the prospective adoptee in a private room that is typically provided by the shelter.

In most cases, the animal's history is unknown, so find out if the shelter does temperament testing to screen for aggression. When spending time with the dog, note if he seems excessively cautious, timid, or fearful. Observe whether the dog is overly aloof, wanting nothing to do with people. If you already have a dog, arrange to have the potential adoptee meet your resident dog (see the section on compatibility in this chapter).

Whether you choose the dog because you like the shelter or you choose the shelter because you love the dog, the important thing is this: you will change the world of one dog forever and fall hopelessly in love. Your world will change, as well, with a dog's unconditional love.

Rescue Groups

There exist many privately run purebred and mixed-breed rescues that save homeless dogs. These groups are usually run by a network of volunteers that take in dogs of a specific breed or mixed breeds of a certain type, i.e. giant breeds, hounds, or terriers.

The volunteers rescue, transport, foster, and adopt out the dogs. A well-run, responsible rescue group will have veterinary screening done before placing dogs in foster care and then adoption. They will also have a behavioral evaluation done before placing a dog, which is an essential step to find out if the dog is showing any signs of aggression.

Some rescue groups consist of well-meaning volunteers that may put their hearts ahead of their heads, rescuing any and every dog that comes their way. Beware of groups whose members are driven by emotion, taking any dog regardless of whether he is behaviorally adoptable.

Reputable rescue groups will have thorough application and approval procedures in place. Volunteers are often highly experienced and knowledgeable about the represented breed. They take extreme care to be sure their dogs are well matched with their adopters and will be supportive after the dog is placed.

Purchasing a Puppy or Dog

Backyard Breeders

Backyard breeders are defined here as those who are in it for the money. This is not the occasional accidental litter of puppies, but a for-profit endeavor with little regard for the wellbeing of the dogs and puppies.

It might be easy and less expensive to obtain a puppy from a backyard breeder, because they always have available litters. They advertise and sell online for easy price comparison. Some make it even easier by having a litter of pups (along with a sad back story) available at the local park or big-box store parking lot. However, the cost to you and the dog may heavily outweigh the convenience in the long run.

There is uncertainty of what you're getting from a backyard breeder. They are surely not in it to improve or even maintain the breed. Potential for medical issues is high, due to the fact that these breeders may be uninformed about health risks common in the breed or simply don't care about the puppies' wellbeing. They may omit expensive health screening and testing in order to increase their profit margin. Likewise, they are unaware or indifferent as to whether the breeding pair is physically and mentally fit. Puppies come from any two dogs of the same breed simply to say that they "have papers." These breeding pairs are not typically from healthy bloodlines.

Backyard breeders do little screening of the buyer, seldom turning anyone away or showing concern for the puppy's future. Often, pups are sold before the advised eight weeks of age, and no health "guarantees" are given. These breeders are not willing or even qualified to take the dog back if problems arise.

Irresponsible breeders are often unwilling to let buyers see the rest of the litter or the parents of the puppies. Accommodations are often improvised or temporary, showing lack of commitment.

Beware of the backyard breeder claiming they breed because it's "a good learning experience for the kids," it's "fun," or the dogs "must earn their keep." These are not the claims of a responsible breeder.

Responsible Breeders

Responsible breeders are dedicated to their breed. Their motivation is more about advancing the breed than making a profit. They thoroughly and carefully screen and approve buyers, turning away those that they deem unsuitable. Breeding stock is screened for health issues and genetic faults, and a reputable breeder will freely produce records as proof. They are knowledgeable about their breed, its history, and standards.

Trustworthy breeders are willing, often insistent upon backing their dogs. They agree to take them back for any reason or assist the owner with problems that arise.

Health is guaranteed. These breeders are willing to show the breeding parents and the facility. Accommodations are clean and in good repair, showing a commitment to the investment.

Responsible breeders do not sell puppies to pet stores, nor do they sell them on eBay or online sites like Craigslist. These breeders do not treat the process as a mere transaction, by selling puppies sight unseen. They make sure that the pups are a good match for the purchaser and that they will live in a healthy, loving, responsible environment.

"Pet quality" dogs are sold with a spay/neuter agreement or limited AKC registration, which means that the dog is registered but no litters produced by that dog are eligible for registration.

Puppy Mills

Puppy mills are factory farms for dogs where profits are priority. Little if any consideration is given to the wellbeing of the dogs or improvement of the breed. There is no concern for genetic quality, including hereditary defects. Accurate lineage documentation may be nonexistent or misrepresented.

Often puppy mills are inhumane environments with dogs living out their lives in cramped, overcrowded, filthy conditions. They live in stacked wire cages with no life enhancing or mentally stimulating pursuits.

Mill dogs are never allowed to be dogs. On no account do they experience playtime, toys, treats, fresh air, or compassion. Females are bred at every opportunity with no recovery time between litters. Adult dogs that can no longer be bred and puppies with obvious physical problems that deem them unsalable are put to death.

Puppy mill puppies taken from the mother and littermates too early (six weeks of age) lack socialization and frequently show behavioral problems. They are often fearful, aggressive, and overly shy.

Pet Shops
Most often, pet shops acquire puppies from puppy mills, usually through a broker or middleman. Puppies are often taken from their mothers and littermates and put up for sale too young. Records may be falsified to avoid suspicious practices.

Finding a Dog on the Internet
The Internet is a great way to research breeds, shelters, rescue groups, and breeders. This can be of great benefit to dogs, because it enables people to make informed decisions. However, bear in mind that it's easy to spontaneously lose one's heart to the photograph posted on the adoption or for-sale page.

Internet advertising is advertising. Beware of euphemisms about temperament, such as "Fido will do best in a home without children." or "Sparky prefers a home without other dogs or pets." This ad could be describing a dog that has shown aggression toward other dogs or children, or a dog with an extreme predatory behavior, which could harm the cat.

Don't be taken in by ads that play the pity card. These ads describe the shocking abuse the dog has endured. It may be true, but these ads can play too heavily on emotion. Adopting a dog out of pure pity could be a risky move.

Beware of breed euphemisms. Unfortunately, certain breeds are discriminated against and even banned in some cities. To increase the likelihood of adoption, some ads will read lab/boxer mix or lab/terrier mix to describe a Pit Bull. Pit Bulls and other banned breeds are usually wonderful dogs. However, whether you are actually seeking one or not, you need to know what you're getting.

Some ads are intended to make you feel guilty. These ads describe how the dog has already been re-homed four times; or he's already been at the shelter for twenty-nine days, and his number is up tomorrow.

In addition to newspaper ads and venues such as flea markets, many puppies sold online come from puppy mills. The only way to be sure that your puppy is not from a puppy mill is to visit the breeder's facility. Responsible breeders want their puppies to go to good homes, so they will screen potential buyers to be sure that happens.

The Dangers of Buying a Dog Online

The federal Animal Welfare Act (AWA) states that commercial breeders selling to pet stores must be licensed by the U.S. Department of Agriculture (USDA). However, the AWA does not regulate breeders that sell directly to the public, including sales made over the Internet. Wholesale breeders, dealers, exhibitors, and research labs are covered but not small retail breeders and pet shops selling only domestic pet animals. Local anti-cruelty laws usually cover these entities.

The AWA was passed in 1966, prior to the Internet boom, creating a loophole that allows many puppy mills to operate without a license and without submitting to inspections.

While the Internet can be a great way to explore different breeds and find a reputable breeder, it can become overwhelming and is filled with traps set by scammers. It's on the Internet, so it must be true, right? There exist many polished web sites loaded with endearing photos and insincere promises. It's easy to be taken in.

Blindly buying online is risky business. You may unknowingly being supporting puppy mills and taking a chance of being swindled. You may not get the dog you think you're getting, or you may not receive the dog at all.

To avoid being scammed, simply never buy a dog that you haven't met.

Visit the breeder, tour the facility, meet the parents, and ask questions. A responsible breeder will ask you as many questions as you will ask her. Check references of previous buyers, and talk to the breeder's veterinarian. Deal directly with the breeder and not a broker. Beware of declarations that all sales are final. A responsible breeder or rescue group will always take the puppy back, regardless of the reason, and will be there to support you should problems arise.

Watch for red flags. Beware of "free to good home" ads or those that offer free dogs with a mysterious "re-homing fee." Take heed of ads that state "moving" or "child is allergic," especially if they are advertising young puppies.

On the other side of the coin, if you need to re-home your dog, don't list him online or anywhere else as "free to good home." Sadly, there are people out there with less than honest intentions. Some are looking for bait dogs to use in dog fighting or engage in a practice called "dog flipping." Dog flippers get dogs free or very cheap (or steal them), and then they sell them for profit, just like house flippers flip houses. Dogs that are flipped may be trained for attack or used for fighting, which changes their behavior. Even if a stolen dog is later returned to the owner, they will not be getting the same dog back. Animals used for flipping are often housed in deplorable puppy-mill-like conditions.

Decisions, Decisions

Size

At first glance, it would seem that a small dog would be the superior choice for a small space, and a large dog would be a better fit in a large space. However, the physical size of the dog and the home don't matter as much as the dog's energy level. Greyhounds, in fact, can live happily in an apartment. They are often referred to as forty-mile-an-hour couch potatoes, because they like to lounge. Many giant breeds like Great Danes, Newfoundlands, and mastiffs do well in small spaces. As long as age- and breed-appropriate exercise is provided, many large breeds can be perfectly happy in apartments.

On the other hand, small energetic breeds like Jack Russell terriers would, in their perfect world, appreciate a yard that could accommodate a full competition agility course. Sporting dogs, like Labrador retrievers and German shorthair pointers, dream of a big yard that includes an Olympic-sized swimming pool.

High-energy dogs can do well in small spaces, provided they have an outlet for their vigor such as dog parks, day care, and adequate playtime. One twenty-minute walk per day isn't even a warm up for the likes of a Brittany spaniel.

Big dogs can do great bodily harm if they pull on the leash during walks or jump up. However, even a medium-sized dog can cause injury, so consider your physical abilities when deciding on the size of the dog you want. Bear in mind that all dogs need leash training, for their safety and yours, regardless of size.

There is a cost differential between small dogs and big ones. Big dogs need big beds, crates, and taller gates. Big dogs cost more to board and groom, and medications are more expensive. And then there's shedding. There is, of course, a lot more hair on a big dog. Big dogs make bigger messes with their large muddy paw prints, larger puddles, and bigger deposits left behind for backyard cleanup.

Coat
Consider the type of coat your new dog will have and whether anyone in the household has allergies. People tend to be allergic to dog dander, not dog hair, but often do better with low-level shedders. Some people have skin reactions to dogs' saliva. Therefore, these folks will want to avoid heavy droolers. Curly-coated dogs such as poodles, Bichon Frises, and Portuguese water dogs tend to be better suited to people allergic to dander. To determine your reaction to an individual dog, see if the rescue or shelter will do a trial adoption or private time at the shelter in a visitation room.

Decide how much time and money you want to invest in grooming. Do you want to and are you capable of doing it yourself? Can you put a 150-pound mastiff into the tub? Do you own a reliable vacuum cleaner? How much dog hair would you be willing to eat and wear?

Other Physical Traits
As mentioned above, some people are allergic to dog saliva, but if you are considering a heavy-drooling breed, decide how you feel about dried dog

spit on the ceiling. Gather your thoughts on dealing with slimy water bowls and having your clothes eternally slimed.

Dogs with beards, such as wire fox terriers or schnauzers, are very messy drinkers; and they often choose to come put their head in your lap right after a visit to the water bowl.

Life Span
Small breeds tend to have a longer life expectancy than large breeds and considerably longer than the giant breeds. What do you expect your life to look like in the next ten to fifteen years, and how does a dog fit into that picture?

Activity Level
If you are a hiker, walker, runner, or cyclist, you might do well with a high-energy breed. Otherwise, your energetic dog will require day care, or you may want to participate in dog sports.

Personality Traits
Depending on your lifestyle, you'll want to consider whether your new dog will be good with kids, compatible with people and other animals, and whether he's more social or independent. Take into account trainability, protectiveness, and whether you prefer a vocal or quiet dog.

What Age?
There are advantages and disadvantages to acquiring dogs at different life stages. However, each person defines advantage or disadvantage differently, so what's considered a benefit to one person may be deemed a drawback to another.

Puppies: Seven Weeks to Five Months
Acquiring a puppy means a minimum ten-year commitment. Puppies require more time (at home) for house training, basic training, and mental stimulation. A possible advantage to getting a puppy: through proper socialization and training we are afforded the most opportunity to shape the temperament.

Puppies seven to nine weeks old must be let out every three hours. A general rule to determine how long a puppy can be left alone is to calculate the puppy's age in months and add one. For example, a three-month-old puppy can be left for four hours. (Note: this does not mean that a ten-month-old dog should be left alone for eleven hours—common sense.)

Some people think that they should acquire a young puppy in order to form a stronger bond and have an optimum training time. Bonding and training occur at any age, not just puppyhood.

Do not acquire a puppy under the age of seven weeks old, as they're not developmentally ready to leave their mother and littermates. If you already have a dog at home, a pup this young may bond more to your dog than to you. Furthermore, consider whether your current dog can handle an exuberant puppy. He may not tolerate the youngster, or the new pup may make him feel younger.

Resist the temptation to adopt two puppies at the same time. Raising two puppies together can be done, but it's an exponentially greater investment of time and training.

Adolescent: Five to Eighteen Months
With an adolescent dog, what you see is what you get. They are almost at their full physical and temperamental development. But be prepared. Dogs this age are like human adolescents, testing boundaries and patience. Resembling human teenagers, they seem to lose their minds at this life stage. Adolescents need plenty of exercise, mental stimulation, and a large dose of our patience.

Adult: Eighteen Months to Five Years
With an adult dog, what you see is what you get in reference to physical attributes, behavioral issues, and temperament. They've passed the seemingly insufferable stage of adolescence and have settled into themselves. They may need a bit more time to adjust to their new home than an adolescent dog or puppy.

Mature: Five to Eight Years

Dogs of this age are rarely surrendered because of behavioral problems and most often come with at least basic training. If you think about it, no one would keep an untrained or un-housetrained dog for years, so these dogs are ready made.

They, too, may need a bit more time to adjust to their new home.

Senior: Nine Years and Older

A senior dog is the complete package. They need the least amount of time invested, unless they have special needs. They tend to be calm and quiet. Again, more time to adjust is likely required.

Purebred or Mixed

Some people prefer purebred dogs, because they want to show them in the confirmation ring or because they just love the look, temperament, and general breed characteristics. Others prefer a one-of-a-kind dog. Shelters are full of mixed breeds, with some purebreds available as well. Many rescue groups rescue one specific breed or mixes thereof.

Adopting or purchasing a purebred dog means predictability in universal physical characteristics and general behavioral tendencies (but there are no guarantees). There can be a greater risk of genetic health issues, however these risks are pretty well known, so you will be aware of these possibilities in advance.

Mixed breed dogs are genetically diverse, meaning they are less prone to health problems specific to a particular breed. They possess qualities of more than one breed, which can make for a more or less desirable temperament, size, and personality, depending on what you're looking for.

There are numerous types of purebred dogs, and an infinite number of mixed breeds. A good source for researching breeds is the American Kennel Club. Their web site lists the breeds recognized by the AKC, along with a description of physical and temperament characteristics: http://www.akc.org/breeds/complete_breed_list.cfm

Many web sites and books list the same information. When deciding what breed you want, visit dog parks and talk to other dog owners. Go to dog shows. Contact breed affinity groups, rescue group volunteers, trainers, groomers, vets, and shelter people. Keep in mind that dogs were originally bred to serve specific functions. This consideration will determine whether you'll both be happy. An objective and trusted individual, like a trainer or other dog professional, can help you make a decision with your head instead of only your heart.

Homecoming Checklist

Now that you've discovered *the one*, you'll want to prepare for his homecoming. Finding yourself with a new dog and no plan will be overwhelming for everyone.

The first order of business is to establish rules and have everyone in the family agree on them. It's easier to implement rules straight away and ease up later than it is to change behavior afterward. That goes for the behavior of both dogs *and* humans. For example, decide whether or not to allow the dog on the bed at night. It's easier to train a dog to sleep on the bed than to not sleep on the bed if you change your mind.

Purchase supplies such as bowls and grooming equipment in advance to have them on hand before bringing your dog home. Collars, beds, harnesses, etc. can be purchased afterward so that they can be custom fit.

If you are bringing home a new puppy from a breeder, take a blanket or towel along and rub it on your pup's mother to get her scent on it. This will help your puppy's transition into her new home by having something familiar to comfort him. Many breeders will provide a blanket or toy themselves for this purpose.

Have a plan for training. You should have already vetted and chosen a private trainer or training program.

Have a plan for health care. You should have previously interviewed and chosen a veterinarian.

Have a potty training plan in place, and choose a place for the dog to eliminate so that you can begin potty training straight away.

Dog proof the house. Get down on all fours for a dog's eye view in order to inspect every detail (especially if you're bringing home a puppy). Remove electrical cords and fragile, expensive, and irreplaceable items with sentimental value. Remember that both ends of the dog can be destructive. The surface of a coffee table can be completely cleared with one swipe of a happy Labrador tail.

Set your schedule so that you have time to spend with your new dog. Vacations and long weekends dedicated to your dog's homecoming make for a great start to acclimate your dog into his new life.

Another Dog?

Getting another dog can increase the love, joy, companionship, and fun in life. There is also the possibility that another dog brings frustration, jealousy, fighting, noise, and dismantled home interiors.

Make the decision of getting another dog based on what will be best for everyone: you, your family, your resident dog(s), and the potential adoptee. This is not a decision to be made by how many likes the idea gets on Facebook.

We've all, at one time or another, been besotted by a cold, wet nose and a pair of soft, sad eyes. However, infatuation can turn to regret if the idea of getting another dog is not given careful thought. The decision is easier to make before bringing the dog home than to change one's mind afterward.

Make the decision based on everyone's best interests. It can be a mistake to acquire another dog simply to keep your resident dog company. Be sure that you and everyone involved want to get another dog.

Avoid thinking that the first dog will alleviate the burden of training and exercise for the second. (If these responsibilities were viewed as burdens, then I would question whether to have dogs at all.)

There is another problem with adding another dog simply to keep the current one company. It is possible that the dogs will bond more strongly with each other than with you. In order to be the leader, there needs to be a concentrated effort to build and maintain a strong relationship between you and your dogs. Dogs need to learn basic obedience, polite behavior, and have boundaries set by their leader, which is you.

Depending on your reliable resident dog to train the new dog is problematic when the reliable dog is not reliable or is not present. (What happens when the reliable dog is at the vet or has unfortunately passed on?)

Points to consider:

- Do I have the time and money to support another dog? (training, feeding, health care, grooming, boarding)
- What life changes do I expect in the foreseeable future? (growing my family, getting married, going to school, moving, downsizing, increased travel)
- Do my resident dogs and the prospective new addition get on well with other dogs?
- Is it physically possible in my home to separate the dogs whenever necessary?
- Are any of my resident dogs overly protective of any family members or me?
- Do any of my resident dogs guard resources such as food, toys, beds, etc.?
- What is my backup plan if it doesn't work out?
- Can the whole family give the same answer to these questions?

Now That You've Decided to Get Another Dog

Gender

People definitely have their preferences as to whether they prefer to live with a male or a female dog. Some are concerned about male dogs marking* and their desire to wander. They worry that male dogs are more aggressive or dominant. Some people prefer female dogs, because they feel they are gentler, maternal, more protective, less likely to roam, and generally easier to live with. Dogs are individuals, and the personality traits described above are not gender specific. Look for these tendencies in breed more than in gender.

If you already have one or more dogs, look at what is most acceptable to your resident dog(s).

Keep your current dog in mind:

- What is his temperament?

- What is his play style?

- Is he submissive or does he tend toward bullying?

Compatibility

Sue Sternberg, one of the foremost authorities on successful shelter adoptions, cites the following general formulas for compatibility in her book *Successful Dog Adoption*. As stated in the book, these general rules are not based on statistical percentages of dog-dog relationships most likely to fail, but on the most common, difficult-to-fix behavioral problems that dog trainers encounter. Difficult dog-dog problems are not necessarily representative of the rate of problems within a particular matchup. Much depends on the individual dog. These guidelines are presented to reduce the risk of dog-dog problems in the multi-dog household.

From Sternberg's book:

Combinations with the best chance for harmony

Resident dog female, older, larger + New dog male, smaller, younger
Resident dog female, larger + New dog male, smaller, younger
Resident dog female + New dog male, smaller, younger
Resident dog male + New dog female

If both dogs are the same gender

Resident dog should be older, larger
Resident dog should be older
Resident dog should be larger

Most risky combination

Resident dog female + New dog female
Both dogs same age, same size, same breed type, same personality with people.

*Marking is not a problem for all male dogs. Neutering usually reduces incidences of marking, but it is no guarantee. Some still engage in the behavior, especially highly territorial dogs. Neutering also helps decrease the urge to stray in the desire to find a female. Territorial marking does occur more in male dogs, but females are not exempt from the behavior.

Evaluating Dog Aggression for Potential Adoptees

General guidelines:

- How does the dog behave when he first sees another dog when he's on leash?

- Can he pass by another dog without whining, lunging, and/or barking?

- Does he get so aroused at the sight of another dog that there is a possibility of redirected aggression, either toward the human or another dog walking with him?

- Can the dog live with another dog? If so what age, gender, and size?

- Is he aggressive toward other dogs?

- For a detailed aggression testing procedures, see *Successful Dog Adoption* by Sue Sternberg.

Introducing a New Dog

Since we only get one chance at a good first impression, it's important that introductions are done correctly, slowly, and carefully.

It is best to have dogs meet on neutral territory. Select a large, quiet area with plenty of space for the dogs to move around. Avoid clustering around the dogs, if multiple people are present.

Start the introductions off leash with a barrier between the dogs, such as a fence. Let them sniff and see each other through the fence for as long as thirty minutes. They need to be comfortable and let the excitement of a new dog wear off before the barrier comes down.

Allow the new dog to meet only one of your resident dogs at a time. Determine the order of introductions by which resident dog makes friends the easiest, and let the new dog meet that one first.

Allow the dogs to sniff for a minute; then, call them away and have them move around. Limit the first playtime to just a few minutes, and be sure to end on a good note. Leave them wanting more.

If you are uncomfortable, acclimate each dog to a muzzle that will be worn during the first encounter (use cage muzzles to allow for proper panting). This will mitigate injuries and give you confidence.

After the neutral territory introductions, have the dogs meet in your yard. Following a successful yard meeting, have them meet in the house. Bring the new dog into the house and allow him to sniff and explore when the resident dogs are not present. Then, let the resident dogs in after the new dog is inside.

If introductions must be done on leash, make sure that the leashes are loose (far easier said than done). Otherwise, if it is safe and you are comfortable, let the dogs drag the leashes. Long lines are good for first-time introductions, but you'll want to practice using them beforehand to become adept at keeping them tangle-free. Always stay within two feet of your dogs during initial introductions.

For on-leash intros, start by walking the dogs parallel, letting them get closer and closer as they become comfortable with each other's presence. Next, let them mutually sniff things, and then let them sniff each other. Keep all meetings brief at first, and don't leave the dogs unsupervised together.

Give special consideration to senior or ailing dogs. Bringing a young, energetic puppy or adolescent dog into the home may be overwhelming. Close management will keep things positive and ensure that both dogs are safe.

Puppies under sixteen weeks of age hold what is often referred to as a "puppy license." This license allows pups to get away with things that they won't be able to get away with after the age of about four months. Therefore, be aware that the puppy license will expire in the eyes of your older dog, and the dynamics will change.

Have a plan for breaking up a dog fight (see *Breaking Up a Dog Fight* in the chapter *Aggressive Dogs*).

Be realistic. Know your limitations, the limitations of your family, and the limitations of your current dogs. Research breeds and know which ones fit best together. Terriers, bully breeds, or high-energy herding or sporting dogs are more challenging as a pack than, say, a pack of greyhounds.

Selecting a Dog for a Multi-Pet Household: Cats and Dogs

Cats and dogs can live peacefully with some forethought and management. Begin by creating a safe haven for the cat to retreat to. Install a baby gate or a chain lock on a door. This allows the cat to retreat to the safe place, but the dog cannot jump the gate or go through the small opening the chain lock allows. The gate allows the cat and dog to get to know each other safely. The chain lock, of course, does not work for small dogs, but the baby gate does. Put the cat food and litter box in the safe place, thus preventing the dog from eating the cat food before or after it's gone through the cat.

I'd rather be pleasantly surprised than fatally disappointed.
—Julia Glass, I See You Everywhere

In conclusion, animals are a proven life-enhancing experience. They don't call a dog man's best friend for nothing. With careful planning and thought, we can find the perfect match and change our lives and the life of the dog forever and for the better.

9

In it for Life

If I was told I could only ask 1 more question ever, I would grab my dog's snout, and say, "Who's the most beautiful dog in the world?"

—Paula Poundstone

I did not think that I was ready, but the teacher did appear. He came in the form of an adorable, lively, Border collie mixed breed puppy. And, Mr. MoJo certainly lives up to his name. His verve is incomparable, living life with unimaginable gusto. Mr. MoJo was, and still is, one of my greatest teachers. He's always known that I am highly trainable and has been teaching me for over thirteen years.

I've had the honor of living with many dogs throughout my life, none of which hold a candle to the inimitable Mr. MoJo. He's been more of a challenge in raising than all of the dogs in my life combined.

I expected that raising this puppy would be no different than raising any other. It would be normal. Mr. MoJo proved what Whoopi Goldberg said to be true, "Normal is nothing more than a cycle on a washing machine."

At the risk of eroding the reader's confidence in me as a trainer, I will share a select few of Mr. MoJo's antics. He has been a better teacher than I could have ever hoped for. He's left indelible paw prints on my memory and in my heart throughout the stages of his life.

The pinnacle of Mr. MoJo's destructive behavior in puppyhood was the tearing down the living room drapes and then shredding them. Lesson learned: active breed puppies need jobs. If we don't provide one, they will choose self-employment and we will not necessarily approve of their career choice.

Mr. MoJo's adolescent achievements ranged from breaking the bedroom window to teaching his canine roommates the art of de-upholstering a couch in less than 17½ minutes. Mr. MoJo developed the ability to shape shift in order to fit between fence pickets, facilitating unauthorized trips through the neighborhood. I've seen that dog climb a wire fence like a ladder, use his teeth as wire cutters to open a Mr. MoJo-sized hole and then, take his leave.

I held the status of teacher where my other dogs were concerned. Mr. MoJo is largely self-taught. For example, I trained my German shepherd, Jude to ring a bell at the back door to signal that he wanted in. One day, I heard the bell ring and headed for the door. I was puzzled when I nearly tripped over Jude. Who's ringing the bell? It was Mr. MoJo, who had evidently learned the skill simply by observation.

Mr. MoJo is a talker and he's verbose. Whenever I return home, he howls, "Where were you?" and then proceeds to tell me about his day. At mealtime, he prods me and micro-directs meal preparation. It's as if he's saying, "Get my dinner on the table, woman!" I think that this is my own fault, because his vocalizations sounded like words, so I shaped them into Mr. MoJo's best trick. I ask him where he lives and he responds with, "Aaa-rooor-a." (we live in Aurora.) As it turns out, I thought I was teaching Mr. MoJo, but he was actually training me.

Just when I think that life with Mr. MoJo will settle down that we'll spend his twilight days taking leisurely walks, and he'll lie at my feet next to the fire, he reminds me that he doesn't take life lying down. Oh, we do take walks, but to Mr. MoJo they're missions. Always on task to mark territory, put wildlife on evacuation notice, and to scavenge.

At the age of nearly 14, Mr. MoJo still keeps me on my toes. On a recent outing, he managed to stealthily retrieve something from the grass—something dead. To my horror, Mr. MoJo was chomping on the corpse of a rabbit. Now, this wasn't a long-dead, flat, dried up rabbit. No, it was a freshly-dead, squooshy rabbit. Now, Mr. MoJo knows "drop it," but the cue fell on deaf ears. He looked at me as if to say, "Are you kidding? This is the best thing I've found in my 13 years on this planet. I am so not going to give it to you!" I then proceeded to extricate the carcass from iron canine jaws. It was quite the spectacle to passers by and I must admit I was not the composed, cool, and collected trainer. I was the gagging, grossed out, and flustered, dog mom.

I managed to extract (most) of the disgusting mass from Mr. MoJo's maw and collect myself enough to see that I'd sustained a superficial cut on my finger. Oh, great! What had we both been exposed to? I didn't know whether to be more worried about my dog or myself. The story ended (or so I thought) with me getting a tetanus shot and on the advice of my vet, keeping Mr. MoJo under close supervision. All seemed to be fine until a week later when I was on yard clean up duty. Sparing details, suffice it to say that I found Mr. MoJo had contracted a parasite. When I asked the vet how that could happen, she cited a couple of reasons, and then added, "Could he have gotten a hold of something dead?" Bingo!

Whenever I reminisce about the challenges of life with Mr. MoJo, I know that I'll miss those things sooner than I'd like to think. What a cavernous hole will be left in my life when this teacher disappears.

When the student is ready, the teacher will appear. –**Buddhist Proverb**

Dogs are a lifelong commitment. Life is dynamic and so is behavior. We ask a lot of our canine companions, yet they ask so little in return. However, raising and training a dog can sometimes leave both ends of the leash confused and frustrated.

To avoid the pitfalls and frustration, it is helpful to dwell *from* the goal and not *on* it. We can take life's ambiguity and turn it to our advantage–start from where we are and work with what we have. We are better equipped to have a dog we can live with if we understand their developmental stages and the behaviors to expect during each:

- Puppy: 8 weeks to 5 months
- Adolescence: 5 months to 2 years
- Adult: 2 to 7 years
- Senior: 7 years and over

Dog Years

A popular belief is that 1 human year equals 7 dog years. More accurately, the first year or two of a dog's life represents the equivalent of some 18 to 25 years in human life. Furthermore, it is an inexact to apply this formula to all dogs, as the ratio varies with size and breed.

Another, formula says that the first two years of a dog's life equal 10.5 human years each, with succeeding years equal to four human years. This equation still falls short of accuracy because it does not address size and breed. There are breed and size specific calculators that factor in these important criteria. They work using the expected adult weight or breed category of small, medium or large and are probably the most precise.

For all intents and purposes, the first year of a dog's life equals 10 to 15 human years. The second year is equivalent to about another 3 to 8 human years, with the years thereafter, equivalent to around 4 or 5 human years.

It is generally accepted that small breed dogs (under 20 lbs. such as Maltese or Yorkshire terriers) become geriatric at around 11 years old. Medium breed dogs (20-50 lbs. such as the Border collie or Portuguese water dog) become seniors at around 10 years. Large breeds (50-75 lbs. such as German shepherds or Labrador retrievers) enter their senior years around 8, and giant breeds (over 75 lbs. such as mastiffs and St. Bernards) at about 6 or 7 years old.

Maturity is a progressive developmental process. It is dynamic and fluid, with overlapping transitional stages. In other words, puppyhood does not expire on the exact date the puppy reaches 5 months old, nor does the dog suddenly take retirement and start drawing his pension on his eighth birthday.

As with humans, life and learning varies for dogs as mental and physical capabilities change over the course of a lifetime. Because it is far easier to learn new skills than to unlearn old habits, we strive to prevent unwanted behaviors, rather than change them. It's easier to be proactive than reactive.

Happiness is a warm puppy. –**Charles M. Schulz**

Puppyhood: Establishing a strong foundation
Note that the puppy section of this chapter is longer and more detailed than those on other life stages. That's because puppies are a lot of work. Furthermore, you will be revisiting the puppy manners section when your pup reaches adolescence, you adopt an adult dog, or any time a refresher is in order.

Puppies do indeed, take a lot of energy, but time and effort invested early on will result in a better-behaved, happier dog. It's totally worth the time; otherwise, we may come completely unmoored when puppies reach adolescence.

Puppies' developmental stages happen at the speed of light. Therefore, we must be prepared to be their pilot and to journey with them. The human/canine bond is unique and the nature of this connection is most impacted in the first year of a puppy's life. By 7 weeks old, puppies are naturally forming strong ties with those in his world. Puppies are always watching and learning, trying to figure out the rules.

Puppies, as social beings need and appreciate structure, leadership, and rules. Ambiguousness results in the puppy testing boundaries. If there is no clear leadership, he may feel that he needs to take the helm, willingly or not. Think about how this happens in human families–the teenager running the show, voluntarily or not, the teen typically does not make a good leader.

A puppy sees you as his leader and caretaker 24/7. He does not know that you have obligations to job, family, and community. He does not understand and is not designed to stare at four walls for ten hours a day while you are at work. He is designed to (and will) play, learn, and proceed through developmental stages no matter what is happening in your life.

Puppies must learn the social skills of impulse control and bite inhibition. They learn this from other dogs, but only in regard to things that are important to other dogs, like don't steal others' bones, don't bite so hard, you're playing too rough. It is our responsibility to teach puppies the rules of the human house such as to stay off the furniture, don't eat the shoes, or dig holes in the yard.

If you watch dogs teaching puppies, you will see how the levels of tolerance and expectations change. There exists what we call a puppy license, which is granted up until the puppy reaches the age of 16-20 weeks. The expiration corresponds with hormonal changes in the puppy's body. At this time, the puppy is taught that the same behavior acceptable in the past, such as charging up like a runaway train and climbing over the dog, is no longer tolerated. Now, the expectations are raised.

Early Socialization
The quality of a pet dog's temperament is of paramount importance. Temperament is largely the result of socialization–the most influential time in a puppy's life.

Periods of Early Socialization:
- Weeks 3-8: puppies learn about interactions with dogs.
- Weeks 5-12: puppies learn about interactions with humans.
- Weeks 10-20: puppies learn by exploring new environments.

Behavioral problems are more likely to arise if socialization does not occur during specific developmental periods. If not exposed to stimuli during the pertinent developmental stages, dogs are at risk of acquiring behavioral problems specific to that developmental period. E.g. if a puppy is not exposed to people when he's between 5 and 12 weeks of age, there is a higher probability he'll become fearful or aggressive because proper dog/human interaction skills were never learned.

Puppies that leave their mother and litter before 8 weeks old do not learn to interrelate with dogs. This includes learning the highly important skills of bite inhibition and communication. This is the time pups learn what is appropriate behavior through body language and gain self-confidence.

Dealing with behavior problems later on is extremely difficult. Inattention to the developmental periods and lack of exposure to relevant stimuli means that the puppy will never be the dog he could have been had proper and adequate socialization taken place.

The most important time for concentrated socialization is between 8 and 12 weeks of age. However, socialization is life long and it's extremely important it continue throughout adolescence. See chapter on socialization.

Fear Periods

A fear period is a developmental stage during which dogs may perceive certain stimuli as threatening. Dogs can go through two fear periods. The first happens during puppyhood at 8-11 weeks old–the second happens during adolescence at 6-18 months. Because the rate a dog matures varies with breed, these time frames are approximate.

Whether it is the first or second fear period we're dealing with, it is extremely important to help puppies through it properly. The second fear period is more difficult because it occurs during adolescence when the dog is exploring his world, pushing boundaries, is hormonally charged, and can feel very insecure.

A clue to recognizing a fear period is to notice that the dog has suddenly become afraid of something that he was previously not. Additionally, he may seem more anxious in general.

It is important to help dogs through these fear periods gently. We must allow them to do it on their own terms and time frame, never forcing a dog to confront the things that trigger his fear. If he is fearful and stressed, he cannot learn. He's in the fight or flight mode and beyond the capacity for rational thought.

Notice that the fear periods coincide with possible major life events. The first fear period at 8-11 weeks is commonly when puppies are separated from their mothers and littermates to go to their new homes. The second fear period occurs during adolescence, a time when dogs are exploring boundaries and are hormonally charged. Adolescence is the age when most dogs are given up due to behavioral problems. Imagine the trauma of a shelter, or even re-homing during this fear period.

Puppyhood: Establish a strong foundation from day one

Congratulations! You have a new baby! As with a human infant, you will be sleep deprived, you will be potty training, and you'll have your schedule rudely rearranged. A notable difference in babies of the human and the canine type is that with puppies everything happens within a few months time instead of years. Depending on your perspective, that is either a good thing or a bad thing.

Choose the right puppy for your lifestyle (see the chapter *Choosing a Dog.*) Remember that puppies require more time for housetraining and learning bite inhibition. Puppies can be destructive, because puppies need to chew (more on that later.) To puppies, the whole world is a toilet and everything in it is a chew toy. Therefore, houses must be puppy-proofed.

Time Alone

It is tempting to spend every waking moment with our new, fuzzy, bundle of joy, but you and your puppy will benefit from teaching him to be alone. Do this by having him enjoy a chew bone in his crate or puppy-proofed room for a minute or two while you leave the room. Be sure to return before the puppy finishes his chewie or starts to cry. Do not return if the puppy is whining or barking, as we do not want him to learn that he has you at his beck and call. Gradually increase the time you are gone, until the puppy is comfortable with being alone. If you have other dogs in the household, make sure the puppy spends time away from them as well.

Socialization

Socialization is so important, that I've dedicated an entire chapter to it.

Socialization is not just about meeting people and other dogs. It's about having positive experiences with many other things including:

- Handling
- Gentle restraint
- Sharing
- Impulse control
- Meeting unfamiliar people
- Appropriate play with humans and with dogs
- Interactions with other pets
- Walking on different surfaces
- New sounds
- New objects
- New locations

Socialization is the underpinning of a good temperament. It builds a solid foundation for a well-balanced, confident, and friendly dog. We hear a lot about the critical socialization period for puppies 8 weeks to 5 months of age. Yet, the reality of socialization is that it's a lifelong process with adolescent socialization having equal importance as that of puppyhood. In fact, if socialization is discontinued, dogs will gradually de-socialize. Consequently, they may become fearful or asocial.

Behavior is ever changing, as life is ever changing. Therefore, attention to socialization and training is essential throughout life. The better job of training and socialization done during puppyhood, the better prepared we will be when our dog hits the dreaded adolescence.

There is no psychiatrist in the world like a puppy licking your face.
—**Bernard Williams**

Teaching Puppy Manners

The rules and boundaries have been determined *before* bringing your puppy home so that his training and socialization can start from day one. Teach your puppy immediately that polite behavior is what works for him. It is much easier to train a puppy than it is to modify the behavior of an adolescent or adult dog.

Chewing, Mouthing, and Bite Inhibition

Bite inhibition, paws down, is the single most essential thing to teach your puppy. Bite inhibition is the dog's ability to control the amount of force applied with the jaws.

Your new puppy will have a full set of deciduous teeth by the age of 6 weeks. Through the process of teething, he will lose all of them, and they will be replaced by permanent teeth at around 4 to 7 months of age.

Puppies bite. It is a normal, natural, and necessary behavior, which develops bite inhibition. With proper training and feedback, puppies learn to control the pressure exerted with their jaws resulting in a safer adult mouth. A puppy's jaws are weak and his mouth full of pins can be painful. He needs to learn that those teeth do hurt and he must learn this before he develops jaws that can do serious damage. Puppies that have been properly socialized will be less likely to bite in adulthood. However, in the event he does bite out of fear or from being hurt, the bite inhibition he learned during puppyhood means he will be less likely to inflict serious injury.

Bite inhibition, the most important attribute in a companion dog, must be learned before the age of 4½ months. Early on, pups learn it from interactions with their littermates and adults. From here, we must take over the role of teacher with socialization and training.

Teaching Bite Inhibition: Mouthing

While it is essential for puppies to mouth and bite, the behavior must be eliminated before they become adolescents and adults. Beyond puppyhood, dogs have the potential to do serious damage with their powerful jaws. Eliminating the behavior should be done gradually and progressively where the puppy first learns to inhibit the force of his bites and then to lessen the frequency.

Inhibiting Bite Force

It is not necessary to use physical punishment or to physically restrain the pup that bites too hard. Punishment can work to immediately stop the behavior. However, punishment is only successful in suppressing the behavior, not changing it. Consequently, in a real-life event where the puppy feels the need to bite someone, he will revert to a hard bite, instead of an inhibited one that he has been taught.

Teaching bite inhibition cannot be emphasized enough. It is so important because accidents do happen in real life. A dog may bite if he's startled, hurt, or under extreme stress. A dog that has acquired bite inhibition is less likely to hurt someone or at least not cause serious damage.

To teach a puppy to inhibit the force of his bite, we can emulate what his mother or littermates do when he delivers a hurtful bite–yelp! When your puppy puts his teeth on you, let out an attention getting, "Ouch!" The puppy will stop play and back off for a moment. Next, ask the pup to come sit quietly for a few seconds, and then resume play.

Some puppies do not back off and will become over stimulated by "Ouch!" Timeouts tend to benefit these exuberant biters. If this is the case, say, "No!" then immediately exit the room and close the door. Wait a 30 to 60 seconds, and then return to the room. Have the puppy come sit and then resume play. If he bites again, repeat the timeout. Your puppy will learn that his biting results in losing his playmate and your attention. Always play with your puppy in an area where you can walk away from him and leave him alone (safely.) This technique is more effective than taking your puppy to a confinement area for a timeout.

For the energetic pup that gets into trouble during the timeout, you can have him on leash during playtime. When initiating a timeout, hold the leash and close the door on it so your puppy won't wander off.

Once the puppy has learned to bite softer, we want to eliminate the pressure altogether. When playing with the puppy, wait for a bite that is a bit harder than the others. Say, "Ouch!" or use the timeout if necessary. This will have the puppy learn gradually to mouth gently instead of biting.

Reduce the Incidence of Mouthing

Now that your puppy has learned to mouth gently, we want to diminish its frequency. He will learn that mouthing is acceptable during playtime, but he must stop on request.

You can teach your puppy "Out," which means that he is not to touch something unless given permission. This is easily done with a treat. Start by holding a treat in your hand. Say, "Out" and wait one second. If the puppy does not touch the treat say, "Take it" and let him take the treat. Once the pup can do this for one second, gradually increase the time he waits for you to say, "Take it." If the puppy goes for the treat say, "No" and start again.

If your puppy ever refuses to stop mouthing on request, remove whatever body part your puppy is holding on to and initiate an immediate timeout.

Play Tug of War: Some believe that playing tug of war with dogs leads to aggression. Done properly and with a little discipline, it's an effective way to teach give and take while the pup also learns to control his mouth.

Have the puppy sit while you hold the tug toy in your hand. You've already taught the puppy to "Out" (see above) which means that he should not touch the toy until given permission. Additionally, you will have taught the puppy "Drop it" (see *The How-To of Training*.) Offer the toy to the puppy and say, "Take it" to begin the game. Let the pup tug for a minute or so, then say, "Drop it" and ask the puppy for a "sit." Repeat.

Take frequent breaks to be sure that you are in control. These breaks are built-in opportunities for reinforcement. When the puppy complies with the request to drop it, sit, and take it, he is rewarded for his behavior by getting the chance to play again.

Chewing

We must teach dogs what is appropriate to chew on and what is not. If we don't we are destined to come home to find the house looking like the last day of Woodstock.

Dogs chew. It's normal. It's one way they explore their world and it's fun. Chewing is necessary to maintain healthy gums and clean teeth. Puppies chew to soothe the inflammation of teething and to explore the world. It's how they determine the difference between sentient living beings and inanimate objects. Additionally, dogs chew out of boredom and some chew to relieve stress (as in the case of the dog with separation anxiety.)

Many believe that puppies will simply outgrow the urge to chew. While the behavior will naturally diminish, a pup continues to see the whole world (including your home) as his chew toy into adolescence and adulthood unless he's learned otherwise. Chewing is fun, and now it's become habit.

It is much more effective and easier to be proactive about chewing. Rather than being reactive and punish the dog for chewing on inappropriate objects, let's teach him what is appropriate to chew. Punishment would mean absolute consistency in disciplining the pup every time he chews on something inappropriate and this is simply not possible when you are gone.

It is impossible to teach dogs not to chew. Therefore, our goal is to re-channel misguided chewing. We will teach him what is acceptable and appropriate to chew on–chew toys. Because chewing is normal and necessary, puppies will choose to chew anything available. Although it may seem he's chosen to gnaw your new, expensive Persian rug out of spite, this is not the motivation. He has no idea about the retail value of floor coverings. He has done it, simply because he could. Maybe he was bored, maybe he was anxious, and maybe he had never tasted Persian wool.

The point is we need to provide appropriate chew toys and we need to teach puppies what they are for. This requires more than dropping him into a pile of toys. He may still choose the Persian rug unless he's shown what chew toys are all about.

The first rule of appropriate chewing is never allowing puppies to have unsupervised free range of the house. Just as we would not have an unattended toddler, we must oversee our puppy's activities, guiding him away from making mistakes.

From day one, encourage the puppy to play with chew toys. Attract his attention by waving one in front of his nose, dragging it, or throwing it. Keep a constant eagle eye on your puppy when you're with him. Praise him every time he makes the proper choice of items to chew and redirect him when it's inappropriate. Your puppy will learn to make good choices because those options get your attention. To redirect, simply say, "No!" and provide an appropriate alternative. Now, praise your puppy and encourage play. Remember that dogs want our attention and that lecturing is an ineffective technique. Scolding without redirection is giving the dog attention. It is negative attention, but to the dog, it's better than no attention at all. Therefore, we must give the puppy feedback by showing him the right choice.

The right choice would be indestructible chew toys. Toys that will not require constant replacement (which is expensive) and toys that the puppy will not consume (which is bad for his health.) Puppies must be supervised when playing with plush and squeaky toys to teach them to play gently and not to eat them.

Puppies should be confined to a small puppy-proof area when they cannot be supervised. This area might be a crate, pen, or small room. Leave him with only acceptable, indestructible toys. Teach your puppy to spend time here when you are at home. Periodically praise him when you see that he has settled and is chewing on an appropriate toy. He is not only learning what's appropriate to chew on, he's learning how to occupy himself during time spent alone.

There are many indestructible, interactive chew toys on the market. To mention a couple, the Kong® company http://www.kongcompany.com/ makes a wide variety and Nina Ottosson offers an array of wonderful dog puzzle toys http://www.nina-ottosson.com/

Learn to be alone

It is important that puppies learn to spend time alone because inevitably you will have to leave your home. Your puppy needs to be okay with that. He needs to know how to amuse himself and be comfortable in his own company.

The first step is to provide your puppy with a place of his own and to settle there when you are present. Whether his place is a crate, an exercise pen, or a gated room, he must have a positive association with it. This is the place where he eats his meals, chews his appropriate chew toys and sleeps. It is not a place of timeouts, isolation, or punishment. Teach your puppy to go to his place on cue and have him spend time there while you are home, but ignoring him. Later, you will have him go to his place and practice departures. See the chapter *Fearful Dogs* for crate training and creating a safe zone.

Teach your puppy to settle with frequent quiet moments throughout the day and work them into the daily routine. Sometimes your puppy is in his place and sometimes he is settled down next to you. During playtime, encourage your puppy to settle with frequent breaks in the action. Play with him, and then ask for a sit and/or a down. Let him settle for a few seconds, then resume play. This helps him learn impulse control as well as to settle on cue. Additionally, he learns that settle is not a bad thing and does not necessarily mean that playtime is over.

Indiscriminate playtime and unlimited access to you while you are home, is a setup for an over dependent puppy who is anxious when you are gone. Once your pup has gained some self-confidence and able to entertain himself in your absence, you can spend unlimited time together, yet know that he's okay while you're gone.

Having the puppy spend time in his place while you are at home, allows you to monitor him and he makes a positive connection with it. If he's only in his place during your absence, he will associate it with your departure and loneliness.

Housetraining

The key to successful potty training is to supervise, supervise, supervise. This means that the puppy is either attached to you with a leash or in his crate or confinement area whenever you are not engaged in playtime or training.

Outfit the crate with a bed and appropriate chew toys. Confinement will prevent the puppy from having accidents and will facilitate his learning about chew toys and time alone. Puppies should not be crated for more than an hour at a time. Short-term confinement allows you to predict when your puppy needs to relieve himself.

The ideal crate for potty training should be just large enough for the puppy to stand up, turn around, and lay down comfortably. This discourages

elimination in the crate, as dogs naturally do not soil the area where they sleep.

Let the puppy out of his crate once every hour (set a timer if you need to) and take him directly outside to the place where you want him to go potty.

Then, reward him for doing so. Make sure you stay to observe whether the pup has done his business. Puppies are easily distracted and might forget why they are there. If you do not observe the act, you will miss the opportunity to reward him for doing the right thing in the right place. Furthermore, you'll be cleaning up a mess when he comes in the house and remembers that he had to go.

When you are not at home, your puppy needs to be confined to his puppy-proof area where he has access to an appropriate area to potty. Perhaps the area is equipped with potty pads, a litter box, or a patch of turf.

Basic Puppy Skills

Following are some basic, essential skills to teach your puppy. They are the foundation for the well-trained, well-mannered adult dog and later advanced training.

Training tip: portion out your puppy's food for the day, and use it for training. This has your puppy working for his meals and prevents treat overload.

Attentive Dog

Paying attention is the keystone for successful training. To teach attentiveness, first sit with your puppy on leash or in a small, enclosed area and let him go about his business of exploring. Ignore everything he does and wait until he looks at you. You may wait a while for that first glance, but don't be concerned about how long it takes or how brief the look is. When your puppy looks at you for even a second, mark the behavior with a verbal cue (the word yes) or a click if you are using a clicker and reward him. Now, break the puppy's attention by stepping away and let him go back to his puppy business. Wait for him to look at you again. Every time he looks at you, mark, praise, and treat. You will notice that he starts checking in more frequently. Raise the bar by gradually lengthening the time the puppy is looking at you before he receives his reward.

This exercises teaches puppies that there is someone else in the room, and paying attention is worth his while. We can also use this exercise to teach the puppy his name. When the puppy looks at you, say his name, mark, and reward. Soon the puppy will learn to look at you when he hears his name.

Greetings

Socialization with other dogs is more than taking your puppy to group play
dates or the dog park (puppies under 4 months of age should not go to the
dog park.) While we want our puppies to meet a variety of dogs and people,
these interactions should be structured, supervised, and educational. If we
allow our puppies to rush up to everyone, we've inadvertently taught them
that they can meet every person and dog they encounter—and it's done by
pulling on the leash, jumping, barking, and lunging. Such greetings are
intensely rude, which can get puppies into trouble, not to mention the
embarrassment we endure. We can teach dogs that we don't meet everyone
and how to do it politely when we do.

Puppies allowed only free-for-all playtime or turned loose in a puppy melee,
do not learn appropriate play skills. Focused only on each other, they do
not learn to pay attention to us. This could set them up for troublesome
overly excited greetings toward other dogs. Teach your puppy pass bys
and proper dog-to-dog on leash greetings. See the chapter *The How-To
of Training.*

Find It

This is an incredibly easy, yet highly beneficial exercise to teach your puppy.
It can be used to help him refocus, avoid distractions and unwanted
behaviors, and diffuse potentially unsafe situations.

It's always a good idea to take treats (or any other high-value rewards) on
walks, especially when training a new behavior. Rewards need to be high
value in order to trump the squirrels, people, other dogs, and blowing
leaves—all things that are endlessly more exciting than the other end of the
leash (you.)

For this exercise, choose high-value treats as rewards that your puppy
absolutely loves. Make a potpourri of these treats so that he never knows
which yummy tidbit is coming next.

Start in a low-distraction environment such as inside the house. Have your
puppy on leash using the same equipment that you use on your walks.
Begin by dropping a treat on the floor right in front of your puppy so that
he sees it. As he moves toward the treat and picks it up say, "Find it!"
Repeat the exercise a few times. Then, make it gradually more difficult by

dropping the treat to the side, then behind the puppy. The goal is to have him put his nose to the ground and search for the treat when he hears, "Find it!"

There are multiple benefits to training "Find It." One advantage is that it diverts the puppy's attention away from environmental distractions. It gets you and your puppy engaged. Additionally, it keeps the puppy calm and cognitive. Sniffing the ground is a behavior that dogs do to calm themselves and others. So not only is the puppy calming himself with his nose to the ground while playing "Find It," he is sending a calming signal to other dogs.

When your puppy is adept at "Find It" in the house, gradually increase the level of distraction. Have him play the game while someone enters the room, have another dog enter the room, take the game to the back yard, and finally take it to the streets for your walks. Remember, to set your puppy up for success by getting him reliable with the game before increasing the level of distraction. Help by giving him enough distance from the distraction. For example, do not try to do the game by walking two feet away from the barking dog behind the fence. Be prepared to raise the stakes when out in the real world by using higher value treats and/or a higher reinforcement rate.

Group Puppy Classes

Well-run puppy classes effectively facilitate socialization and help build confidence with other dogs. Many classes start pups as early as 9 or 10 weeks of age. It is important to enroll puppies before they reach the age of 4 ½ months of age, as this is a crucial juncture in a puppy's development. This is when he turns from puppy to adolescent. Guidance through this challenging transition by a skilled, professional dog trainer will serve you and your puppy well.

Effective puppy classes allow puppies to gain their canine social skills through constructive playtime in a controlled environment. Dogs that learn to play as puppies, are more confident and less likely to be fearful or aggressive as adults. Dogs that have learned proper canine social skills in puppyhood are better equipped to handle the occasional fearful situation or scuffle in adulthood.

Puppy classes should be organized and educational for both pups and owners. Free-for-all classes or unstructured play dates might do more harm than good–even be downright traumatic for puppies. By no means should we take a puppy to the dog park to "let him learn the ropes" or "be put in his place." Ushering a young puppy to a dog park would be like taking a youngster to a frat party. A good puppy class teaches canine communication skills, attentiveness toward owners, impulse control, appropriate play, and how to be relaxed around other puppies.

In the past, owners of new puppies were advised never to take their pups out of the house before their series of puppy vaccinations were complete. This advice was based on the fear that young puppies would contract diseases. Even though puppies' immune systems are still developing, we mustn't wait. If we delay socialization until a puppy has all of his shots, we will miss a vital, one-time opportunity. With commonsense precautions during socialization, we can minimize the risks. The probability of infection is quite low compared to the much higher risk of puppies developing serious behavior problems such as fear and aggression later in life.

Bite inhibition is far and away the most important reason for puppies to attend puppy class. Play fighting with other pups provides an excellent opportunity for him to improve control of his mouth. He learns that if he bites too hard, no one wants to play with him. Puppies provide appropriate, immediate feedback to one another if their sensitive skin is bitten too hard– much better than what we humans can do. These valuable lessons are generalized to humans, facilitating training and control during playtime.

Even if they are well socialized, it is unrealistic to expect dogs will never squabble or need to use their mouths as a warning if startled or hurt. However, a well-socialized dog that has learned good bite inhibition as a puppy, will settle issues without doing serious damage or any damage at all.

He had the appeal of a very young dog of a very large breed -- a kind of amiable absurdity. **–Dorothy L. Sayers,** *Gaudy Night*

Adolescence
Surviving canine adolescence is comparable to surviving the human teenage years. Maybe better, at least we shouldn't have to worry about most dogs breaking curfew or denting the car.

Adolescence is a time when dogs push their boundaries and push our buttons. However, their button pushing is not intentional, even though it would seem so. Adolescence is a time to gain independence. It's a time when everyone loses his mind and impulse control seems but an unattainable dream. This frustrating and exhausting time (frustrating and exhausting for us) is a sensitive learning period, in which dogs are vulnerable to sudden environmental changes and adverse experiences with dogs, people, or events. Adolescence is when the real work of training begins.

Sadly, more dogs are given up for behavioral problems during adolescence than at any other age. Adolescent dogs may suddenly become unreliable in their training and manners. They may revert to old puppy behaviors and leave us thinking that all the hard work of early training was for naught. They seem completely independent one minute and cling like Velcro® the next. They may have lapses in house training, refuse to comply with cues, and have serious selective hearing. And, on top of it all, like the human teenager, he thinks he's smarter than we are.

Large breeds develop slower than small breeds. Small breeds' temperaments will begin to stabilize at around the age of two years. Large breeds tend to enter adulthood around their third birthday.

Dogs experience similar developmental stages as humans. The puppy, like the human 2-year-old stays willingly beside mom at the store. The 7-year-old may venture over to the toy aisle. The teenager doesn't want anyone to know that she even has parents!

Between four and eight months, dogs begin to exhibit their independence and become more adventurous. This is time is often referred to as the flight instinct period. In other words, he is testing his wings. He's becoming more confident and develops a strong desire to explore the world.

Puppies experience a fear period between 8 and 11 weeks. The second fear period, the adolescent fear period, takes place between 6 and 18 months of age. This is a stage when the dog may exhibit fearful behavior in the presence of things that gave him no pause before. For example, he may now become fearful around people or other dogs, or novel experiences.

Adolescents need plenty of physical exercise and mental stimulation. Group classes are a good source of support because training during adolescence often seems futile. It appears our dogs have become irretrievably distracted and daft. Group classes offer structure and encouragement from a professional trainer and other owners. They provide an outlet for your dog's adolescent energy and a learning experience for both of you. It is a bonding experience as well. Perfect timing, as this is when we may need to rekindle and strengthen our relationship.

It is important to revisit the basic puppy skills your dog has learned previously. If you have adopted your dog as an adolescent, he may be undertrained or lacking these skills altogether. Take your newly adopted adolescent through the puppy basics of socialization, learning to be alone, greetings, and paying attention. Furthermore, get him into a group class.

Socialization and bite inhibition are apt to decline during adolescence. To keep his bite inhibition in tact, provide plenty of opportunities for your dog to play with other dogs. Hand feed your dog. Examine and clean his teeth and continue practicing "Take it" and "Out."

We've worked hard to socialize our puppy, but there is a tendency to become complacent when he reaches adolescence. We are inclined to take the same route for walks and attend the same dog park to play with the same dogs. We tend to slack off on having him meet new people. Consequently, adolescent dogs can de-socialize toward unfamiliar people and dogs. They come to trust only their inner circle of canine and human friends. To avoid loss of confidence and social skills, we must continue to socialize our dogs. Puppy socialization was an overture to adolescent socialization. Adolescent socialization is a prelude to adult socialization.

That said we must know that it's unrealistic to expect our dogs to like every other dog or person. Good bite inhibition and socialization will have the dog handle anxious or unfriendly situations in an acceptable manner.

It's kind of fun to do the impossible. — **Walt Disney**

Tips for Adolescent Success

- Take your adolescent back to the puppy basics. Start from the beginning, as you would with a new pup on his first day home. (It's not really starting over, but a refresher course.)

- Revisit potty training if necessary

- Provide occupational therapy in the form of appropriate chew toys and interactive toys

- Practice short training sessions daily

- Continue bite inhibition exercises

- Take daily walks varying the time and route in order to meet new people and dogs

- Visit different dog parks (providing your dog enjoys dog parks)

- Take your dog along on various outings to dog friendly destinations like the pet supply store, the local bistro with outdoor dining, or home improvement store that welcomes dogs

- Continue his regular play dates with his core group of canine friends

If you've raised your adolescent from a pup and done a good job of socializing and training, you are better prepared for the challenges ahead. Adolescence does not last forever, but it will seem so if there is a lack of direction and no boundaries and rules set. As challenging as adolescence is, with patience and understanding, you'll come out on the other side having a stronger relationship with your well-behaved dog.

Choose the right adolescent

Many people choose to adopt puppies in order to raise them up right from the beginning. For various reasons, others choose to adopt an adolescent dog. There are some pros and cons to be considered with adolescents in need of plenty of exercise, mental stimulation, and a large dose of patience.

Pros:
- What you see is what you get—adolescents are almost at their full physical and temperament development.

• The adolescent dog is most likely potty trained.

• Adolescents most likely have some basic training.

• Adolescents have already gone through the first chewing stage.

• Adolescents may have already gone through the first fear period.

Cons:

• The first, all-important socialization period has passed.

• If the dog has not learned proper bite inhibition, it is far more challenging to teach it. The dog will likely revert to a hard mouth if ever he bites in a moment of fear or pain.

• Adolescents have unlimited energy and (seemingly) limited brains.

• Adolescents have likely developed some bad habits or never learned many good ones.

• Although the first fear period and the first chewing stages have past, the second ones that occur during adolescence are more challenging to handle.

Setting boundaries and making rules is a must for adopting a new adolescent or transitioning the puppy into adolescence. If transitioning a puppy, you've already done this, but be prepared to stand your ground with the onset of adolescence. Some puppy behaviors carry over, some will be outgrown, and others require additional guidance.

Dogs need (and want) structure to make the world manageable and predictable. Establish leadership so that the dog doesn't have to. They don't want the leadership position and neither do you want them to have it. Abdicating leadership to a dog would be like renouncing leadership to a human teenager—we most likely wouldn't care for the decisions made.

In adolescence, we must pay close attention to environmental management and control resources. Manage attention-seeking behavior and reinforce calm conduct. In other words, be proactive, not reactive. Set your adolescent up for success and allow him to learn. Do so by reinforcing the good stuff.

Motivation and Attention

Adolescent dogs have difficulty maintaining focus and food lures may temporarily lose their effectiveness. If this is the case, try raising the value of the food treat. This may or may not work. If it doesn't, try using toys instead. Fetch or tug-of-war can be highly rewarding for the adolescent dog. Remember, that anything a dog wants can be used as reinforcement, so instead of rewarding your dog with food, have a rousing game of fetch or tug instead, if that what floats his boat.

If you've taught your puppy to pay attention with the Attentive Dog exercise described in the puppy section, you can strengthen it with your adolescent. If you have adopted an adolescent dog, start with the Attentive Dog exercise. Once the Attentive Dog exercise is learned, proceed as described below.

The Attentive Dog exercise taught your dog that it's worth his while to look at you and be calm. When he's learned this, you will notice him checking in with you more often. Now it's time to get more specific.

Praise and reward your dog for voluntarily checking in by looking at you. After rewarding him, step away to break his attention, but this time, turn your back to him. Wait for him to figure out that you want him to look at you, but that he must come to face you in order to do so. It may take a minute, but when he comes around and looks at your face, mark, reward, and praise. Repeat the exercise a few times until your dog is reliably coming in front of you and looking at your face.

Now, we want to put the behavior on cue. Turn away from your dog, wait for him to come around to look at your face, and then say, "Watch" as he makes eye contact. Once he associates the cue word with the behavior, you will be able to say, "Watch" as you turn away. Next, put the behavior in motion by asking your dog to "Watch" as he is heeling. Ask for "Watch" during other exercises such as stay or wait.

Dogs have given us their absolute all. We are the center of their universe. We are the focus of their love and faith and trust. They serve us in return for scraps. It is without a doubt the best deal man has ever made. **–Roger A. Caras**

Adulthood

If considering adopting an adult dog, do so carefully, as carefully as choosing a pup. An adult dog's temperament has been established and his habits are entrenched. This is not to say that you can't *teach an old dog new tricks*, but doing so can take copious amounts of time, effort, and patience as an adult dog has been rehearsing the unwanted behavior for longer. However, he's been practicing desirable behaviors for longer as well. Undesirable behaviors are more difficult to extinguish, but good ones will remain if they continue to be reinforced.

Adopting an adult dog:

Pros:

- An adult dog is more likely to be housetrained
- Adult dogs typically need less exercise
- An adult dog's habits are more entrenched
- An adult dog is likely to be less destructive
- Adult dogs have better focus in training

Cons:

- Adult dogs take longer to adapt to their new environment
- An adult dog's habits are more entrenched

An inherent danger in rescuing an adult dog is to get caught up trying to compensate for the unfortunate life he had before. Whether he comes from a mill dog situation, abuse, or neglect, we feel compelled to rectify the situation. A noble gesture, but we must still set boundaries and rules and stick to them—especially in the first couple of months. One or two months is typically the time it takes an adult dog to settle in to his new home.

Set the rules before you bring your new dog home and implement them from day one. He may have gotten away with things in his former home that are not acceptable in yours. It's easier to set the rules from the beginning and relax them later than it is to tighten them or fix the unwanted behaviors.

Even though your adult dog is probably housetrained, he doesn't know where the acceptable toileting area is or how to get there. As you would do with a new puppy, take your adult dog outside to the designated location, observe, praise and reward him for his success.

An adult dog has developed adult interests, like sniffing other dogs' butts and putting backyard squirrels on notice to evacuate—activities that compete with training. The adult dog must be given time to adjust to new environments and situations. Continue socialization throughout adulthood. Your new adult dog must explore his physical and social environment, experience new ones, and continue to meet unfamiliar people and dogs. Older dogs generally become more cautious of unfamiliar stimuli. Therefore, take care to make new experiences pleasant ones.

If you are transitioning with the adolescent into adulthood, then you will be blissfully aware of this fact: At long last, by the age of two or three years, your dog has reached his social maturity. Adulthood is the time to reap the benefits of all that early training and you can thank yourself for staying with it. Adulthood is the time to celebrate the fact that you both survived adolescence! But, all relationships, take continued work. Dog training is not like programming a computer. Alas, it's never done.

Keep your training guide handy and your skills honed. There may be times when an adult dog needs a training refresher on basic skills. This could be brought on by a traumatic experience, a major life change such as moving, divorce, the birth of a baby, adopting a new dog, the death of a resident dog, or major schedule changes.

Tips for Adult Success
Use the puppy basics as a guideline with your newly adopted adult dog.

- Establish a routine
- Teach your adult dog to pay attention
- Enroll in a group class to learn the basics or as a refresher
- Enroll in a group class for the bonding experience
- Socialize
- Do handling exercises

Aging has a wonderful beauty and we should have respect for that.

—Eartha Kitt

Seniors

I've come to accept the fact that longevity is only accomplished through aging. However, it happens much faster than expected. Recently, I was talking with a childhood friend, when I suddenly burst out laughing. I asked, "Do you realize that just yesterday, we were playing Barbies together, and now we're talking about Social Security?" What happened? I still feel like playing Barbies!

A shared opinion among dog lovers is that our furry companions don't live long enough. Accepting the velocity of my own aging process is difficult, but it's even tougher to see it happening to my dogs. I've adopted a perspective of acceptance and appreciation of the process. I'm happy to have shared my life with so many wonderful dogs and I'm honored to have spent their twilight days with them.

When my dog Mr. MoJo is being his pushy, sometimes annoying self, I remember that he is 13 years old, an advanced age for a large dog. I remember that I did not have this time with other dogs that went too soon, and I imagine how I will miss MoJo's pushy, annoying behaviors sooner than I'd like to think.

Living with a senior dog has it's own set of privileges and challenges. Older dogs sleep more and they sleep more soundly. They are under foot more.

Dog walks with seniors are different than with younger dogs. We now let the dog set the pace and length of the walk. Older dogs are less tolerant of extreme temperatures because their body temperature may not be regulated as efficiently. Therefore, we must be Goldilocks for our senior companions. We must be sure that walks, living quarters, and sleeping areas are not too hot or not too cold.

Pros

- Senior dogs are wiser as well as older.
- Senior dogs are calmer and require less exercise.
- Senior dogs may be more affectionate.
- Senior dogs are independent, requiring less attention.

Cons

- Senior dogs are independent, requiring less attention.

- Senior dogs have more health issues.

Health Issues

As humans do, dogs develop health issues as they age. Arthritis and joint pain are common, among a myriad of other age-related maladies. Health issues can cause changes in behavior. Unlike, my uncle Marty, who shares his ailments ad infinitum, dogs tend to be stoic and very good at hiding pain. Consequently, it can be difficult to recognize when a dog is hurting. Discomfort can cause dogs to become moody and irritable and even cause them to aggress, especially if pain is sharp or intense.

Oftentimes behavioral changes in dogs are attributed to senility, but let's not be hasty with this assumption. Behavioral changes can stem from pain or diseases that produce chemical imbalances affecting brain function. Aging pets can experience increased anxiety due to Canine Cognitive Dysfunction or age related vision or hearing impairment.

Decreased reliability in housetraining may occur due to physical reasons for incontinence. The fact that the dog is now incapable of the old routine can also be a factor. For example, the physical requirements of getting to his toileting area may be impossible. He simply can't hold it if it's a long trip or physically traverse the stairs.

Mobility issues are common in senior dogs. There are harnesses designed for large breed dogs to help them climb stairs or to lift them. Ramps and steps are also available to assist dogs in loading into the car or getting up on to your bed.

We often must deal with pain management for senior dogs. Know the signs of pain, some of which are not as obvious as yelping, whining, or difficulty getting up. These less apparent signs include loss of appetite, decreased activity, and reduced sociability. Seniors may become more defensive of their personal space when they are in pain and may display aggressive behavior. Visit your vet to determine the best way to manage your dog's pain. Schedule more checkups and follow her recommendations on diet and exercise. Do frequent physical inspections of your own on a regular basis.

Incontinence

Incontinence can be due to neurologic or muscular control issues. Senior dogs must be allowed more opportunity to go out and be provided potty pads if they need to be left for long periods of time.

Incontinent dogs require the same close supervision as that of a puppy. Resist temptation to keep the dog outside or constant crating to keep the house from being soiled. Proper use of the crate can be helpful, but take heed. Separating the dog in the name of saving the house may result in his feeling isolated. The family member who is suddenly excommunicated is now lonely and stressed. Separation can lead to behavioral changes such as barking for attention or destructiveness.

Your vet can prescribe medication to address the issue of incontinence after she's ruled out other causes such as diabetes, kidney disease, or urinary tract infection. Close supervision and frequent potty breaks will help reduce the number of accidents and doggie diapers are available for times when your dog cannot be supervised.

Obesity

Obesity, a common problem in senior dogs, can cause adverse health conditions. As in humans, a dog's metabolic rate slows with age. A slower metabolism combined with orthopedic or other age-related health problems, can lead to weight gain. The formula for weight control with dogs is (ah, don't we know it?) to reduce caloric intake and/or increase the expenditure of energy. Another fact that holds true for human weight control is true for dogs: the majority of caloric intake should be from healthy food–not treats. We need not eliminate treats altogether, but it is wise to choose healthy, low calorie ones. Consult your veterinarian for your geriatric dog's special dietary needs.

Mobility, Lameness and Weakness

There are obvious physical manifestations of lameness such as limping or showing signs that sitting is uncomfortable. Additionally, a dog might develop an unwillingness to jump on or off of furniture or traverse stairs.

Mobility issues can have a psychological effect on dogs. Ambulatory difficulties that disallow the dog to follow his people may result in feelings of isolation. In this case, provide a resting place near the center of activity where the dog can be safely out of the way, but hear and see what's going on.

Seniors need a softer place to sleep. Orthopedic beds available on the market can provide a comfortable resting place. Older dogs may have trouble negotiating uncarpeted floors. Strategically placed non-skid rugs will maximize comfort and minimize pain, giving dogs the ability to navigate the home more easily.

Decreased mobility can cause behavioral changes in how dogs react to stress. Whereas in previous stressful situations, the dog would have moved away, he may be unable or less willing to do so given his mobility issues. He might become fearful and even resort to aggression instead.

Changes in Vision

Seniors often experience deterioration in vision due to cataracts and glaucoma among other things. Oftentimes there is a decline in both vision and hearing or complete blindness and deafness. Keep the dog's environment and routing stable. Avoid rearranging furniture so that the dog can navigate the home by memory. If it is necessary to alter the environment, allow the dog to sniff and hear the modified surroundings while escorting him on leash.

Changes in Hearing

Hearing loss can be gradual and go unnoticed. It may be difficult to distinguish whether the dog's hearing is impaired or whether he chooses not to respond due to other reasons such as pain.

Deaf or hearing-impaired dogs are easily startled. Therefore, they need warning when approached (especially when sleeping) as some dogs may respond to surprises with aggression. Helpful tips for deaf or hearing-impaired dogs include teaching hand signals, stomping on the floor when approaching, and the use of a vibrating collar (NOT a shock collar) for training. Make sure that the dog can see you when you approach and teach hand signals for basic cues like sit, down, and stay.

Deaf or hearing-impaired dogs are more vulnerable to dangers such as traffic, which requires extra supervision and leashes–always.

Changes in Routine

Elderly dogs can be resistant to changes in routine, location, and social situations. Give the dog plenty of quiet time alone in short-term situations, like when small children are visiting or workmen are in the home.

Give senior dogs plenty of time to adjust to unavoidable alterations in schedules or major life changes such as moving. In the new home, show the dog where he is to eliminate, sleep, and eat. Help him to generalize basic behaviors by revisiting fundamental training exercises such as sit, stay, and down in the new environment.

Changing Hierarchies

Aging can mean status change in the multi-dog household. This is most evident when the aging dog is the one holding the highest rank. Whereas many dominant dogs abdicate their position graciously, some hierarchies experience conflict. Oftentimes dogs work it out, but we may need to assist by stepping in as the benevolent leader that we are (see how to establish leadership in the chapter *Living at Peace in the Pack*.)

Other resident dogs know when one of their housemates is ill and aging, so close supervision of their interactions is necessary to prevent bullying. Practice solid management by separating dogs, especially at feeding time and when you are away. Make sure the elderly dog has a private safe place to escape when necessary.

Ensure that all dogs are getting age appropriate exercise, manage resources closely, and know what to expect. If there is imminent status change in the works, the dog trying to overthrow the king may become possessive of chew bones, beds, food, and you.

Require polite behavior before dogs get food or attention and avoid taking sides in rivalry. When conflicts occur, intervene, and redirect (see how to establish leadership in the chapter *Living at Peace in the Pack*.)

Dementia

Geriatric dogs can experience dementia or Canine Cognitive Dysfunction. With this cognitive decline, dogs can experience changes in awareness and deficits in learning and memory. Dogs experiencing dementia may exhibit symptoms of disorientation, anxiety, irritability, and fecal/urinary incontinence. Your vet can prescribe medication to reduce the severity of the symptoms.

Heaven goes by favor. If it went by merit, you would stay out and your dog would go in. **–Mark Twain**

Oftentimes we must make the decision to assist our dog in passing from this life. This is a heart wrenching and difficult decision. My dogs have always told me when it's their time, but I inevitably second-guess myself. I expect it. It's part of the process. I've lost most of my dogs to cancer, and no matter how much I wanted someone else to make the decision for me, I know that ultimately, I had to do it for myself.

If I could say that money is no object, I would, but unfortunately, money is a consideration. However, in regard to dogs lost to incurable forms of cancer–if the chemotherapy had been free, I would have opted out. I could not subject my dogs to weekly hospitalization, hooked up to machines and successive days suffering the side effects of chemotherapy. All of that physical and emotional stress endured to extend life by *maybe* 4 months? I did not consider that as quality of life. I opted instead, to make my dogs as comfortable as possible at home with his canine roommates and me.

The decision is about the dog. Though I might want radical treatment to extend our time together, I must think of the quality of my dog's life. I want his last days to be as comfortable and peaceful as possible.

The decision of *when* is emotionally trying. Your dog will give you clues. Monitor his appetite, pain, mobility, and participation and interaction with other household members, both human and canine.

Is the dog eating his normal amount of food? Is he missing meals? Is the dog in chronic pain and how is that affecting mobility and daily life? (Your veterinarian can advise and give you options for pain management.) How is he interacting with members of the household? Are they pleasant? Is the dog seeking attention or being withdrawn?

The Final Vet Visit: Euthanasia
Choosing whether the final vet visit takes place at home or at the clinic is a personal decision. I prefer to have it take place in the privacy of my own

home where my dog and I are most comfortable. This also allows the other dogs in the household to say goodbye, to see and sniff the body afterward, and to understand what has happened.

I would like to take a page from my dogs' book on handling death. Each time, when allowed to approach the body, they've sniffed, then went casually about their business, as if to say, "OK, now what?"

The other dogs will grieve, but as humans do, they will do it in their own way. Other pets in the home may experience differing levels of behavioral changes after the death of a dog. Some may become withdrawn and depressed, while others show no apparent signs of grieving or any behavioral changes.

Animals form attachments to their housemates and anecdotal evidence indicates that they mourn the loss of their companions. Especially for older dogs, grieving can be more difficult. They may experience a decrease in appetite and activity, restlessness and altered sleep patterns. Changes in eating and drinking habits may signal health problems, so seek veterinary attention if necessary.

To help with their grieving, uphold your regular routine with the other dogs. Maintain the same level of attention they receive, but don't force interaction if they seem to want more time alone. You may want to increase the number of walks and playtime the other dogs are getting.

What you do with your dog's physical remains is another individual decision. You may choose cremation and to scatter or keep the ashes. Alternatively, you may choose burial. City regulations vary and most prohibit burying pets in the back yard and require interment in pet cemeteries. Your veterinarian can help you find these services.

End of life care for your dog and the decisions made are highly personal. I've shared my own experiences here, but your choices may be very different. I cannot tell you or even suggest what is right for you. Follow your heart and listen to what your dog is telling you. Allow yourself time to grieve and be compassionate toward yourself. Gather strength from friends and family or a pet-loss support group.

Another Dog?

Some people want to get another dog right away. Some people get another dog before their elderly dog passes. This is another very personal decision and you will make the right one for yourself.

Assisting dogs in passing is the most humane and loving thing we can do for our unfailing friends. Each time I go through it, I swear I don't ever want to do it again. But, I do. I do it because I cannot imagine my life without dogs. End of life care is part of what we sign up for when we choose the pleasure of a dog's company in our lives.

No matter where our dogs are in their life journey, the most important things we can do is to understand them, teach them well, love them, and let them be dogs.

If there are no dogs in Heaven, then when I die I want to go where they went. **–Will Rogers**

It has been difficult to say goodbye to each of my dogs. I have loved them all from the bottom of my heart. I could share each story, but I'd like to tell you about one—the tale of Bob. Bob danced into my life as the happiest dog in the world. He left in the same manner. Even as the doctor arrived for the final house call, Bob summoned the energy to greet him at the door with a smile and a wagging tail. After the doctor administered the injection, Bob walked over to me, lay down in my lap, and drew his last breath. Even the doctor was moved by Bob's last gesture of goodwill.

Before Bob's passing, a friend had told me the story of how she'd acquired her dog. The breeder told her the pup was too small to sell and offered him to my friend. When she heard that the puppy weighed only 2.5 pounds she said, "Perfect. That's just how much my heart weighs!" My heart weighed 90 lbs.

10

Wish You Were Here

Coping with and Treating Separation Anxiety

Paul came home after a long day to find his Border Collie lying smugly atop a heap of trash and displaced household goods. She was quite pleased with her artful redecorating. Home alone, she'd spent quality time rearranging select pieces of furniture, relocating garbage from the bin, and sorting the dirty laundry.

Fortunately, Paul's phone had not become part of the wreckage, so he called me with his concerns about his dog's tendencies toward demolition. "Could my dog be suffering from separation anxiety?" he asked.

After some discussion, we determined that Bonnie did not have separation anxiety, and that she was not suffering from anything other than boredom. Bonnie was experiencing something more like separation fun. Bonnie needed more mental stimulation, adequate physical exercise, and environmental enrichment. This plan would relieve the tedium and extinguish her penchant for interior redecorating.

Jenny works from home. Her French Bulldog, Emmett, is a constant fixture by her side. Jenny takes Emmett with her whenever possible, but French Bulldogs are not allowed at the English Tearoom (no politics, just state health code), where she often meets clients. Jenny may possibly be the Expedia.com of booking guilt trips, especially for herself. She can't bear the thought of Emmett being in doggie solitary confinement (crated) while she's away.

Jenny's home departure theatrics are unmatched by any television daytime drama. In reality, Emmett is quite the independent little Frenchman and does pretty well when home alone. Jenny, on the other hand, needs to unpack from her guilt trip. She can help Emmett by dispensing with her theatrics and enhancing his alone time with a few brain teasing interactive toys. With a little planning and some letting go, Emmett and Jenny will be able to relax and enjoy time spent together as well as time spent apart.

Don't let separation anxiety be an excuse for an ill-mannered dog—or one that's bored silly. Let's not create problems where they do not exist. This chapter will help identify and address the real issues: separation anxiety, separation fun, or the theater playing in our own heads.

We've all gotten those whimsical vacation postcards emblazoned with the sentiment *Wish You Were Here!* If dogs with separation anxiety had the money for postage, they'd be sending one with each of our departures.

Dogs are not genetically designed to be isolated. However, most dogs, the adaptable creatures that they are, do just fine staying home alone. A small number of dogs do not. These are dogs with true separation anxiety.

What is Separation Anxiety?

We are quick to label a dog's destructive, loud, annoying behavior as separation anxiety. In reality, true separation anxiety is uncommon. Behaviors such as destructive chewing, house soiling, howling, and incessant barking can be symptoms of separation anxiety. They can also be signs that dogs are simply filling their uneventful free time with the canine equivalent of Angry Birds. If these dogs had thumbs, they'd be twiddling them. In other words, they're bored, and their alone-time antics are simply something to do.

Dogs suffering from genuine separation anxiety (SA for short) are in a state of terror the entire time they are alone. They panic at our departure and remain so until our return. These dogs may soil the house, chew on the furniture or themselves, attempt to escape, pant, drool, tremble, bark, or howl during our absence. It's heartbreaking that they spend so much of life in a state of panic.

Causes

We often wonder if humans can cause SA in dogs.

"Does letting my dog sleep with me cause SA?" you ask.

"My dog never lets me go companionless while on a simple mission to acquire a tissue. Does this mean he has separation anxiety?"

The experts say, "No."

Over-attachment issues may not be the cause of SA, but they can exacerbate the issue. Some dogs have a genetic predisposition for SA. Dogs have different personalities. Some have an outgoing, friendly nature; while others are less secure and shy. It stands to reason that the unconfident dog may have more trouble staying home alone.

• **Traumatic events:** A traumatic event experienced while home alone can precipitate the onset of SA. Sudden loud noises, thunderstorms, alarms, attempted break-ins, and harassment from unsavory passersby are but a few frightful happenings that could trigger SA.

• **Abandonment:** Dogs that have been abandoned suddenly or re-homed to a dramatically different environment may have difficulty making the adjustment. Candidates for SA are dogs that have been dumped and left to fend for themselves; the owners move, they are left alone, for whatever reason, without food or water. Additionally, dogs left in an unfamiliar, stressful place, such as an overcrowded shelter or boarding facility, can develop separation anxiety.

• **Never alone:** Dogs who have never been left alone can be candidates for separation anxiety. If show dogs, competition dogs, or puppy mill breeding stock have spent their entire lives surrounded by other dogs, a new, quiet home can actually be very disquieting, even terrifying—a situation rife for the onset of SA.

Sudden changes during a dog's assimilation period into a new home can contribute to the development of SA. For example, a dog is adopted during the summer when the kids in the family are out of school. There is always someone at home. Then, August rolls around and suddenly the dog is alone.

In the Meantime: Management
SA is fixable. Yet, there is no quick fix. Treatment takes time and dedication. However, life happens in the meantime, so we need solid management in place while we work through the gradual treatment process. Following are some tips for management in the meantime:

Don't Leave your Dog Home Alone
You're asking if this isn't the point. Yes it is. However, if we leave our dog home alone before he is ready, we run the risk of undoing all of our hard work. Treatment of SA includes desensitization, which is a gradual process, and we don't want to interrupt our progress by moving ahead too quickly.

Take your Dog Along
When running errands, take your dog along. This works well if your dog is

comfortable staying alone in your vehicle. Of course, we must be sure that it's not too hot or cold for our dog to spend some alone time in the car.

Dog Care Swap

Find a friend or trusted neighbor who would enjoy the company of your dog. Better yet, if your friend has a dog that gets along well with your dog, swap dog sitting.

If you don't have a friend who can help, get creative. Advertise. There are likely others in your area with the same need. Check the senior market. Many senior citizens can't have their own dog, but they would love spending time with yours. Do your homework and choose sitters and daycare for your dog as carefully as you would choose your childcare.

Doggie Daycare

If your dog loves a good romp with his canine friends, then find a reputable dog daycare facility. An added benefit: your dog gets plenty of exercise.

To Crate or Not to Crate

A crate can be a happy place or a terrifying prison cell. If you are considering crating your dog with separation anxiety, first learn the art of proper crate training. It can be an effective management tool.

Another Dog?

With this option comes an important caveat: don't get another dog unless you want another dog for yourself. The responsibilities and costs of having multiple dogs grow exponentially, so give the idea careful thought. Consider whether your dog will be comfortable with another dog in the home and if his anxiety would be reduced or relieved. Some dogs get anxious merely by *your* absence, and it wouldn't matter if 101 Dalmatians surrounded him. He will still be afraid.

Treatment

First, let's discuss what does *not* work in treating SA. Leaving toys or chew bones with a terrified dog would be like asking a fellow airline passenger for a friendly game of bridge as your plane plummets to the ground. Dogs with SA rarely show an interest in food or toys when home alone.

Reprimands do not work. If you return home to find destructive chewing or house soiling, simply clean it up. Reprimands occur hours after the fact, rendering them ineffective. Dogs will *not* connect scolding with the previous undesirable behavior, but they *will* associate the punishment with your return. Now you have a dog that is afraid to be alone *and* afraid of your homecoming.

Techniques that Work

Leave the drama to Hollywood. If you turn on the theatrics during your arrivals and departures, your dog will play the supporting role. If you're emotional, your dog will be as well.

Build Confidence

Dogs with SA are often globally fearful and/or insecure. Teaching confidence-building exercises and implementing solid leadership is helpful in treating separation anxiety. Leadership is not about dominance, force, or intimidation. Leadership is more like being a parent than a dictator. We want to instill confidence by leading with compassion and assurance; use only positive, gentle training methods, and open the lines of communication between you and your dog. This will establish that you are someone your dog can depend on, thus building his confidence. Teaching even basic behaviors such as sit, stay, down, and recall will develop your dog's self-reliance.

Teach Stay Out of Sight

Teach your dog to stay while you leave his line of sight. This helps to build his self-assurance, and he'll learn that you can leave but you will then return.

Dog Sports and Extracurricular Activities

You and your dog will be amazed at what he can do. Dog sports such as agility, free style, fly ball, and nose work are great confidence builders. Explore these options, but be sure that your dog enjoys them. Don't be a stage mom or dad here. This is about your dog's wellbeing, not your competitive ego.

Desensitization and Counter-conditioning to Triggers

It seems that dogs know what we are thinking and what we're going to do before we do it. They are much attuned with our body language and behavior patterns. Therefore, they can predict our departure when certain triggers are presented.

Does your dog start to become nervous when you pick up your car keys or pour coffee into your favorite travel mug? If so, desensitize him to these triggers by randomly performing them at home *without* leaving. Better yet, give them new meaning by following up with a stuffed chew toy, walk, or game.

Safe Place

Create a safe place in your home for your dog. This could be a crate or a cozy gated area. There is more to creating this safe place than simply redecorating. First, determine the best setup for your individual dog and floor plan. Is Dinky happier in a closed-sided crate or a wire-mesh one? Is there a room in your home that can be conveniently dog proofed? Consider what type of flooring is easiest for you to clean and hardest for your dog to destroy. Interior rooms are usually quieter, both for the dog and for the neighbors, in case Dinky vocalizes his loneliness.

Helpful Tools

Some management tools that we've found helpful in coping with SA are flower essences, dog appeasing pheromones, anxiety body wraps, and soothing music, all designed to calm the canine. These tools are described in detail below.

Crate or Gate?

Properly trained, many dogs with separation anxiety do well staying alone in a crate. Dogs with mild to moderate SA may fall into this group. Dogs with severe separation anxiety are at risk of injury if they attempt to escape. At best, they are destined to spend their time in a panic and puddle of drool. One caveat: just because a dog is generally comfortable in a crate does not mean he'll be comfortable in it when left alone.

Crates and gates are good management tools to keep your house and dog from going to pieces in your absence. SA dogs often do well if they are securely enclosed in a "safe place." Usually a small, quiet, cozy room is best. You'll want to dog proof it by removing anything harmful or valuable (harmful to the dog and valuable to you). Bathrooms and laundry rooms make good safe places. Use a gate rather than closing the door, as dogs usually do better if they can see out of their cozy, safe place.

Whether using a crate or a gate, there are some preparations and helpful hints in creating a successful safe place for your dog:

- **Leave a Little Bit of You Behind:** Put an article of clothing with your scent on it in the safe place. An old T-shirt or towel works well, provided your dog is not prone to consuming textiles.

- **Music or TV:** Many people leave music or the television playing as a calming presence for their dog. Calming is the key word here. Music without a strong beat is best (lullabies are preferable to Led Zeppelin). Studies show that piano music alone is more soothing. Music is preferable over the TV. Remember what was said earlier in the chapter about drama? The soaps, CNN, or daily doses of The Jerry Springer Show may not have the desired effect.

The music should be predictable, so use recorded music (radio has blaring commercials). A wonderful resource for soothing music is *Through a Dog's Ear*. *Through a Dog's Ear* is clinically researched music with practical solutions for canine anxiety issues. This psycho acoustically designed music is downloadable from the website: http://throughadogsear.com/

It is a good idea to play this music when you are home and an even better idea to couple it with some snuggle time and calming massages for your dog. He will learn to associate the calming music with peaceful times with you.

- **Hide and Seek and Interactive Toys:** When your dog's level of anxiety has been reduced and he's showing interest in food while alone, introduce food-stuffed Kong® and puzzle toys like Buster Cubes, Kong® Wobblers™, etc. Hide some of these toys, and scatter kibble around the safe place. The time your dog spends searching out food will keep him occupied. Mental stimulation is beneficial in lowering stress levels. Be careful. If you want to keep your sofa in tact, don't hide a Kong® under the cushions!

- **Flower Essences:** Based on the healing power of plants, flower essences are often successful treatments for anxiety in dogs. A popular flower essence combination called Rescue Remedy is available at many pet supply stores and natural grocers. Rescue Remedy was originally formulated for humans. The discovery of its benefits to other species led to development of a pet-specific formula. There are individual flower essence tinctures available for anxiety and related issues. Use them individually or create your own customized combination.

• **D.A.P.:** The acronym D.A.P. stands for Dog Appeasing Pheromone. These products, available in diffuser and spray form, are a synthetic equivalent to the chemical produced by a lactating female dog. The natural chemical produced by the female dog has a calming effect on her puppies. D.A.P. is designed to have the same effect on dogs of all ages.

• **Body Wraps:** The concept of gentle, uniform pressure applied to the body to produce a calming effect is not new. Babies have been swaddled since the beginning of time. We've since adopted the idea to help dogs with anxiety.

Create your own body wrap from a T-shirt or purchase a ready-made variety from sources like the Thundershirt Company (www.thundershirt.com).

If you do it yourself, find an appropriately sized T-shirt for your dog. Place it upside down on your dog so that the front of the shirt is on the dog's back. Gather the excess material so that it fits snuggly (not so tight as to restrict movement or circulation). Knot the material with a rubber band, being careful that the knot does not ride on the dog's spine.

Be sure that your dog is comfortable "suiting up" by using slow, gentle movements coupled with praise and treats. Get your dog used to wearing the wrap when you are home. If you put the wrap on only when you leave, you may turn it into a trigger that signals your departure. Create an even more positive association with the wrap by having your dog wear it during his meals, snuggle time, and on walks.

Desensitization to Departures
After determining which of the aforementioned tools and tips are best for your dog, we are ready to start the work of desensitization. Have Lucy go to

her safe place (that has been stocked with interactive toys as described above). Gate or crate her there, and then sit quietly where she can see you. Read a book or update your Facebook status, completely ignoring Lucy. After a few minutes, casually get up and allow her to leave the crate or room. Be sure that Lucy is not crying, barking, or doing any attention-seeking behavior when you release her.

Repeat the exercise above, gradually increasing but varying the amount of time Lucy spends in her safe place. When she is able to remain calm, begin to leave her sight for very short periods, just a few seconds at first. Departures and arrivals should be unceremonious. Lucy will learn that her safe place is a good place, and that you will always return.

Once Lucy can remain calm with your departures from the room, you are ready to simulate leaving the house. With Lucy in her safe place, nonchalantly leave the room, pick up your car keys, go to the door, open it, close it, but don't leave. Wait a few seconds (be sure Lucy isn't crying), then open the door and "come back home." Without fanfare, release Lucy from her safe place.

Repeat the above exercise and gradually increase the time you are "gone." You can even desensitize Lucy to other departure triggers like the garage door opening, the ring of the elevator, and the car starting up. The key to successful desensitization is to do it in baby steps. The more steps you can break the process into, the better the results. Slower is faster in the treatment of separation anxiety.

With patience and training, separation anxiety is solvable and has a high treatment success rate. It is not an easy or quick fix. However, unlike many behavioral problems, when SA is fixed, it stays fixed. Success, like the treatment, is defined by each individual case. For instance, a dog who is genetically predisposed to SA may never be a complete canine couch potato in your absence, but he can reach a healthier acceptable level of relaxation. Home alone time is no longer *Wish You Were Here* time.

11

Bone of Contention
Resource Guarding in Dogs

I can relate to resource guarding all too well. I've been known to bark and growl at passersby for sifting through my recyclables left at the curb for pickup. My friends and family know to give me a wide berth when I possess anything containing even trace amounts of chocolate.

It is said that when the student is ready, the teacher will appear. My teacher appeared when I adopted my dog, Bob Barker. In addition to teaching me about barking, as his name implies, Bob taught me a great deal about resource guarding.

Bob was one of the most enthusiastic resource guarders I've met. He was the happiest, most carefree dog—unless you met him at his food bowl. Had it been within his power, Bob would have had a machine gun nest at the entrance to the pantry where the dog food was kept. Neither man nor beast could enter the room where Bob dined. If they dared, Bob would turn instantly to the dark side with a display of teeth and temper. Surely one risked dismemberment or death if they were to be so foolish as to approach Bob's coveted kibble.

I knew I had to call in my think tank of trainers and colleagues on this one, the travelling circus of trainer friends, if you will.

I worked Bob through the food bowl and the object guarding exercises with diligence. I considered consulting my zookeeper friend on the protocol for feeding hyenas, because Bob was, well, scary in his resource guarding behavior.

Finally, with diligence, a good plan, a bit of bravery, and a large dose of compassion, Bob learned the virtues of sharing.

When we teach, we learn. I learned from Bob how to help others whose dogs are resource guarders. I also learned not to bite you if you come near my chocolate.

The nose of the bulldog has been slanted backwards so that he can breathe without letting go. —**Winston Churchill**

I was recently out for dinner with a group of dog trainers. Everyone was famished. Because we were dining at an Ethiopian restaurant, there were no eating utensils on the table, but for one serving fork. One person commented that the fork had better be moved before someone got stabbed! In dogs, this behavior is called resource guarding.

Sharing is a respectable trait among humans. Dogs: not so much. They are not genetically programmed to share. Unlike the hungry aforementioned diners, dogs are demonized for this natural behavior. We take it so seriously with dogs, because of their potential to do bodily harm to those who threaten their critical resources. In the case of the eager diner, the fork would have been the weapon with which to guard the resource. Dogs might use their single choice of armament—their teeth.

Food is not the only thing that dogs guard. Some dogs will guard objects like toys, beds, and stolen items (e.g. dirty socks). Other bones of contention might be locations, such as feeding areas and preferred resting spots, even crates. Some dogs will protect their own body parts from being handled, and some will guard their people.

As the hungry dog trainer warned her fellow diners about the risk of being maimed by flatware, dogs warn us of their intent. If they perceive their valuable resource to be threatened, dogs will give us the gift of growl. There are other signals that are perhaps more subtle precursors to a snap or bite. These signals include freezing, accelerated consumption (of food), placing the chin or paw over the object, and snarling. Dogs make use of one or a combination of these signals before resorting to a bite.

We expect dogs to guard our property, but not theirs. (Guard my state-of-the-art sound system and my vintage kazoo collection, but not your rawhide bone.) We might think that we can solve the problem by simply taking the dog's bed or food away, putting our hands in his food bowl while eating. By doing so, we think we're showing the dog that he must allow it. In reality, we're merely teaching the dog that we're going to mess with his stuff.

There are some myths surrounding resource guarding that need to be dispelled before making a plan for treatment. Some of those myths are as follows:

RG is a genetic predisposition, therefore unalterable.

Resource guarding is a natural behavior in dogs used as a measure to preserve the species. It can also be learned (i.e. the dog is always punished after dropping an object). In either case, there are effective behavior modification techniques available for treating RG.

RG is aberrant behavior.

Not true. As previously stated, RG is natural, even essential to an animal's survival in the wild. A resource-guarding dog, if left to his own devices, would stand a better chance in sustaining life than the non-guarding dog.

RG is about dominance.

A pervasive discussion in dog training culture is the concept of dominance. Unfortunately, the hierarchy model of dog behavior lists dominance as the universal explanation for all too many canine behaviors.

Dominance is a state, not a trait. We have a high success rate with counter conditioning and desensitization in the treatment of resource guarding. One cannot counter condition or desensitize a personality trait. This fact should render the question of whether or not RG is about dominance a moot point.

RG is a result of spoiling the dog.

A "spoiled" dog is often a description of (or an excuse for) a dog with bad manners. RG may be lumped into a plethora of other undesirable behaviors believed to be caused by spoiling a pet. This dog gets what he wants by being pushy, rude, and annoying. However, RG is seen in dogs with varied histories and sterling manners. Both scenarios can be successfully treated, so it follows that spoiled dogs do not necessarily make resource guarders.

He's protecting me from harm.

One type of resource guarding is that of a dog guarding his person. Most people interpret the behavior as the dog protecting them from, say, the terrorist lurking in the alley. This could very well be the case, but with true

RG dogs, the behavior is more about guarding his person as his resource (the person who feeds him, etc.) than fending off danger.

He'll be cured, because he'll learn that resources are abundant.
We wish it were this easy, but human logic doesn't seem to apply here. We can even make matters worse. In our erroneous thinking, we provide unlimited access to food, furniture, toys, or anything the dog guards. This recipe for disaster would have the unsuspecting victim in harm's way at any given moment.

He won't bite.
If pushed beyond his limits, even the most affable dog can and *will* bite. Period.

Avoidance: Management as a permanent solution
Management and avoidance are not permanent solutions. They *can* and *will* fail. Period.

He'll outgrow it.
No, he won't. Period.

Management

The dog's kennel is not the place to keep a sausage. –Danish Proverb

Management is essential for safety and the treatment of resource guarding behavior. Some management tools may be useful on an ongoing basis as additional safety measures, but no amount of management should substitute for sound training. Furthermore, management preserves the integrity of the training program. If the dog is not allowed to fail, there will be no backsliding in his training.

Set your dog up for success by removing all resource-guarding triggers possible. Pick up toys, chew bones and food bowls when not in use. If the dog guards furniture or locations, disallow access to them.

Make sure that the dog stays under threshold at all times. If he growls when you come within three feet of his food bowl during meals, then don't get that close. For now, we don't want the dog to rehearse the guarding behavior, so avoid the conflict.

If an unavoidable situation does arise, such as the dog finding something on the street when out on your walk, do what you must do within the realm of safety. This scenario would be a good time for bribery. Offer your dog something of higher value to him in exchange for the found item. This is a very good reason to carry super yummy, to-die-for treats on walks.

If you find yourself in a situation where management has failed and your dog has gained access to a guarded location, like your bed, just ignore him until he gets off. Another plan would be to casually call him to another room for a tasty treat. These management mishaps are not training moments but merely a means to stay safe and avoid conflict.

Fixing it: The Treatment Plan

Note: This chapter is intended to help the reader understand resource guarding and deal with the challenges of having a resource-guarding dog. Treatment methods should be done in conjunction with and under the supervision of a reputable, professional trainer or behaviorist, especially for severe cases and households with children.

Variables

After identifying the actual triggers, we need to look at variables that exist surrounding the given triggers. It's important to identify these variables so that we can predict the intensity of the RG behavior and design a treatment protocol in which the dog will be kept under threshold.

Approach

Some dogs are more reactive to certain types of approaches than others. Distance, angle, and speed of approach can trigger a more intense display of aggression. Determine whether a straight on approach, eye contact, approach from behind (fast or slow), entering from an out-of-sight location, or close up has a greater effect on the dog's reaction.

Another variable to consider is *who* is approaching. Dogs know whom it is safe to be around. Thus, it is extremely important that all capable family members work with the dog's treatment. In addition, dogs need our help to generalize the new behavior. If the dog is not comfortable around children, then he will likely regress if an unfamiliar child approaches.

Note: The presence of children in the home with a resource-guarding dog raises the stakes exponentially. Due to their short stature, children are more likely to be bitten in the face. Management is difficult, if not impossible, in a busy family household, and young children cannot be expected to follow protocol. In serious resource guarding cases, tough decisions need to be made. Re-homing a dog to a childless household or even euthanasia could be the most humane choice.

Duration

It's much easier to take possession of that chew bone when the dog has had possession of it for only five seconds as opposed to five minutes. Once he is in *the zone* with an item, relinquishing it becomes more difficult. Occasionally, dogs will lose interest in an item when the novelty wears off (i.e. a new toy), but usually the former rather than the latter scenario holds true.

Finders Keepers

Many dogs cherish found items more highly than, say, the mundane, every day, always-available toy. The sock that escaped from the dryer or the pizza crust lying in the gutter is a treasure to be vigorously guarded.

Escalation

Treatment involves rising above the conflict and remembering that aggression begets aggression. In any of the aforementioned situations, aggression will likely escalate if the dog is challenged once he presents resource-guarding behavior.

Basics of Training a New Behavior

When teaching a new behavior to a dog, remember the following basics in order:

1. Get the behavior: This can by done by luring, shaping, or capturing.

2. Markers: Mark the desired behavior instantly with either a clicker or a verbal marker.

3. Establish reliability: Once the behavior is reliable, you're ready to attach the cue word.

4. Put it on cue: Say the cue word immediately as the dog is presenting the behavior. For example, the instant the dog's belly hits the floor say "down."

Behaviors to Teach

Following are some useful skills and behaviors for resource guarding dogs to learn which will help to facilitate the treatment.

Hand Feeding

For the food-guarding dog, you will want to teach him, literally, how to eat out of your hand. Cue the dog to sit, then take a small handful of kibble and hold it one or two feet in front of the dog's nose in your open hand. If the dog breaks his sit and moves toward the food say "no" and quickly take your hand away.

Repeat the exercise, this time holding the handful of food a bit further away. Let the dog hold his sit for a few seconds, then say "okay" (or an established release word) and allow the dog to take the food. Vary the time the dog waits for your permission to take the food.

Once the dog is reliably waiting for permission to take the food, put the behavior on cue. As the dog is waiting in a sit, say, "wait." After a few seconds, release him so that he can take the food.

Touch

Teaching a dog to "touch" or to target your hand is a great way to move your dog from place to place without the use of the leash or force. Touch is a great tool for moving a dog away from the resource that he's guarding. See the chapter *Fearful Dogs* for instructions on teaching touch.

Off

Teach "off" by starting with furniture that the dog is not interested in guarding or has never guarded before. Let's say that's the sofa. Using the word "touch," cue the dog to get up on the sofa. Once he is up, immediately cue him to get off using "touch" and then mark and treat the behavior. When the behavior is reliable, add a cue word such as "off."

Note: If the dog guards all furniture, you may want to start this exercise by removing one sofa cushion and placing it on the floor at a distance from the sofa where he will not guard. When successful at this distance, begin to move the cushion closer until you are able to place it on the sofa.

Move Out of the Way

Teaching a dog to move out of the way can be done with "touch" as previously described. Following are additional handy cues to move your dog out of the way:

Go

This cue means that the dog should move away from you in the direction you are pointing or moving your hand. To teach "go," simply toss a treat in the direction you want the dog to move. Use a sweeping motion with your hand as you toss the treat, ending by pointing toward it. As the dog moves toward the treat, say "go."

Back

It's handy to have a dog know how to back up on cue. This can be easily taught by standing in front of the dog, then stepping toward him. As he moves backward, say "back," then treat him for backing up. It's helpful to do this in a narrow hallway and on leash, so that the dog does not simply wander off or step around you.

Leave It and Drop It

See the chapter *The How-To of Training* for instructions on teaching "Leave It" and "Drop It."

Retrieve

To teach a dog to retrieve, start by waving a ball in front of his nose. The movement will get him focused on the ball. Now, toss it just a short distance (two or three feet) away.

If the dog goes to it and puts his mouth on it, clap your hands and run the opposite direction, encouraging him to move toward you. Wait to clap until the ball is in the dog's mouth. Do not call him or say his name, as this will likely cause him to drop the ball.

If he comes only part way back with the ball and then stops and tries to get you to chase him, back up again. Clap your hands again and run away so that he'll move toward you. Always have the dog move toward you; don't move toward him. If the dog grabs the ball and runs, run in the opposite direction to entice him to chase you.

If the dog does bring the ball toward you and drops it anywhere near your feet, pick it up and throw it *instantly*. Don't wait. The dog wants the ball back, and if we spend time praising him or interrupting the game to ask for a sit, he'll lose interest.

Many dogs will only fetch a few times, especially outside where distractions abound. If the dog retrieves two times and then ignores the ball, calmly go get it and end the game. If you notice a pattern (say, the dog fetches five times in a row and then quits), the next time, stop the game after four throws. As they say in show business, "Always leave them wanting more."

If the dog brings the ball back but then refuses to give it up, use the "drop it" cue that's been previously taught. Some dogs lose interest in the ball if they know you're packing treats. If that is the case, use a second ball or another toy of equal value to the dog. Soon you can eliminate the treat or toy altogether, because chasing the ball is enough of a reward.

Here's another way to teach dogs to give up the ball. As soon as he gets close to you with the ball, fold your arms and turn away from him, refusing to face him or take the ball. He should eventually drop the ball. When that happens, pick it up and throw it immediately. If the dog won't drop the ball no matter how long you ignore him, try throwing a second ball once he has retrieved the first one.

Practice Exercises

After establishing the variables, making a list of items guarded, and teaching the necessary behaviors described, you are ready to begin treatment with some practice exercises.

An axiom in dog training is that if he can't do it when it's easy, he can't do it when it's difficult. Therefore, training will begin with objects and locations of neutral or low value. Practice trials will be set out of context; never attempt to train in the heat of the moment when the dog is presenting resource-guarding behavior.

Object Guarder Exercise

First, teach the dog to drop objects on cue using neutral-value items. Practice the behavior with various uninteresting items in a neutral, out-of-context location. For example, if the dog guards his favorite squeaky toy while on his bed, then practice with a no-value toy in the backyard.

For a serious object guarder that will guard anything (for him, zero-value items don't exist), you will want to tether the dog and work at a distance to avoid mishaps. With the dog on tether, place a low-value guarded item on the ground. Next, pick up the item and toss the dog a treat. Repeat this until the dog is anticipating the treat when you pick up the object. You will gradually be able to move closer with the object.

Food Guarder Exercise

Prior to this exercise, you will teach the dog to eat hand-fed meals. Do this by measuring out the portion of kibble for his meal. With the dog in a sit, take a small handful of the kibble and hold it several inches from his nose. If he gets up to take the food, take your hand away. Ask the dog for a sit, and then present the food again. If he gets up again, remove the food. Repeat this until the dog can hold his sit for a second or two while you're presenting the food. Release the dog from his sit using the release word that's been previously taught, and let him eat the handful of food. Hand feed the entire meal.

When the dog can sit and wait reliably, put the behavior on cue by saying, "wait" while he's sitting and waiting for the food.

Once the dog is savvy to hand feeding, give him the first half of the meal by hand. For the second half of the meal, hold the empty food bowl in your lap, cue the dog to wait, and place a handful of food in the bowl. Now, give the release word and allow the dog to eat the food from the bowl. Continue these steps for the rest of the meal.

Location Guarder Exercise

Practice moving your dog from place to place by playing the touch game. (See the chapter *Fearful Dogs*.) Do this out of context or in places that he's not interested in guarding. If the dog guards his bed when it's in the bedroom, try moving it to another room or to the yard. Additionally, practice "off" with furniture that the dog does not guard.

The point of the practice exercises is to condition the dog to have a positive response to the resource guarding triggers. Instead of feeling threatened when someone approaches his beloved bed, your dog will accept the approach with eager anticipation. Growling and snapping will be replaced with, "Woo hoo! Here comes something good!" When the dog reliably gives the anticipatory response (woo hoo!), you are ready to begin working him through the range of his resource guarding triggers.

Tips for Success

Following are some tips for successful treatment of resource guarding.

Timing

Timing is everything. To establish a strong anticipatory response, the first event (e.g. approaching the food bowl) must reliably predict the second event (yummy treat delivered to the food bowl). If the treat is offered on or after the approach, the dog does not learn that the first event predicts the second, and you'll never see the anticipatory (woo hoo!) response.

Only the Best

Use only high-value treats, and use them exclusively for treatment. Special treats result in a quicker, more reliable response from the dog.

Be Predictable

Consistency is the key to establishing a strong anticipatory response. Remember that event A always predicts event B. Always.

Identify Triggers

The first step in treating resource guarding is to make a list of all items, locations, and food that the dog guards. Do this in order from lowest to highest value. In addition to known RG items, experiment with items or locations that the dog has potential to guard, but have never been tested. The untested items will be tested, and the unguarded items will be used in practice exercises before working up the scale.

Muzzles

If the dog does not have a strong bite inhibition or this fact is unknown, a muzzle (preferably a basket muzzle) is recommended. Testing can be done using an artificial hand, heavy-duty leather or Kevlar gloves, or a tether, but exercises should be done with the dog wearing a muzzle. The dog will need to be desensitized to it, so that the muzzle is not a distraction or an aversive element in treatment.

Desensitizing to the Muzzle

1. Show the dog the muzzle several times during the day. Each time he looks at it, reward him with a generous portion of treats. When the dog is reliably displaying an excited anticipatory response to the muzzle (as he does when he sees his leash), you are ready for the next step.

2. Play the "touch" game with the muzzle. Once the dog is readily and quickly touching the muzzle, begin to reward only the prolonged touches. This gets the dog used to having the muzzle in contact with his nose for longer periods of time.

3. Now, hold a treat at the end of the muzzle with the opening facing toward the dog's nose. Allow the dog to put his nose inside the muzzle, and then give him the treat. You can also put a smear of peanut butter inside at the end of the muzzle to entice the dog to insert his nose.

4. Gradually increase the time that the dog's nose is inside of the muzzle by delaying delivery of the treat a few seconds.

5. Adjust the straps on the muzzle so that they fit very loosely. When the dog is acclimated to having his nose inside the muzzle for a few seconds, start to handle the muzzle straps while he waits for his treat. When he is comfortable with this, put the straps very loosely behind his ears.

6. When the dog is comfortable with the loosely fitting muzzle, gradually adjust the straps for a tighter fit. The muzzle fits correctly when the straps remain in place right behind the ears.

7. Make sure that you do not progress too quickly through these steps. You want the dog to be comfortable and happy throughout the desensitization process. Be sure that the dog has only pleasant experiences while wearing the muzzle.

Desensitization and Classical Counterconditioning

The first step in the desensitization process is to determine the dog's threshold. You will work just below the point that the dog presents the resource-guarding behavior. The threshold and its variables will have been previously determined in the practice exercises before working through the scale.

Classical counterconditioning applies the Pavlovian technique in which one event reliably predicts another, and the subject develops an involuntary, anticipatory response to the first event. This theory is demonstrated every time a dog shows excitement when his leash is brought out. He has learned that the first event predicts the second...a walk.

Counterconditioning changes associations. A dog that previously became tense when someone approached his food bowl will happily anticipate the event after counter conditioning.

In treatment, the dog is presented with low-level triggers followed immediately by high-value rewards. This process is repeated (always keeping the dog sub-threshold) until the dog shows an excited anticipatory reaction to the trigger.

Tips for Success
For successful counter conditioning to happen, careful attention needs to be given in establishing the anticipatory response. Remember that this response happens because event A consistently predicts event B. Therefore, the order of events during training must remain consistent. For example, dogs have a strong anticipatory response to the appearance of the leash, because the appearance of the leash (event A) is always followed by a walk (event B). If the leash appeared simultaneously or after the walk, no anticipatory response would be established.

Successful resource-guarding treatment means predictability, consistency, and high motivation. The anticipatory response will only be learned if the payoff is of higher value than the item guarded. Reserve the high-value treats for the resource guarding treatment.

Working through the examples will require the ability to think on your feet and be flexible. If at any point the dog presents resource-guarding behavior, go back to the previous step and adjust previously established variables. For instance, increase the distance between you, the dog, and the guarded item.

Only proceed to the next step when the dog presents no resource-guarding behavior *and* a strong anticipatory response at the current level of the scale.

Food Bowl Guarding Example

1. Begin with an empty food bowl. Approach the dog and empty bowl from a distance of at least six feet, drop some treats into the bowl, and then walk away. (If the dog guards the empty food bowl, increase the distance of the approach, tossing the food toward the bowl. Then, decrease the distance until you can toss the treats into the bowl.) Repeat the approaches varying the angle, speed, and intervals between.

2. Gradually increase the distance from which you approach. Increase the approach from six feet to ten feet, then ten feet to twenty feet.

3. Approach the empty bowl from ten feet away, and then bend halfway down toward the bowl, as if to pick it up. Drop the treats in and walk away.

4. Approach the empty bowl from ten feet away, and then bend all the way down to the bowl, as if to pick it up. Pause for a second or two, then drop the treat in the bowl, and walk away.

5. Vary the distance, speed, angle, and time intervals of the approaches.

6. Approach the empty bowl from ten feet away, bend down reaching toward the bowl. Drop the treats into the bowl with the opposite hand, and then walk away.

7. Approach the empty bowl from ten feet away, bend down, touch the bowl for one second, drop treats into the bowl with the opposite hand, and then walk away.

8. Repeat Step 7 and gradually increase the time your hand is touching the bowl before dropping the treats into it. Work up to having your hand touch the empty bowl for twenty to thirty seconds before dropping the treats into it.

9. Vary the distance, speed, angle, and time intervals of the approaches with the twenty-to-thirty second bowl touches.

10. Approach the empty bowl from ten feet away, bend down, take hold of the bowl, and move it for one second. Drop the treats in with the opposite hand, and then walk away.

11. Repeat Step 10 and gradually increase the time you are moving the bowl to ten seconds before dropping the treats in.

12. Approach the empty bowl from ten feet away, pick it up to waist level, drop in the treats, and then return the bowl.

13. Approach the empty bowl from ten feet away, take it away, place it on a counter or table, drop in the treats, and then return the bowl.

14. Once the dog is reliably presenting no resource-guarding behavior and a positive anticipatory response to Step 13, begin the process again. Work through Steps 1 through 13 using dry kibble instead of an empty bowl. Remember to always deliver a higher value treat than whatever is already in the bowl.

15. Work through Steps 1 through 13 using half dry kibble and half canned food.

16. Work through Steps 1 through 13 using canned food.

17. Work through Steps 1 through 13 using bits of real meat. Since real meat may be hard to trump with a treat, deposit bits of another type of meat or the same meat that is of equal value.

Object Guarding Example

Gather together the guarded and unguarded items on the list made previously. If the dog compulsively guards any item, you will want to tether him and begin with the lowest-value item. With the dog tethered, stand ten feet away from him, pick up the low-value item at your feet, and toss the dog a high-value treat. Once the dog is no longer resource guarding particular items, or if there are existing items that the dog does not guard, begin as follows:

1. Using an unguarded item, approach the dog from several feet away, pick up the item, deliver a high-value treat from your pocket, pouch, or behind your back with the opposite hand. Return the item, and then walk away. Repeat this process several times approaching from varied distances, angles, and speeds. Alter the interval between trials and amount of time spent near the dog.

2. If the dog has no issues with being touched, approach him, pat him on the back for a second or two, and then take the object away. Repeat and gradually increase the time that you can pat the dog, working up to five or six seconds.

3. Now tether the dog, if you haven't been doing so. Practice exchanges outside of his reach using unguarded items. Do this by placing the item on the floor at your feet, pick it up, and then toss a treat to the dog.

4. Now proceed to the lowest-value item and repeat Step 3.

5. Once the dog is no longer presenting resource-guarding behavior with the lowest-value item, you will hand him that item without letting go of it. As soon as the dog's mouth touches the item, take it back in exchange for a high-value treat. Repeat this step several times.

6. Hand the same low-value item to the dog again, but this time let go for a second. Now, take the item back in exchange for a high-value treat and lavish praise. Repeat this step several times. Gradually increase the time the dog has possession of the item to ten seconds.

7. Hand the same item to the dog, and then walk ten feet away for one second, return, and take the item back in exchange for a high-value treat.

8. Repeat Step 7 gradually increasing the time the item is left with the dog to thirty seconds.

9. Begin to vary the distance that you walk away from the dog, starting back at one second. For example, walk twenty feet away from the dog for one second, and gradually increase the time the item is left with the dog to thirty seconds. Repeat this by walking five feet away from the dog and so on.

10. Hand the same item to the dog, leave the room for ten seconds, and then return, approach the dog, and take the item back in exchange for a high-value treat. Repeat this step increasing the time you are gone from the room to thirty seconds.

11. Place the same item somewhere in the room and let the dog, unprompted, take possession of it. Immediately approach and take the item back in exchange for a high-value treat. Repeat this step,

gradually increasing the time the dog has possession of the item to thirty seconds, and then work up to two or three minutes possession time before approaching.

12. You are now ready to work this scale with the list of the dog's guarded items. Using the lowest-value item, start at Step 3 and work through Step 11. Next, work through Steps 3 through 11 with all medium-value items, and then all high-value items. Finally, work these same steps with novel, high-value items.

Location Guarding Example

For this exercise, you will first teach the dog to "touch" on cue, in order to move him from place to place without leash or force. (See the chapter *Fearful Dogs* for instructions on teaching touch.)

1. Using "touch," cue the dog to target your hand and get him onto a piece of furniture that he does not guard. (If all furniture is guarded, place a sofa cushion on the floor, have the dog get on and off of it, and then gradually move it back to its rightful place. The dog is now willingly getting on and off of the sofa.) Use a verbal cue such as "up" or "on the sofa" before the dog targets your hand. It's important to teach a verbal cue for use later with guarded items.

2. Once the dog is on the furniture, praise him (do not treat him), and immediately have him target your hand to move him off the furniture. Give your verbal cue (such as "off") before the dog targets your hand. Reward him with praise and a treat. Repeat this step until the dog is happily getting on and off the same piece of furniture.

3. The dog should begin to get on and off the unguarded piece of furniture when only the verbal cue is given, and the targeting behavior will become unnecessary. When this happens, you are ready to move on to locations that are mildly guarded.

4. Start working the scale with a location that the dog has previously guarded. Do not attempt a cold trial (spontaneous, in-the-moment trial) here. In other words, don't begin working if the dog happens to be settled into his spot on the previously guarded sofa. Start by cuing the dog to go to a guarded area, and then cue him to move away. Begin at a distance from the guarded location, where the dog remains under threshold. If the dog displays guarding behavior at a

distance of two feet from the sofa, then stand three feet away to cue him on and off.

5. Once the dog is readily moving toward and away from (on or off) the location, begin to practice cold trials. When the dog spontaneously goes to the previously guarded location, ask him to move away immediately. Then begin to increase the time the dog is allowed to settle in. Let him remain at the location for one minute, cue him to move away, and then allow him to go back to his original agenda of, perhaps, napping on the sofa. Gradually increase the settle-in time to fifteen minutes.

6. Cue the dog to an unguarded location. Keeping the dog under threshold, reach toward him with your hand, and then praise and treat him for allowing you to do this. Gradually decrease the distance between you and the dog, literally one step at a time, until you are able to reach out and touch the dog. (If the dog has a history of body-handling issues, you will have worked through them prior to doing this exercise.) Touch the dog for one second, praise, treat, and then cue him away from the unguarded location.

7. Repeat Steps 4 through 6 with all low-level previously guarded location.

8. Repeat Steps 4 through 6 with all medium-level previously guarded locations.

9. Repeat Steps 4 through 6 with all high-level previously guarded locations.

10. Do cold trials repeating Steps 4 through 6 with all locations.

Resource Guarding People Example

Some dogs will resource guard their people–their resource; the person who feeds and provides for them. The behavior might be presented when on walks, when a person enters the home, and/or anytime there is interaction between the owner and another person. You will use classical counter conditioning to treat this type of resource guarding. Before beginning, pinpoint specific interactions with people that trigger the dog. For instance, the dog may react when another person enters the same room as the owner, or when a person touches the owner or speaks to them. It may also escalate if the dog is on a leash. Determine all variables before working through the scale.

1. Position the dog at a distance from the person where he is alerting to them, but not reacting.

2. *While* the dog is looking at the person but not reacting, generously treat and praise him for several seconds.

3. Have the person leave the dog's sight, and stop delivering the treats.

4. Repeat Steps 1 through 3 several times.

5. Bring the person back into the dog's line of sight at the same distance as before. This time, wait a second or two longer before treating the dog to see if he will look back at you. The dog should seem to be asking, "I'm looking at the person. So where's my treat?" If this happens, generously praise and treat him.

6. Repeat Step 5 until the dog is happily looking at the person, then looking back at you for his reward. You should see that this exercise has become a game to the dog. He will soon be wagging his head back and forth between you and the person, playing the Look-at-the-Nice-Person Game.

7. Repeat this process until the dog is playing the game immediately upon seeing the person. When this is happening reliably, repeat the exercise, gradually having the person move closer, until the person can be within arm's length.

8. When the dog is comfortable with the person being in close proximity, repeat the exercise, working through the predetermined variables that trigger the dog. For example, if someone touching you triggers the dog, start by having the person reach slowly toward you while you play the Look-at-the-Nice-Person Game. Gradually work up to having the person touch you while the dog plays the game.

9. Put Look-at-the-Nice-Person Game on cue. Now that the dog is happily playing the game, put it on cue by saying a word like "friend" when the dog first looks at the person. This will help in alerting him to the person's presence and to elicit the positive anticipatory response.

Body Handling Example

Dogs that have issues with having certain body parts handled will need to go through a desensitization process before working through the resource-guarding scales. If a dog does not like to be touched on his hindquarters, he will react more aggressively if touched near or on his hindquarters when in possession of a resource.

To begin the desensitization process, make a list of the dog's body part sensitivities, listing from the lowest (zero) sensitivity to the highest (ten.) For this example, let's say that we're working with a dog that does not like to have his back paws touched but has no other body part sensitivities.

1. Place your hand on the dog's shoulder for one second and treat the dog with your other hand. Pause and repeat at varied intervals. Gradually increase the time that your hand is on the dog's shoulder until you're able to hold your hand there for thirty seconds and the dog shows a positive anticipatory response.

2. Repeat step one, moving your hand to the dog's midsection, then to his hindquarters, and eventually to his back paws. Progress to the next step only after the dog is comfortable with the duration and pressure of your touch and presents a positive, anticipatory response.

Help the dog to generalize by practicing in different locations and with different people working him through the exercises. If there is specific equipment involved with the dog's sensitivities, such as nail clippers or brushes, be sure to work through the exercises without the equipment present. Then, start back at the beginning, working through each step with the equipment.

It is tempting to skip ahead and move quickly through the described desensitization process. It might seem painfully tedious, but remember slower is faster in behavior modification and desensitization. The more steps you can break the treatment into, the more successful you'll be.

Incompatible and Alternative Behaviors

It can be helpful to teach the dog an incompatible and/or alternative behavior to replace the resource guarding. For the object guarder, it's a useful substitute for the dog dropping the object. We've already done this with the location guarder by playing the touch game to have him move away from the location. We've turned the previously contentious situation into a fun game in which the dog willingly participates.

Some alternative behaviors for the object-guarding dog are lifting his head from the object, moving away from the object, or retrieving it. These behaviors can be shaped starting with zero-value objects and then working through the object scale.

Shaping an Alternative Behavior

In this sample exercise, you will teach the dog to come away from an object in his possession. Begin this exercise with an object that he is interested in but doesn't guard.

Tips for Success

After working through the scales, the dog must generalize the behavior. Once the primary trainer has successfully worked the dog through treatment, all capable family members need to work the dog through the scales. Furthermore, anyone else who interacts with the dog on a regular basis, such as dog walkers or frequent visitors, should work with the dog.

There are some common trouble spots in the treatment of resource-guarding behavior. These include pushing the dog too hard, skipping intermediate steps, or starting too high on the scale. Likewise, lack of generalization, socialization, and management failure during treatment will quickly make the plan fall apart.

The most important thing to remember is that the absence of resource guarding is not sufficient criterion for proceeding to the next step. You need to see no resource-guarding behavior *and* the positive anticipatory response before moving to the next rung of the scale.

Dog-to-Dog Resource Guarding

Dogs can be allowed to work out normal resource-guarding behavior between each other if no harmful fighting is happening. Here, we must define normal behavior in order to determine whether intervention is necessary. There is no need to put the kibosh on the occasional kafuffle over resources if the guarding dog simply gives a quick warning growl, air snap, or inhibited muzzle grab to another dog. However, owner beware if the dog displays other signals like freezing, accelerated consumption (of food), or placing the chin or paw over the object and snarling. Dogs make use of one or a combination of these signals before resorting to a bite.

Management and Prevention

It's helpful to maintain calm, polite behavior in a multi-dog household in order to prevent resource guarding. Dogs who are allowed to jump up, whine, and stand on their heads during meal preparation or opening of the cookie jar are headed for trouble in this over stimulated state.

Teach your dogs to sit politely and accept treats individually in the presence of the other dogs. First, have the dogs sit at a distance from each other where they are able to maintain calm in the presence of food. Stand between the dogs and ask each of them for a stay. Now, say the first dog's name as you hand him a treat; next, say the second dog's name and hand him his treat. You may want to hold your hand up in a "stay" signal to the dog that is not receiving the goods. Release the dogs from their stays after the snacks have been eaten. Practice this regularly, mixing up the order in which the dogs get the treats. Gradually move the dogs closer to each other until they can sit next to each other for handouts.

For dogs with serious resource-guarding behavior, strict management must be employed during the treatment program. Dogs should be crated, gated, and separated in the presence of the guarded resources. This means at mealtime or chew-bone time. If toys are the guarded resource, then playtime must be separate and all toys picked up when they are not in use. If locations like beds are guarded, then dogs should be crated, gated, and separated.

Note whether tension between the dogs escalates around mealtime, walk time, etc. If dogs are always fed their meals upon return from their afternoon walk, anxiety may start to escalate well before the food bowls show up. If this is the case, a change of schedule and routine is in order.

Dog-to-Dog Food Bowl Guarding Example

Before working this exercise, each dog should be able to hold a stay reliably, even under distraction and in the presence of guarded resources.

1. Begin with empty food bowls. Place the dogs far enough away that guarding will not occur, using tethers if necessary. First, place the non-guarding dog's bowl on the floor, and then drop a treat into it. Then, immediately and generously treat and praise the guarding dog. Repeat this several times at varying intervals until the guarding dog is showing a positive, anticipatory response to the treat being dropped into the non-guarding dog's bowl.

2. Next, begin to replicate mealtime. Start with the empty food bowls on the counter, or wherever the dogs' meals are normally prepared. Place the dogs far enough apart that guarding will not occur. Put a few pieces of kibble into the non-guarding dog's bowl, asking both dogs for a "stay." Place the non-guarder's bowl on the floor, keep the guarder in a "stay," and generously treat him while the first dog eats the kibble. Repeat this having the non-guarder stay while the guarder eats his kibble.

3. Once the guarder is showing a positive, anticipatory response to the first dog being served, increase the amount of kibble put into the non-guarder's bowl. While the non-guarder is eating, put the guarder's bowl down, allowing both dogs to eat simultaneously. If one dog finishes, before the other, have him stay by his bowl until the other dog finishes. Immediately pick up the bowls and release the dogs from their stay. Do not allow the dogs to go "shopping" in the other dog's bowl, even if both bowls are empty.

4. It is helpful to teach dogs to go to their respective feeding stations on cue at mealtime. Feeding stations should be a safe distance apart, and the dogs must be waiting there in a "stay" before delivering their meals. This alleviates tension between the dogs during mealtime preparation.

Dog-to-Dog Object Guarding Example

This exercise is done with food bowl or object guarding. The point of this training method is to change the way the guarding dog feels about another dog being in proximity to his resource. In other words, the presence of another dog while in possession of the resource predicts good things.

1. Sit in a closed room with the guarding dog and simply ignore him. There should be no guarded resources in the room. Read a book or update your Facebook profile, just pay no attention to the dog for a half an hour or so. If you have someone to help you, have that person bring the non-guarding dog into the room on leash. If you

are working alone, tether the guarder while you bring the non-guarder into the room.

2. Next, have the non-guarder sit and treat him. Now, generously treat and praise the guarder for several seconds. Remove the non-guarder from the room and go back to ignoring the guarder.

3. Repeat this process until the guarding dog is presenting a positive anticipatory response to the non-guarder's entrance into the room. When the anticipatory response is happening reliably, repeat the exercise in different rooms of the house, working up to the kitchen, feeding area, and play areas, where the most severe resource guarding is likely to occur.

4. Work through the exercise again in each of the different rooms, and gradually work the non-guarding dog in closer proximity to the guarder.

5. Next, work through Steps 1 through 4 while the guarding dog has access to guarded objects. Begin with the lowest-value object that the dog guards. When you are ready to bring the non-guarding dog into the room, be sure the guarder and his resource are as far from the door as possible. Use leashes and tethers.

6. It is helpful to teach dogs to go to their respective beds or any separate designated area on cue when given chew bones or treats. The beds should be a safe distance apart, and the dogs must be waiting there in a "stay" before chew bones are delivered.

Tips for Success
Make sure that you use high-value treats. The treat needs to trump the guarded object and hold the guarder's interest. Jackpotting (liberal amounts of treats fed one by one in rapid succession) can raise the stakes and the level of success. This is hard work for the dog, and he should be paid well. Using high-value treats over dry kibble is like the difference between paying minimum wage or rock-star wages.

Never dial up more than one criterion at a time. For instance, when you are ready to move the non-guarder closer to the guarder, use a low-value guarded resource. When you are ready to move up to a higher-value resource, increase the distance between the dogs.

Always be sure that the guarder is showing a strong, positive, anticipatory response to the non-guarder's entry into the room before moving to the next step. Jumping too quickly up the scale is a recipe for failure.

Dog-to-Dog Location Guarding Example

Another dog's entrance into a room can often be the true source of anxiety for a location-guarding dog. These dogs are sometimes comfortable with the other dog once that dog has been in the room for a while, or if the other dog is already present when the guarding dog enters the room. In this case, you will work specifically on desensitizing the guarder to another dog's entry into the room. You will need two people to conduct this exercise.

1. Sit in a closed room with the guarding dog, and simply ignore him for several minutes.

2. Have the other person bring the non-guarding dog into the guarding dog's sight, remaining outside of the room. The non-guarding dog should remain at a distance where the guarder is alerting to, but not reacting to him.

3. *While* the guarder is looking at the other dog but not reacting, generously treat and praise him for several seconds. Remove the non-guarder from sight and go back to ignoring the guarder.

4. Repeat Steps 1 through 3 several times.

5. Bring the non-guarding dog back into the guarder's line of sight at the same distance as before. This time, wait a second or two longer before treating the guarder to see if delaying the treat has him look back at you as if asking, "I'm looking at the dog. Where's my treat?" If this happens, generously praise and treat the guarder.

6. Repeat Step 5 until the guarder is happily looking at the non-guarder, then looking back at you for his reward. You should see that this exercise has now become a game to the guarder. He will soon be wagging his head back and forth between you and the other dog, playing the Look-at-the-Nice-Dog Game.

7. Repeat this process until the guarding dog is playing the Look-at-the-Nice-Dog Game every time the non-guarder appears. When this is happening reliably, repeat the exercise, gradually working the non-guarding dog closer to the doorway, then through the doorway and into the guarded room. Be sure to have the guarder at the

farthest distance possible from the doorway to ensure success and safety.

8. It is helpful to teach dogs to go to their respective beds or any separate designated area on cue when either dog enters a guarded room. The beds should be a safe distance apart and not near the doorway.

Dog-to-Dog Resource Guarding People Example

Some dogs in multi-dog households vie for attention of human family members by guarding that human as a resource against the other dogs.

1. Have the guarded person sit in a closed room with the guarding dog and simply ignore him for several minutes.

2. Have another person bring the non-guarding dog into the room. The non-guarding dog should remain at a distance where the guarder is alerting to, but not reacting to him.

3. The person with the guarding dog should talk to the non-guarding dog in a praising, cheerful tone. *While* the person is talking and the guarder is looking at the non-guarder without reacting, generously treat and praise him for several seconds. Remove the non-guarder from sight and go back to ignoring the guarder.

4. Repeat Steps 1 through 3 several times.

5. Bring the non-guarding dog back into the room, keeping the same distance as before between the dogs. This time, wait a second or two longer before treating the guarder to see if the delay of the treat has him look back at you as if asking, "I'm looking at the dog. Where's my treat?" If this happens, generously praise and treat the guarder.

6. Repeat Step 5 until the guarder is happily looking at the non-guarder, then looking back at you for his reward. You should see that this exercise has now become a game to the guarder. He will soon be wagging his head back and forth between you and the other dog, playing the Look-at-the-Nice-Dog Game.

7. When the Look-at-the-Nice-Dog Game is happening reliably, repeat the exercise, gradually working the non-guarding dog closer to the person with the guarding dog.

10. Put the Look-at-the-Nice-Dog Game on cue by saying the non-guarder's name when the guarder first looks him. This will help the dog to develop a positive, association with the appearance of his roommate.

11. Once the dogs are comfortable in close proximity, begin to pet and praise the non-guarder while treating the guarder. This should be done only if there is no food guarding between the dogs.

After dispelling the myths, analyzing the source of the behavior, and exploring adjunct measures, a plan for treating resource guarding can be made. With the help of a reputable, professional trainer or behaviorist, the issue of can be safely resolved for most dogs.

12

Fearful Dogs

Traversing the forest on the yellow brick road, Dorothy and her motley companions were startled by the Cowardly Lion. He suddenly darted onto the path, growled and snarled, then made a hasty retreat back behind the tree where he had been hiding. He acted tough, but ran in terror when challenged by the pint-sized, cat-chasing Toto. The Cowardly Lion was exhibiting a classic case of fear aggression.

Fear has many faces. Some dogs are globally fearful, the paranoid Barney Fifes of the canine world that sweat and fret every minute of the day. These nervous dogs tremble and shake as if they start each day with a triple shot espresso.

Showing another face of fear are the seemingly intrepid dogs; otherwise courageous until the appearance of the dreaded, sinister vacuum cleaner! This comes in handy if ever attacked by a cleaning appliance, but otherwise it's a useless behavior in your guard dog.

My German shepherd, Jude, was the superficial model of the big, brave German shepherd. Yet, he was a drama king, forever expressing his underlying insecurities with incessant whining. In fact, I named him Jude, after the Beatles song "Hey Jude" because I always had to take his sad song and make it better.

For the first five years Jude lived with us, he envied my dog Bob because Bob slept on the bed with me. A lack of confidence and athletic ability had Jude believing he was incapable of jumping up on the bed. Thus, he settled for putting his front paws on the edge, then gazing wishfully at me. This endearing pose made him look as though he was praying, and I decided to put the behavior on cue. After that, prompting Jude to say his prayers became part of our nightly bedtime ritual.

Then one night, he surprised me (and himself) by suddenly and confidently springing up onto the bed. From that night on, Jude slept on the bed, and there was nothing I could do to remove him! While I enjoyed Jude and Bob's company and bed-warming services, I missed our little prayer meetings. It occurred to me that for five years maybe Jude had been praying for the courage to jump up on the bed!

Jude also had an irrational fear of getting into the car—not riding in the car, mind you, but specifically the act of getting into the car. I tried all of my proven tricks, which included littering the back seat with slimy bits of hot dog. (This activity resulted in the purchase of an industrial-strength, vegetarian-approved air freshener). I also tried getting into the back seat of the car ahead of Jude, hot dogs in hand. I tried getting into the back seat, hot dogs in hand, with Bob the dog. I made a step to assist this nonathletic dog. Note: Jude was a physically fit, 90-pound German shepherd. I drove a small sedan. It's not like he needed an escalator to reach the back seat of my Ford Focus! Alas, none of my genius ideas worked.

Then, one day I was unloading groceries from my car, which was parked in the garage. On the second trip, I noticed Jude happily sitting in the back seat! I'll never know what switch suddenly tripped in Jude's mind that gave him the courage to hop into the car. Maybe another of his prayers had been answered!

It took a kindly wizard to grant the wishes of the Cowardly Lion and his character-deficient and homeless friends. We may not be wizards, but there is help for the anxious dog. A treatment plan is a yellow brick road of sorts where there is no other place to start than at the beginning. With our eyes on Oz, we are aware that the beginning of the journey is the point where we have the farthest to go; yet it is ultimately the point where we have the most to gain.

The key to success is understanding and appreciating the journey. Anything worth pursuing is worth the courage it takes to do so.

Courage is resistance to fear, mastery of fear, not absence of fear.
—**Mark Twain**

It is unrealistic to expect dogs (or us, for that matter) to evolve to a place where fear is completely absent. However, it is possible to come to a place free of the limitations that fear imposes, a place where fear neither dictates life nor distracts from learning.

Fear of a real and immediate danger is a normal and necessary function for survival. But, emotional behavior tips into the realm of abnormal with the following conditions:

- When anxiety is global

- When there is fearfulness in the absence of a trigger

- When the response is profound and disproportionate to the actual or perceived threat

It's hard to imagine life for the globally fearful dog. It must be like living in a Stephen King novel, always looking over his shoulder waiting for "It" (the inter-dimensional predatory life form that exploits its victim's worst fears) to come and drag him down into the storm drain.

Dogs may be fearful of sentient things such as people, other dogs, or animals. They may be afraid of inanimate things including sounds, or have situational fears such as riding in the car or being left alone.

Fear can also be learned. Take riding in the car for example. The dog may become afraid of car rides if he was present during a negative experience, such as a fender bender. Or maybe the only place the car takes him is to the pet clinic, and he is fearful of the vet.

Reinforcing Fear
The only thing more heartbreaking than the sight of a dog cowering and trembling in fear is that of a frustrated owner scolding him, believing that domination is the solution to the problem. At the opposite end of the spectrum, there is the coddling owner who believes that they can talk their dog out of being scared. For many dog owners, it's difficult to know how to help their fearful friend.

When a dog is in the throes of fear, most people would naturally comfort, soothe, and even pick up small dogs. It's been said that this only reinforces fear. Actually, the *emotion* of fear cannot be reinforced, but behaviors surrounding fear can.

In this discussion, it is important to differentiate between emotion and behavior. Reinforcement increases the frequency of *behavior*. It is difficult, if not impossible, to affect involuntary behavior and *emotions* through reward and punishment (reinforcement).

The question is whether it's helpful to comfort a frightened dog. Reinforcement by definition increases the frequency of the *behavior*. Soothing a thunder-phobic dog may reduce the intensity of the *emotion*, thus indirectly decreasing the resultant behavior. If the thunder phobic dog stops trembling, lies down, and relaxes while you stroke him, you are reinforcing the *behavior* of lying down, not the *emotion* of fear.

Identifying the motivation behind the behavior is important. If a dog is barking at someone because he is fearful, then comforting him does not reinforce the barking. Instead, comforting reduces the emotion, which in turn, reduces the behavior. If the motivation is not fear, then you may reinforce the barking when you comfort the dog. For example if barking is an attention-seeking behavior, then giving the dog attention *will* reinforce it.

Some folks would have their fearful dog simply suck it up, get over it. Some would go even further, insisting upon strict obedience in a frightful situation. I once saw a woman forcefully command her fearful dogs to stay in a down position while other dogs passed by. In my opinion, this was heartless. By the looks of the dogs, it was as frightening for them as snakes on a plane are to me. I couldn't take that lying down!

Wild animals live in an alert, yet peaceful state of mind. They notice danger and react if necessary. In the wild, mothers do not send their babies out to suck it up and deal with it. They comfort them. We must listen to our dogs when they tell us they are afraid. We cannot simply talk dogs out of their fear with human logic; we can comfort them with a calm, quiet, gentle voice and touch. Soothe them, and then promptly and coolly remove them from the situation, if possible.

There is a caveat. If you only use this calm, soothing demeanor in an emergency, you risk getting the opposite of your intended result. Your dog may begin to associate your tranquil state with imminent danger. To avoid this pattern, use your calming technique when the dog is not afraid. Put calm on cue by saying a word like "easy" while petting your dog. The next time your dog is in a tense situation, he will associate this word and gentle touch with being in a calm state.

Chronic Anxiety and Health Problems

Anxiety is a symptom of stress, which can manifest as behavioral or physical problems. Triggers of stress may be:

- Change in environment
- Illness
- Change in hierarchy (addition of or loss of another pet)
- Change in family dynamics (addition or loss of a family member)
- Reintroduction of a dog or person after long absence
- Change in noise and activity levels
- Change in hormones
- Change in human stress level
- Change in schedule

Whether physical or emotional, chronic or acute negative stress weakens the dog's responsiveness and immune system. Dogs under stress might chew or ingest things that are harmful to them. They may eat or drink excessively or not at all. Stressed dogs sometimes demonstrate obsessive-compulsive behaviors, such as incessant licking that may result in an ulcerated area called a lick granuloma. When stress begins to compromise a dog's health by weakening the immune system, he becomes more susceptible to infection, allergies, viruses, parasites, toxins, and more serious diseases such as cancer.

Some physical signs of stress:
- Excessive shedding
- Dandruff

- Diarrhea

- Vomiting

- Sweaty paws

- Drooling

- Dilated pupils

Some behaviors associated with stress are:
- Panting

- Pacing

- Trembling

- Digging

- Chewing

- Excessive licking

- Excessive barking or whining

- Aggression

Some stressors are obvious. Just as the dentist's office is low on my list of travel destinations, a trip to the vet or groomer can be stressful for some dogs. Chaotic and unfamiliar situations or being left alone are worrisome, even terrifying for the fearful dog. Some say that other, not so apparent, conditions can stress dogs as well. These conditions include long periods of highly active play or too much competition, where adrenaline runs high over prolonged stretches of time. The production of stress chemicals in the body is cumulative and can take days or even weeks to adjust back to normal. Therefore, to avoid stress, a dog's activity schedule should be balanced with sufficient down time. Nature designed dogs in the wild to have brief periods of stress for hunting and plenty of down time for eating and sleeping. Remembering this fact helps us uphold a natural balance for domestic dogs and prevent undue stress.

The trainer's axiom of "a tired dog is a good dog" holds true, but it should not be taken to extreme. The key to avoiding stress is to maintain equilibrium between physical activity, rest, and mental stimulation tailored to the individual dog.

Defining Anxiety, Fear, and Phobia

Fear is innate—a natural behavior designed to preserve life, limb, and the species.

The continuum of fearful behavior is then broken down into its characterizations: anxiety, fear, and phobia. Anxiety and phobia fall under the broad term of fear. Fear is defined specifically as the state of being afraid in the presence of the trigger.

Anxiety, at the low end of the fear spectrum, is about future events. It is worry about what *might* happen, not what actually *is* happening. It may be situational, or its source may be unknown. Anxiety is not dependent on the presence of the fear-inducing trigger. For example, a dog that is afraid of children may become anxious approaching an empty playground.

By definition, fear is reliant on the presence of that which triggers the emotion. It is a perceived threat. Some dogs are afraid of people, sounds, specific locations, objects, or certain environments.

Phobias, at the high end of the spectrum, are extreme, irrational aversions that are disproportionate to the perceived threat. Reactions are intense, perhaps so intense as to endanger the dog. Phobic reactions escalate quickly, whereas fearful responses are more gradual.

How Dogs Communicate Fear

If we can recognize the signs of fear early, before a full-blown outburst, we can diffuse the situation and capture the moment as a teachable one.

Dogs use body language and vocalizations to communicate their emotions to us and to one another. Sounds used to convey fear might include whining, barking, growling, yelping, howling, and screaming. They may be used in combination and escalate on a continuum. Of course, vocalizations express things other than fear, too. A dog may whine for attention or yelp in excitement, so we must look at the whole picture to determine what he's telling us. From there, we can formulate the right solution to the problem.

Dog body language can be very subtle. The chapter on canine communication describes the signals in detail. Regarding signs of fear, some are so subtle that they are often misunderstood or go altogether unnoticed.

Subtle signals include:
- Sweaty paws
- Excessive shedding and dandruff
- Loss of appetite
- Refusal to drink water
- Diarrhea
- Compulsive chewing or licking themselves (i.e. paws)

Obvious signals of fear include:
- Trembling
- Drooling
- Vomiting
- Expression of anal glands
- Loss of bowel control
- Urination
- Shutting down (unable to move)
- Hypoalgesia (decreased sensitivity to pain)

Fear or Aggression?

One can look at body language to decode whether a dog is acting out of fear or aggression. A fearful dog can lunge and bark. Here the behavior is designed to put space between him and the perceived threat. Aggression can also involve lunging and barking, but there are differences in the posture that reveal the intent.

A fearful dog distributes his weight on the back legs with his energy moving away from the trigger. He may be barking and lunging, but he does so with trepidation. He may bark, then quickly move away, or bark while moving backward. Ears are most likely pinned back, and his tail lowered.

A dog motivated by aggression intends to do harm. His posture differs from the fearful dog's posture in that he distributes his body weight on the front legs. His energy moves forward, and he may bark and lunge. The aggressive dog's ears are forward and tail held high.

The aggressive dog may also retract his lips to display the front teeth in what is called an agonistic pucker. The fearful dog's mouth is closed, with the corners retracted and no teeth showing. The agonistic pucker may be accompanied by a low, guttural growl. Both the fearful and the aggressive dog may bark, but only the aggressive dog growls.

Identifying a behavior as fearful or aggressive can be complicated when the dog is feeling conflicted. He may lunge and then flee. He may approach cautiously to accept petting or to interact with another dog, but then become afraid and snap in defense.

Fearful dogs should be allowed to choose whether to approach the object of their fear. Never force them to accept petting or to interact with another dog. If we attempt to lure the fearful dog into a an uncomfortable situation before he's ready, he may be just brave enough to approach, but then realize he's in over his head and snap.

Similarly, leashed dogs should be allowed to make their own choices about whether to meet people and dogs. Forcing an approach when a dog is feeling uncomfortable is a setup for leash aggression. Given the choice, dogs usually prefer flight to fight in the presence of perceived danger. Dogs on leash, particularly a tight leash, don't have the option of flight, so they may feel that the only alternative is to fight.

Dos and Don'ts of Human Body Language

Like us, dogs use body language and vocalizations to communicate feelings and intentions. Understanding how they interpret our body language will help us help the fearful dog to be more comfortable in our presence.

It is natural for humans to approach a dog, lean over, look him in the eye, and pat him on the head. This is uncomfortable for many dogs and downright terrifying to the fearful dog. Think of a twenty-foot tall person dressed like the Grim Reaper doing that to you. Scary?

A less threatening approach is to stoop down with your side to the dog and turn your head away. No need to reach out; just keep your hands down and to your sides. Let the dog approach and sniff. If he is comfortable enough to let you touch him, pet him lightly and slowly under the chin and talk in a soothing tone.

Dogs make us smile, and that's a good thing. However, the sight of teeth can be threatening to a dog, so go ahead and smile, but do it with a closed mouth.

I tend to scare myself. –**Stephen King**

Causes
Fear doesn't just happen without a reason, and it doesn't simply go away without treatment. Many factors can contribute to fearfulness. They might occur separately or in combination. In order to establish an effective treatment plan, it's helpful to determine the cause.

Heredity
What happens at the breeders can affect a puppy's predisposition to fear. A mother's stress during pregnancy will have an effect her puppies. Therefore, puppy mills, irresponsible, and accidental breeding are situations rife for producing fearful dogs.

Certain breeds are predisposed to fearfulness. Breeding allows for selection of certain traits, such as wariness of strangers in guard dogs and hesitancy in herding dogs (they will not bite the livestock). These traits are valuable to a certain extent, but problematic in excess.

Different levels of fearfulness are evident within a litter of pups and within a breed line. Here's where nature and nurture come into play. A responsible breeder will carefully select dogs for desired traits and provide socialization and life enriching activities for the puppies. They will spay and neuter genetically fearful dogs to prevent another generation of anxious animals.

Training dogs that are genetically predisposed to fear is difficult and may not be fully effective. In fearful situations, these dogs often revert to their previous behavior, because genetics has overridden training.

Generally speaking, dogs that are not genetically predisposed to fear, are properly socialized, and experience no trauma or abuse in early life have no reason become overly fearful. Conversely, dogs that are genetically fearful, not suitably socialized, and have been traumatized or abused will likely become the most fearful of the fearful.

Lack of Early Socialization

This may be the principal reason dogs become fearful. Fearfulness is often attributed to abuse in dogs with unknown history, but the cause is more likely a shortfall in socialization.

The crucial learning period for puppies occurs in the first twelve weeks. If not exposed to novel situations, people, and things, they may be fearful of them later on. Socialization is more than meeting new people and dogs. It involves having a wide array of new experiences interacting with the world, so it becomes a familiar, friendly place. For more information, see the chapter on socialization.

Abuse

Dogs that have been mistreated are understandably afraid of people. If a dog has been kicked or punched, he will likely become shy of hands and feet. If he has been hit with an object, such as a bat, or whipped with a leash, it's probable that he will fear these and similar objects.

Dogs may become fearful of locations where the cruelty occurred. For instance, a dog beaten for soiling the carpet in the bedroom may become afraid of that room.

Trauma

Fear can develop after an intensely distressing experience, which might affect a dog's future behavior. Even milder experiences can cause a disproportionate response later on. Also, if a dog experiences something while already under stress, their response may be more intense. For instance, a loud noise at the vet's office may cause a more fearful response than a loud noise while in a calm, relaxed situation at home.

Learned Association

Dogs learn by association, which is helpful in obedience training, but not when it's fear that is learned. As in the aforementioned example, a dog may become afraid of car rides if the only place the car takes him is to frightening destinations.

Physical

Pain and discomfort due to illness, injury, or other medical conditions can cause anxiety for dogs. This can be a symptom of the medical condition itself, such as hypothyroidism, or the anticipation of pain from being touched (i.e. hip dysplasia or arthritis). Talk to your vet or veterinary behaviorist about these conditions and their effect on behavior

Dogs that have endured harsh training methods and pain-inducing equipment (i.e. pinch or shock collars) may become fearful of people, equipment, and locations because of the anticipation of pain.

Prevention
An ounce of prevention is preferable to developing a pound of cure. In the case of the fearful dog, it's much easier to learn courage and composure than it is to unlearn fear. Following are some helpful tips for preventing fearfulness in dogs.

Breeding
Choose a responsible breeder who breeds dogs with solid temperaments, and it will save you the heartbreak of living with a fearful dog. Buying a puppy from a pet store is risky, because many of these dogs come from puppy mills and irresponsible breeding.

Socialization
Socialization is probably the single most important element in preventing fearful dogs. It should be started early (during the crucial learning period of three to twelve weeks) and continue through adolescence. Life is always changing, so socialization should continue throughout every dog's life.

Positive and Compassionate Training
Positive training and rearing means setting dogs up for success and rewarding them for it. It means catching them "doing it right" and reinforcing those behaviors, rather than waiting for them to "do it wrong" and then correcting them. Harsh corrections and constant scolding make for a timid dog that is hesitant to offer behaviors for fear of making punishable mistakes.

Safety
Life is unpredictable, but through vigilance and management, we can help prevent traumatic experiences for our dogs. Good management, equipment, and common sense prevail.

Maintaining Good Health
Maintain good health in your dog with regular, preventative checkups.

Manage pain and existing conditions. Engender physical wellbeing by providing age and breed appropriate exercise and mental stimulation.

Physical Exercise and Mental Stimulation

Physical exercise inhibits stress hormones and induces endorphins, the feel-good chemicals. With adequate exercise, the mind and body are physically tired and more relaxed, which makes for an open learning environment. Check with your veterinarian to be sure that your dog is healthy and able to participate in the chosen venture. Activities should be breed and age appropriate for the dog, and he should enjoy them:

- Walks, jogging, and hikes
- Play dates or doggie daycare
- Games (tug, fetch, catch)
- Chewing
- Swimming
- Dog sports

Mental stimulation prevents anxiety by calming the mind and tiring the body. Think about how we feel after attending a lecture or learning a new computer application. Even though the experience did not involve physical exercise, we are exhausted afterward. The same happens for dogs. Here are some examples of activities to promote mental stimulation:

- Interactive puzzle toys
- Hunt for food
(fling kibble on the floor instead of serving it in a bowl)
- Hide and seek (hide toys/food)
- Road trips (take dog along on errands)
- Learning basic behaviors and tricks

Zen Time

The fact that the body and mind are connected holds true for both humans and dogs. Humans can calm the body and mind through meditation and other relaxation techniques. With *Zen Time*, or teaching dogs to calm on cue, can help them to relax even in the midst of bedlam. We can show them that they can maintain a calm state, and that their emotions need not reflect the environment. This is helpful in multi-dog households, because having one dog relax will send a calming signal to the others.

A calm mind is receptive to learning, but Zen Time is more than obedience (as in sit, down, and stay). It is about changing the dog's internal emotional state. In obedience training, a down stay has the dog in a specific position, remaining alert, and waiting for his cue to be released. Zen Time has the dog settled into a comfortable position of choice, even napping. It's relaxation on request.

When the body is relaxed, so is the mind. Dogs can be taught to relax through shaping and capturing relaxed behavior.

Begin training for Zen Time when the dog is naturally calm, say after an outing or at bedtime. Highly active or nervous dogs can be tethered if they can't remain in one location (only if the dog is okay with being tethered and separated from you). They do not need to be taught to relax in one particular spot.

Sit calmly nearby; ignore the dog; and wait for him to show any signs of relaxing, such as standing still or sniffing calmly instead of zooming around the room. Mark the behavior with a calm verbal marker ("Yes!") or a click (if doing clicker training). Calmly praise the dog, and then ignore him again. If the dog knows how to lie down on cue, you can ask him to lie down. If not, wait for the next indication of relaxation, such as a sit or a sign of intent to lie down.

When the dog is in a down position, wait for the dog to relax even more, maybe by rolling on to one hip. Mark, reward, praise, ignore. You will shape the behavior by capturing each progression toward total relaxation. With each step, you will protract the behavior by rewarding it every few seconds. Once the dog relaxes, reward, wait a few seconds, and reward again.

The dog will begin to relax more readily. When this happens, it is time to put the behavior on cue. Each time the dog settles into a comfortable down position, say your cue word. I use the word "settle." Once the dog has associated the cue with the behavior, you can ask him to "settle" when he is sitting or standing, and he'll know he's being asked to lie down and relax.

Help the dog to generalize the behavior by practicing in different locations. Have him settle in different rooms of the house, the yard, and other quiet locations. Gradually work toward having him relax in more distracting situations, such as a quiet park or in the presence of another dog. You will eventually have a dog that can settle at the vet's office or in a group training class.

Zen Time Challenge

Now that the dog has learned to settle on cue in mildly distracting situations, we can practice calm on cue by setting up a game. Using a toy, get the dog excited by being very animated and enticing him to play. While he's excited, ask for a sit (the dog has been trained and reliable on sit). Mark and reward the behavior with a treat and/or throwing a toy and allowing the dog to play for a minute. Once he can do this with sit, do it with down. These exercises teach the dog that he can go from chaos to calm on cue.

Remember that slower is faster here. Do not push the dog, or he may digress. With each step, we will ask for a shorter settle period at first. Don't expect a dog that can settle for twenty minutes at home in the family room to settle for twenty minutes at the vet's office.

Zen Time is helpful in assuaging mild anxiety, but at no time should you ask a dog settle in the face of strong fears. Remember the woman who forced her fearful dogs into a down stay and asked them to focus on her while other dogs passed nearby? This was in no way relaxing for her dogs. It would have the opposite effect by putting them in a vulnerable position.

Go to Bed

Teaching a fearful dog to go to a safe place on cue is a helpful management tool. It builds his confidence, keeps him cognitive, and provides a plan for when anxious situations arise. For example, the dog can learn to go to his safe place at the sound of the doorbell when visitors arrive.

Follow the instructions for teaching dogs to "kennel up" in this chapter. A safe place can be the dog's crate or bed in a quiet location away from the front door. When the dog has learned to go to his safe place on cue, have someone ring the doorbell, then ask the dog to "kennel up" or "go to bed." Repeat this exercise until the dog associates the doorbell with going to his safe place.

If the dog runs to the front door upon hearing the doorbell, you'll want to do a bit of desensitization. With the dog on leash, have someone stand in plain sight and ring the bell. If the dog barks, wait for him to quiet down. Then, cue him to go to his safe place and escort him on a loose leash. Repeat this exercise until the dog is able to go to his safe place independently and on cue.

Leadership and Support

Strong and benevolent leadership engenders a sense of safety for dogs. Dogs that are afraid of unfamiliar people may bark and act aggressively to anyone coming into the house or passing by on a walk. They do this in order to scare people away or warn them not to approach. Dogs often feel a sense of relief when we take charge as the one deciding who comes into the house or who to greet on a walk.

Dogs don't do well with ambivalence. They feel more secure with the rules and boundaries we provide through good training and leadership. Furthermore, strong, benevolent guidance builds confidence on both ends of the leash. When the human end of the leash is feeling calm and confident, so will the canine end. For more details, see the chapter *Is My Dog Winning?* on leadership and the alpha theory.

Management

Maintain a peaceful home environment. Without turning your lifestyle upside down, you can be aware of your dog's fears and manage the situation accordingly.

Schedule and routine give dogs a sense of security. It's helpful if walks, feedings, and your arrivals and departures are predictable. (In the case of separation anxiety, avoid predictable departure triggers. See the chapter *Wish You Were Here.*) However, schedules need not be so rigid that the slightest variation would cause anxiety. Dogs need a regular routine, but they also need to know that it can vary.

Establish a place of refuge for your dog, such as a crate or a cozy bed in a quiet room (see creating a safe place in the chapter *Wish You Were Here.*)

Avoid situations and locations that cause the dog anxiety. Exposure only sensitizes him to being fearful of these things. If your dog becomes nervous when people come into your home, then have him go to his safe place when you answer the door. If the dog is fearful of passersby, limit his view by closing blinds or having him in another room. If he is not exposed to the event that triggers the anxiety, he will not rehearse the fearful behavior and be reinforced for it.

Terms of Agreement

We must meet the fearful dog where he is emotionally and work from there. Help him to meet his fear with an open and engaged presence. Allow him to relax by giving him the opportunity to investigate the source of his fear on his own terms.

Enthusiastically pushing a dog into an uncomfortable situation to show him it's okay is not likely to work. I can illustrate this reality with an episode in my personal life involving my fear of enclosed places suspended in space by a thin thread of cable.

Two friends wanted me to accompany them on a gondola ride to the top of Sandia Mountain in Albuquerque, New Mexico. I was reluctant. My well-meaning friends decided to encourage my participation by physically removing me from the car. The scene was reminiscent of putting a cat in the shower! My friends gave in to my panicked scratching and clawing when they realized that they were only making matters worse. Consequently, I watched their gondola ascend to the peak from the comfort of the visitor's center bar, glass of merlot in hand. With time, counter conditioning using a glass of merlot, and allowing me to operate on my own terms, I would have calmly ridden that gondola. These methods help dogs as well, although I'd suggest using liver bites instead of alcoholic beverages.

Treatment

Treatment of fearful dogs requires a toolbox of valuable skills. These tools include the following, which are detailed in the Beyond the Basics chapter:

- Counter conditioning

- Desensitization

- Classical conditioning

- Operant conditioning

- Teaching adjunct behaviors

- Relaxation exercises

Treatment

Power is of two kinds. One is obtained by the fear of punishment and the other by acts of love. Power based on love is a thousand times more effective and permanent than the one derived from fear of punishment.
—**Mohandas Karamchand Gandhi**

Punishment and Flooding

Dominance-based training theory abounds in today's training culture. This philosophy interprets much of canine behavior as the dog's need for a dominant role in the "pack." In this theory, the owner is included in the pack, and the owner establishes dominance by sometimes by using punishment.

Punishment has no place in the treatment of a fearful dog when punishment fosters fear. A dog's decision to engage in a behavior based on fear is not lasting. The use of force or intimidation merely results in the dog learning to avoid or submit. Behaviors offered in this circumstance are like confessions made under torture.

Tolerance and understanding foster learning. Not despot leadership but confident and compassionate guidance is the key to successful treatment of the fearful dog.

Punishment can make matters worse, because it causes the trigger to bear a double meaning: the elicitor of fear and the antecedent to punishment. If he is always punished for fearful behavior in the presence of the trigger, the dog has learned by association that there is, in fact, a basis for his fear. Punishment will simply overwrite one fear with another, and that new fear might be of you—the punisher.

Humans can rationalize fear and be present with it in order to work through the emotion. We choose when and exactly how we face our fears. But, we are the ones choosing when and how our dog faces his, so we must be sensitive to what he's feeling. We need to know when to advance and when to back off.

Some would say, "Dog up and deal with it. He needs to learn the ropes," and then, proceed to throw their dog into new situations. However, taking a fearful dog to a dog park is akin to taking a wallflower to a frat party. This sink or swim attitude can do more psychological harm than good, increasing a dog's level of anxiety. Furthermore, it might damage the relationship between dog and owner, as the dog cannot trust his owner to support and protect him.

A word about flooding: Flooding is an immersion technique used in both human and animal psychology. It involves exposing the dog to the fear eliciting stimuli with no option of escape. The dog is made to endure the stimuli until he gives up, exhausted. The theory is that if he is can be calm in the presence of the trigger, he will learn that the trigger is not a menacing thing after all, and his fears are baseless.

In strict scientific theory, administered by a skilled professional in controlled circumstances, flooding can work. However, the risk of creating extreme fear and damaging the owner-dog relationship far outweighs the slim chance of success.

Before the Treatment Begins
In the treatment process, we want to do everything possible to avoid accidental setbacks or inadvertently making matters worse. There are some things we can do in advance to set ensure success.

Identify the Cause
Be sure that the behavior is, in fact, prompted by fear. This is important if the dog is behaving aggressively. If fear is not the motivator, then we need a different plan.

Break the Pattern
The dog should not be exposed to the trigger for two weeks before beginning behavior modification. Breaking the old pattern of behavior prevents the dog from rehearsing the former fearful behavior and begins to abate the negative association.

Easy Does It
Successful treatment is based on slow, incremental steps. Use good management to prevent exposure to the trigger and gentle, effective

equipment. Shock collars, choke chains, and prong collars have no place in the treatment of fearful dogs.

Avoidance

During treatment, the dog's environment must be managed in order to prevent or at least minimize exposure to what triggers his fear. This prevents the dog from practicing fearful behavior and having it reinforced.

Muzzles

Use a basket type muzzle in the treatment of fear aggression. The basket muzzle, as opposed to the sleeve type, allows the dog to pant, drink, and take treats while wearing it.

Identify Specific Triggers

Make a list of individual triggers, so that you can address them individually in treatment. Determine whether the triggers have become generalized. For example, if a dog has had a frightening experience around a man wearing a hat (even if the event was not precipitated by the man), the dog may have generalized the incident and be fearful of all men wearing hats. This can happen especially if a similarly fearful event happens in the presence of men in hats.

Find the Highest Motivator

In counter conditioning, we will be changing the dog's inner emotional state by having him associate the unpleasant thing (the trigger) with a pleasant thing (food, toys, fun). The pleasant thing must be of the highest value to the dog, so that it will get his attention when he is near threshold. Remember my glass of merlot?

Specific Fears

Fear of Noise
Fear of loud noises, such as slamming doors, loud voices, etc. can be treated with counter conditioning, desensitization, and relaxation exercises. Recording the sounds in order to control volume and duration is helpful in the process. *Through A Dog's Ear* (http://throughadogsear.com/) offers downloadable recordings of common noises that dogs fear such as traffic, city noises, thunder, etc.

Thunder phobia is much more difficult to treat than fear of other loud noises. This is due to the perfect storm of visual and audio triggers, as well as other intangible and uncontrollable elements like barometric pressure changes, static electricity, and ozone level.

To reduce the effects of static electricity, try a Storm Defender cape (http://www.stormdefender.com/) or rub the dog down with an anti-static laundry sheet. Complementary therapies include Thundershirts (http://www.thundershirt.com/), pharmaceuticals, herbal supplements, and flower essences. Provide a safe refuge where the dog can retreat during storms and treat with counter conditioning, desensitization, and relaxation exercises. *Through A Dog's Ear* recordings are helpful in treatment of thunder phobia.

Fear of the Inanimate
Sound, sight, and smell can trigger a fearful response. Often a traumatic event is the source of these fears, a sort of post-traumatic stress syndrome where encountering an inanimate object becomes a trigger. For example, if a dog had his tail caught in a car door, he may develop a fear of cars. Fear of inanimate objects will be treated with counter conditioning and desensitization.

Fear of Children
Children are unpredictable. They are prone to running, screaming, and roughhousing. Furthermore, they do these things at the dog's eye level—a very frightening situation for some dogs.

Treatment with counter conditioning, desensitization, and relaxation exercises, is the same as for dogs that are fearful of adults. However, exercise extra caution and teach children how to safely interact with dogs (see the chapter *Kids and Dogs*).

Fear of Familiar People
The fearful dog can even have issues with family members or close friends. Frequent visitors to the home, such as the nanny or cleaning service staff, may also trigger fear. Fear associated with people who clean houses may be because they use dreaded, noisy machinery like vacuum cleaners. A treatment plan that includes counter conditioning, desensitization, and relaxation exercises is the key to successful treatment.

Fear of Veterinarian Offices or Grooming Salons

A trip to the vet's office or to the grooming salon can be unsettling to many dogs, but to the fearful dog, it can be a nightmare. Prepare your dog for these visits by desensitizing him to the handling that he will receive during services (see handling exercises in the socialization chapter). Plan a friendly visit to the vet's office or grooming salon. For this visit, take some high-value treats and simply greet the groomers or the doctor and staff. Have these friendly folks give your dog his treats and pet him gently. Let the dog sniff and explore.

Train your dog to wear a muzzle when necessary and to accept gentle restraint. Doing so will help him to be more comfortable during exams. (See the chapter *Aggressive Dogs* for information on acclimating dogs to muzzles.)

Confidence Building Exercises

These exercises will help the fearful dog feel more confident about meeting new people. Work on them slowly, with the dog achieving a calm, comfortable level at each step before moving to the next. Work the dog through the exercises with each new person.

First, make sure that the dog knows basic obedience. This gives confidence to both human and dog, because they are engaged and communicating. It gives the dog self-assurance through structure, concentration, and the ability to perform familiar, routine behaviors. It also puts the owner in a position of compassionate leadership and guidance.

The treatment will begin at home with people who are familiar but not comfortable to the dog. **These exercises are not for dogs showing fear aggression.** You will find that specific treatment in the chapter on aggression. Work with a reputable trainer or behaviorist for treatment of fear aggression.

Touch

It is helpful to redirect a dog's attention during mild anxiety. (If a dog is in a complete panic, he should be removed from the situation.) Keep the dog cognitive. This prevents anxiety from escalating and builds confidence when interacting with people and objects. A nice way to accomplish this is by teaching the dog to touch (target) your hand and other objects. Touch is something that the dog is *doing*, as opposed to something that is being done to him. For instance, the dog approaches and touches a person's hand instead of the person reaching out to pet him.

Start by facing your dog. Sitting is helpful to make the dog more comfortable, but not necessary. Slowly move your relaxed hand to within a couple inches of the dog's nose with palm facing away. Be careful not to hold your hand over his head if he shows any shyness to the movement. When he naturally sniffs and touches your hand with his nose, mark the behavior with "Yes!" or click if using a clicker, and then deliver a treat with your other hand.

When the dog is readily touching your hand, put in the cue by saying, "touch." Do this every time the dog puts his nose to your hand. Soon he will associate the word with the behavior.

Now that the dog is touching your hand reliably and on cue, begin to move your hand around, so he must move farther to touch it. Next, begin taking a few steps, so that the dog follows you to touch your hand. Keep things interesting and exciting for the dog, and keep moving. He should be happy about playing the touch game.

Practice the touch game on leash inside the house, then in the yard, so that the dog generalizes the game for playing it in other situations later on.

Meeting New People
This exercise will acclimate dogs to regular visitors to the home or family members that they feel uncomfortable around. It is not for the occasional or one-time visitor. In those cases, the dog should be crated or in his safe place in another room. **This exercise is intended for dogs whose anxiety is mild and not for dogs with severe anxiety or those showing fear aggression.**

Brief your visitor before their arrival, so they are aware of your specific plan. As elementary and unnecessary as it might seem, explain what it means to ignore the dog. Everyone thinks they are the exception to fearful dog behavior, because they love dogs and dogs love them. These folks will want to coax the dog to interact with them. Tell them that you understand their perspective, but your fearful dog will not. Explain that ignoring the dog means to not look at, talk to, or reach for him, even if he approaches to sniff.

Many fearful dogs will bark hysterically when the doorbell rings, alerting the household to perceived danger. They feel it is their job, even if they are not comfortable doing it. The following exercises will show how to ease their anxiety by relieving them of this duty.

Grabbing the dog's collar at the door can exacerbate the problem. Collar grabbing puts him on the defensive by removing his option to flee. It can cause him more stress and could even result in fear aggression. Picking up a small dog that barks and races to the door stops the assault but could intensify the problem by increasing the little guy's confidence. In your arms and in his mind, he feels mighty and ferocious when he's high in stature and backed up by his human.

Step 1: Dog approaches person

Start by having the dog gated in a back room with a view of the person entering the home. The person will come in, sit down, and ignore the dog.

After the person has entered, release the dog from the back room and allow him to investigate. Most dogs will feel conflicted and waver between approaching and retreating. The dog should not be on leash. On leash, he will feel vulnerable with no means of escape.

The person will continue to ignore the dog, resisting the temptation to lure him closer. The owner should also avoid trying to force or entice the dog. Luring or pushing a dog into a stressful situation would be unfair and punishing. Let the dog decide whether to approach or not.

The visitor will sit still with his or her side to the dog, not directly facing him. The visitor should not talk to or make eye contact with the dog. Hands can be folded in the lap or hanging down by the side. Ignore the dog's retreat. The owner will praise and give treats for approach.

Next, remove the dog from the room, have the person leave, and then let the dog sniff where the person was sitting. Sniffing allows the dog to get information about the person—meeting them without *meeting* them, so to speak.

Step 2: Making contact

When the dog is feeling confident enough to approach the person, have them dangle their hand down to let the dog come take a quick sniff. The person should not reach toward the dog, talk to him, or make eye contact. The owner can praise and treat the dog for sniffing.

Once the dog is comfortable approaching the visitor, we can begin enticing the dog to get closer. Without looking at or talking to him, the visitor can toss an occasional treat toward the dog. The motion should be a slow, underhand toss in the dog's general direction. If the dog is comfortable, allow him to take a treat from the visitor's outstretched hand. Without bending over or looking directly at the dog, the visitor can then hold their hand closer and closer to their side, until the dog takes the treat from their hand when it's relaxed down at their side.

At this point, the owner is ready to play the touch game (previously taught) with the dog. Start with the owner sitting beside the visitor and asking for a few touches from the dog.

Step 3: Transfer touch

The owner sits next to the visitor (between the visitor and the dog), asks the dog to touch her hand, and treats the dog. Repeat this several times until the dog is happily touching the owner's hand.

Next, have the visitor place his hand under the owner's hand. The owner asks the dog to touch her hand, and then treats the dog. Repeat until the dog feels comfortable with this step.

Finally, the visitor places his hand over the owner's hand. The owner will ask the dog to touch the visitor's hand and treats the dog.

Repeat the above steps but with the visitor giving the verbal cues and treating the dog.

Step 4: Playing touch

In step four, the visitor and owner have an opportunity to play the touch game with the dog. The owner sits beside the visitor and asks the dog to touch her hand. Then, the visitor sits with one hand placed palm down on his knee while holding a treat in his other hand. The visitor quietly asks the dog to "touch" the hand on his knee. When the dog does so, the visitor calmly praises the dog and offers the treat. Repeat several times until the dog is readily, even happily taking treats from the visitor.

Next, the owner positions herself a few feet away from the visitor and asks the dog to come touch her hand. In turn, the visitor calls the dog to come touch his hand. Ping-Pong the dog back and forth a few times until the dog is happily playing the touch game. Then, do it with the visitor standing up. From here, begin to play the game at various locations in the house.

Make sure that the dog gets lots of breaks, and watch him for signs of stress. If he is showing nervousness, stop the exercise. It is better to do several short successful sessions than to push the dog to the breaking point. Pushing him beyond his limits only sets him back by proving (in his mind) that strangers are indeed scary and untrustworthy.

The touch game should be just that—a *game*. The dog is happy, cognitive, and engaged instead of concentrating on his fear.

Step 5: Visitor pets the dog
This exercise will increase the dog's comfortable level in approaching visitors and accepting petting.

The visitor sits with one hand, palm up, on his knee and holding a treat in his other hand. He quietly asks the dog to "touch" the hand on his knee. Repeat this a few times until the dog is comfortable taking the treat.

The visitor then positions the treat so that the dog must reach across the hand on the knee to take it. Let the dog nibble on the treat with his chin touching the visitor's upward palm that is resting on his knee. Repeat until the dog is comfortable with this step.

Next, as the dog takes the treat, the person gently scratches the dog under the chin. Repeat this a few times. If the dog is relaxed, the person may slowly and gently move his hand from under the dog's chin toward the dog's shoulder.

Step 6: Visitor approaches and pets the dog
Next, we acclimate the dog to being approached and petted by a visitor. The visitor stands (for small dogs, start by stooping down), asks the dog to

come touch his hand, scratches the dog under the chin, and treats. Then, the visitor takes a step away from the dog, approaches, asks for a touch, and scratches the dog under the chin.

Repeat the exercise, having the visitor retreat and approach from a progressively greater distance. The dog may want to follow the visitor as he moves away. This is good news, because the dog is now approaching the visitor. If he follows the visitor, the owner asks the dog to stay or gently holds him while the visitor approaches and retreats. Remember that the dog is comfortable approaching the visitor at this point. If he were not, holding him or having him on leash would put him in a vulnerable position and compromise training.

Practice this step at different locations throughout the house, then again outside.

Once the dog readily accepts the visitor's approach, have the visitor leave through the front door and immediately return to repeat the exercise.

Fear of Family Member
Some dogs are fearful of a particular family member. This is not uncommon, but it makes life uncomfortable for both the dog and the person. It can also cause feelings of rejection for the person who doesn't feel the love from their canine family member. Oftentimes dogs are afraid of adult male family members, and sometimes they're afraid of children, particularly adolescent boys (see chapter *Kids and Dogs* for more information on healthy child/dog relationships).

The following exercises, done slowly and carefully, are designed to assuage the dog's fears so he can live comfortably *all in the family*. **Seek help from a reputable dog trainer or behaviorist for dogs with severe fear or fear aggression.**

Below are some tips to help the fearful dog acclimate to the family member—we'll call him Dad—with whom he is uncomfortable.

For the dog that is mildly or acutely fearful, follow the directives for visitors described above. Dad should ignore the dog completely at first. It can be difficult to be the odd man out, but ignoring the fearful dog and letting him operate on his own terms will engender trust and prove that he is in safe, predictable company.

For the dog that is mildly fearful, Dad can feed him, walk him, play with him, and participate in any activity that the dog enjoys. The dog may not be ready for physical contact, such as petting, from Dad, thought. So, forgo that at first.

It is important to allow the dog a comfortable distance from Dad during these exercises. If Dad is doing the feeding, be sure that the dog has adequate distance at mealtime. If the dog is not comfortable enough for Dad to walk him, have another person walk the dog as Dad strolls nearby. Playtime can have Dad gently throwing a ball or toy at a comfortable distance for the dog.

For the dog that is mildly fearful, have Dad and the dog spend a lot of alone time. They need these moments to bond. Have Dad be the trainer by working privately with a professional trainer in-home or by taking the dog to a group class. If the dog is comfortable with it, have him tag along with Dad on errands.

If the dog is still too nervous to be alone around Dad, do the above exercises with another family member whom the dog is comfortable.

Use treats to help the dog build a positive association with Dad. Find a very special high-value treat that is used only for this training. Have other family members dispense these treats to the dog only when Dad is present. Dad can toss an occasional treat toward the dog with a slow underhand motion. When the dog is comfortable, allow him to take a treat from Dad's outstretched hand while Dad is not looking at or talking to the dog.

After the dog has learned the touch game, and when he's happily taking treats from Dad as described above, go through the transfer touch exercises. After that, you are ready to have him play touch with Dad.

Taking It to the Streets

The following exercise is designed to help the fearful dog be more comfortable about passing by and meeting people during walks. It is important for the dog to be comfortable walking on leash and have good leash walking skills first, so that he'll be able to pay attention and take cues.

If he is not comfortable on walks, practice in familiar areas like the backyard or immediate neighborhood. If the dog is uncomfortable walking in a new area, simply go to a park and sit on a bench. Let him look and sniff, discovering the new location at his own pace. People may want to pet your dog, but he's not ready, so avoid it for now.

Take along plenty of high-value treats and toys to help the dog make a positive association with the places you go. Get some friends to help, and have the dog start meeting "friendly strangers," which are people he's actually met before. Have your friends go through the approach and touch exercises that the dog has already learned.

These exercises will engender confidence in the dog by proving that there are friendly strangers in the world. Remember that your dog does not have to meet and like every person he encounters. Support your dog, watch his body language, and back his decision about whom he wants to meet.

Emergency Stay

The emergency stay is a helpful tool to support your dog when people approach or pass by. It also sends a signal to the well-meaning stranger who insists that all dogs love them or the child enthusiastically asking to pet the doggie. The message is that you are in training, and that your dog may not be comfortable with approaching strangers.

First, teach your dog to stay. (See *The How-To of Training*) When he can do a solid stay at home in comfortable surroundings, teach him to do it while walking in familiar territory.

Step 1: Sit in the heel position

Most dogs have learned to sit on cue in front of us. It's helpful to teach dogs to sit beside us, so that they can wait at street corners and execute the emergency stay.

With the dog standing in front of you, take two steps backward. As you do this, hold a treat out to your side to lure the dog next to you. Next, take two steps forward, still luring with the treat to bring the dog to your side. You are now both facing the same direction, and the dog is walking beside you. Stop and ask him to sit.

Step 2: Stay in the heel position
Ask the dog for a stay while he is sitting beside you. Then, take one step forward. You and the dog are still facing the same direction, so your back will be to the dog. Next, step back, treat the dog, and release him to walk beside you.

Step 3: Stay behind you
Once the dog is comfortable with doing the stay while sitting beside and slightly behind you, he's ready to learn to stay directly behind you. Ask him for a stay, step forward one step, then step in front of the dog with your back to him. It may be helpful to use your hand signal for stay for the duration of this exercise.

Next, practice the emergency stay while a person walks by. You can start with one of your "friendly stranger" friends. Avoid setbacks by progressing slowly and keeping the dog under threshold. Give him enough space from the trigger, so that he is alert to it but able to remain cognitive and calm.

Practice this exercise in places with no distractions, like inside the house. Then, gradually work up to more distracting situations, such as the park.

Teach a Turnabout
In a perfect world, dogs would not be exposed to fearful situations during treatment. Alas, it's not a perfect world, and the unexpected will happen. We can teach dogs some coping skills to help navigate the unexpected and prevent setbacks. One handy skill is to turn on cue. This allows the dog to exit a situation with the least amount of anxiety. Rather than tighten the leash to drag him out of a situation (which is a natural reaction but escalates anxiety), we can give the dog a functional, even fun alternative.

Start by teaching this skill in a safe place and **not** in the presence of the trigger.

Walk with your dog at your side. Put a treat in front of his nose and do an about turn, luring him along on a loose leash. Be very animated and happy.

Say "turn" as you come about. Happily, jog several yards, and then treat the dog.

Repeat the exercise until the dog is happily turning with you and the event has become a fun game. The dog is readily following with a **loose leash** on his own volition.

For this exercise, practice turning both to the left and to the right, as sometimes there will be no choice in which way to turn. For example, a right turn would put you in the street. If you've never practiced a left turn, you'll be unprepared and possibly unsafe.

Note: Do not do the turnabout when encountering a stray dog. Running away from an off-leash dog will likely entice a chase. Instead, throw a handful of treats in the stray dog's face or slightly behind him, and move away quickly and casually without running.

Accepting Gentle Restraint

Gentle restraint is not in any way to be confused with alpha rolls. Alpha rolls, used in some training methods, involve rolling the dog on his back and holding him there until he shows "submission." This exercise is not about dominating the dog; it is simply teaching him to accept gentle restraint.

It's best to teach gentle restraint to young puppies, but older dogs will benefit from this training as well.

Hold the puppy gently but securely. If he wiggles, continue to hold him quietly until he settles, and when he does, praise and release him. Continue this exercise by gradually increasing the time (by a second or two) you hold the puppy. This exercise teaches the pup to accept gentle restraint and to relax, because when he relaxes, he will be released.

Help small and medium sized dogs to be comfortable standing on a table, as they will need to do for vet exams and grooming. You may want to place something like a rubber mat on the table so that the dog doesn't slip. First, put the dog gently on a table. If he is at ease, pet, praise, treat, and then remove him. When he is comfortable being on the table, practice the gentle restraint exercises below. Finally, practice the exercises without the mat, because most vet exam tables do not have them.

If you have a large adult dog, sit on the floor to practice this exercise, place small to medium sized adult dogs on a table. Position yourself at the dog's side, placing one arm over his back and the other under his neck. Hold him gently but securely against your chest for one second. Praise, treat, and release when he relaxes. Gradually increase the time holding the dog by one-second increments.

Remember, as with all training for fearful dogs: working slowly is the key. Let the dog set the pace. Make sure that he is comfortable with each step before moving on to the next. It may seem as though you are moving at a glacial pace, but advancing too quickly and pushing the dog risks setbacks or even worsening his fear.

Fear of Novelty (Neophobia)

Neophobia is the extreme or irrational fear or dislike of anything new, novel, or unfamiliar. Neophobic dogs are fearful in new environments and new things, people, sounds, and other experiences. Their anxieties may manifest into other anxious behaviors or compulsive habits, such as obsessive licking, chewing, or tail chasing. The cause of neophobia is often under-socialization or complete lack of socialization.

Note: Fear of unfamiliar dogs or people is not classified as neophobia, because the dog has met other dogs and people before. Neophobia is specifically the fear of events or things never before experienced.

Neophobia is best managed with a firm, predictable schedule. Because neophobic dogs don't deal well with change, stability and a quiet environment are helpful in their treatment. Treatment is best done during puppyhood, as rehabilitation of adult dogs tends to have varying levels of success. See your veterinarian or veterinary behaviorist for extreme cases that may require medication.

The treatment of neophobia involves good environmental management, counter conditioning, desensitization, and relaxation exercises.

Fear of the Car

The car can be a scary, enclosed, vibrating place where dogs become over stimulated by movement and sound. Some dogs experience carsickness, and others feel anxiety. Furthermore, it can be difficult for owners to distinguish motion sickness from anxiety. Anxious dogs may drool, be restless, and have a glazed look about them. Nausea can appear the same. To confound the situation, dogs that experience motion sickness may associate car rides with feeling sick and become anxious, about feeling nauseous. For carsickness, consult a veterinarian about medications and/or herbal, homeopathic remedies.

The following steps will help anxious dogs to learn that car rides can be pleasant and often end at a fun destination.

Step 1: If the dog is afraid to be anywhere near a car, begin by playing with him close to a car without asking him get in. Playtime in the garage (dog proof the area to make it safe) or driveway becomes a positive association with the car and prevents stress from building.

Step 2: If the dog is comfortable getting into the car, start by loading him in and sit in the back seat next to him without the engine running. If he is at ease with his seat belt, buckle it. Sit with the dog and feed him treats or a chew bone or play with his favorite toy. When he is comfortable, quietly take him out of the car.

Note: If the dog will not accept a treat or toy, he is over threshold and not in a cognitive state. This is not a teachable moment. Go back to Step 1 and progress at a more gradual pace. You may also want to try a higher value treat or toy.

Step 3: Load the dog into the car, snap him into his seat belt, and give him a food-stuffed toy or chew bone. Sit in the driver's seat and start the car. If the dog is comfortable enough to enjoy the toy or chew bone, sit with the engine idling until the dog has finished the treat. While he is still comfortable, calmly take the dog out of the car.

Step 4: Repeat the above step, and then back the car to the end of the driveway. Return to the starting point. While he is still comfortable, calmly take the dog out of the car.

Step 5: Repeat the above steps until you are able to drive around the block. Then, you will be able to gradually go longer distances.

During training, always make the destination a pleasant one, like the dog park or doggy day care (providing the dog enjoys these places). If a dog is only taken where he feels uncomfortable, i.e. the vet's office or groomer, he'll associate car rides with these spots that are frightening for him.

For extremely fearful dogs that become over stimulated by movement, try using a crate or calming cap, D.A.P., and/or a Thundershirt anxiety wrap. See supplemental remedies in this chapter for descriptions of these products.

Sometimes static shock is a factor that makes riding in the car unpleasant. If so, wipe the dog and car seat down with an anti-static laundry sheet.

Some dogs do not get carsick and are not anxious during the ride, but they are reluctant to load up. They may be fearful of jumping in, or even the beeping sound that occurs when the door is open. You may need to see your vet to make sure the dog is physically able to jump.

If loading is the problem, try a ramp or steps into the car. Play the touch game to move the dog up the ramp or steps. (See Teaching the Dog to Touch in this chapter). Acclimate the dog to the ramp by having him walk on it while it's lying flat, and then gradually increase the incline to the correct height for getting into the car.

Safety first: Dogs can ride safely with the use of seat belts, secured crates, or barriers. Dogs should not ride in the front seat for the same reason small children shouldn't—air bags. Do not allow the dog sit on your lap and/or hang out the window. NEVER let a dog ride in the back of an open pickup truck.

Fear of the Crate or Enclosed Spaces

Some dogs are afraid of the crate, but with proper use and training, they can learn to accept it as a place of comfort and security. **Dogs with extreme separation anxiety that panic in enclosed places should never be crated.**

Crate training

First, choose the type of crate that best fits your dog's needs. There are two main styles: ventilated, enclosed crates made of hard plastic; or the wire cage types. The enclosed crate engenders a cozier, den-like feeling for the dog, while the cage type feels more open and allows added ventilation. Make the wire crate to feel snug by draping it with a blanket.

To begin training, place the crate in a high traffic area. Afterward, it should be put in an out-of-the-way place where it is quiet and a comfortable temperature. The crate should be big enough for the dog to stand, lie down, and turn around comfortably. A crate that is too large will not provide coziness.

Step 1: Place the crate in a common area of the house with the door either detached or propped open so that it will not accidently close on the dog if he goes inside. Put bedding that the dog has slept on inside, along with an article of clothing or a towel that contains your scent. Ignore the crate and let the dog explore it in his own time. This time will vary among individual dogs. It could be minutes or days until the dog accepts the presence of the crate.

Step 2: Place the dog's meal inside the crate just inside the door. Once he is comfortable eating his meal here, begin moving the bowl, little by little, farther inside. Continue the process until the dog is eating his meal completely within the crate.

As an alternative or in addition to the above exercise, attach a chew toy inside at the back of the crate so the dog must enter and stay inside to enjoy it. Do this only after the dog is comfortable going inside the crate.

If the dog is extremely afraid and you are using an enclosed crate, remove the top before conducting Step 2. Gradually replace the top by propping it up, then sliding it further and further into place. If using a wire crate, remove the flooring and have the dog stand on it outside of the crate to eat his meals.

If you're having trouble with Step 2, place an extremely high-value food treat like chicken or hot dogs inside the crate, close the door, and leave the room. If the dog is showing interest in getting the food, open the door and leave the room. The dog may decide to enter the crate for the food.

If the above steps are not working, sit beside the crate and toss treats so that the dog will come as near the crate as he feels comfortable. If he even looks at the crate, mark the behavior with a verbal marker or a click, then treat. Gradually work the dog closer and closer to the crate, and then toss treats just inside the door. Mark and treat if the dog places a foot into the crate. Gradually toss treats further inside so that the dog has all four feet in the crate.

Step 3: Once the dog is comfortable entering and eating treats inside the crate, calmly and quietly swing the door shut and immediately open it again.

Step 4: Repeat Step 3 until the dog is comfortable with the crate door being closed and opened. Next, leave the door closed for a few seconds while the dog is eating his meal or chewing his chew toy. Do these steps without fanfare and do not praise the dog for exiting the crate. Gradually increase the time the door is closed. A word of caution here: if the time the door is closed is increased consistently, the dog will become suspicious, so it's best to vary it.

Step 5: Once the dog is comfortable having the door closed for several minutes, close it, and let him chew on a chew toy or eat his meal. Sit down within sight and ignore the dog. This is a good time to catch up on your reading or update your Facebook status, but don't get carried away and forget the time. Open the door while the dog is still comfortably engaged with his food or chewy.

Step 6: Start leaving the room for short intervals while the dog enjoys a meal or a chew toy in his crate. Next, you can begin to leave the house for short periods of time. Here again, remember not to consistently increase the length of time you're gone. Vary the length of your absence to avoid having the dog become distrustful of your departures.

Do these steps gradually and be sure that the dog is completely comfortable with each step before moving to the next. Do not let dogs out of the crate while barking or whining. Work slowly to avoid nervous vocalizations.

The last step is to teach the dog to go into his crate on cue.

Kennel Up

Step 1: Stand next to the crate. Using a broad, sweeping motion with your hand, toss a treat inside. (The sweeping motion consequently becomes a hand signal that you will use in addition to the verbal cue.) As the dog steps inside, cheerfully say "Kennel up!" or whatever cue phrase you choose.

Step 2: Once the dog is readily going in the crate for the treat, begin to give the verbal cue and hand signal without tossing the treat inside. Now, treat to the dog *after* he enters the crate.

Step 3: Repeat Step 2 and gradually increase the distance you're standing from the crate. It's handy to be able to cue your dog to go into his crate from a distance, even from another room.

Fear of Stairs (Open and Closed)

Dogs may be afraid of stairs if they've had a traumatic experience or if they've never been exposed to them. Fear may be rooted in the lack physical ability (if painful) or coordination to navigate stairs. Fear of heights is another reason stairs are challenging for some dogs.

Dogs that are mildly afraid may overcome their fear of stairs with a little creative effort of their own. Ten-week-old Bella, the yellow lab puppy, figured her best bet for descending stairs safely was to slide headfirst on her belly. Dogs that are more fearful will need a bit of help from us.

Be careful using food as a lure. Make it easy enough for the dog to take the lure comfortably, because pushing the dog too far could ultimately make the situation traumatizing.

Dogs are more often afraid to go down stairs than up. With this in mind, we'll begin at the bottom and work our way up.

Step 1: Stand at the bottom of the stairs a few feet from the last step. Toss treats on the floor and excitedly ask the dog to find them. Gradually toss the treats closer to the bottom step.

Step 2: When the dog is enthusiastically taking treats from nearby the stairs, toss a treat on the bottom step. Repeat this until the dog is comfortable taking the treats from there.

Step 3: Repeat the above exercises for the second, third, and fourth steps and so on. Make sure the dog is comfortable with each step and enthusiastically taking treats before moving upward. Vary where you toss the treats (which step). For example, when the dog has worked his way up to the fourth step, toss the treat to the bottom step, and then the second step. Variation keeps the dog from becoming wary of the exercise getting progressively harder.

Practice on different types of stairs, such as stairs in enclosed places, stairs that have risers, and those that are open. Practice on carpeted stairs and those that are not.

If stairs are not carpeted, place a runner on them to help the dog keep his footing. If the stairs are open, place a piece of cardboard behind them so that the dog cannot see through the stairs. When he is comfortable, remove the cardboard one piece at a time beginning at the bottom.

Sometimes the support of a canine friend can help. Try having another dog that is unafraid of stairs assist.

Superstitious Fears

Superstitious fears develop through association and have no logical foundation.

Superstitious fears develop when a traumatic event occurs, such as the loud, sudden noise of a car backfiring. The dog's fear response becomes connected to other environmental factors that in turn become triggers for the fear. These triggers are environmental cues that prompt the fight/flight/freeze mechanism. They can be inanimate objects, locations, or specific activities that happened during the traumatic event. For example, if the dog was in the backyard when frightened by a car backfiring, he may become afraid of the backyard (location), the swing set (inanimate object), or picnics (activity).

Superstitious fear lingers as long as the dog avoids that which triggers his fear. Furthermore, if he barks at the trigger making it go away, he will continue the behavior, because it works. Barking is reinforced. Desensitization and counter conditioning show the dog that his fear is unfounded, and that the source of his superstitious fear is not dangerous.

Supplemental Remedies

There are complementary therapies available to enhance treatment for fearful dogs. Different dogs may experience varying results with individual or a combination of the following:

• **Flower Essences.** Flower essences are often successful treatments for anxiety in dogs. There are individual flower essence tinctures available for anxiety and related issues. Use them individually, or create your own customized combination with the help of an herbalist.

• **D.A.P.** The acronym D.A.P. stands for Dog Appeasing Pheromone. These products, available in diffuser and spray form, are a synthetic equivalent to the chemical produced by a lactating female dog. The natural chemical produced by the female dog has a calming effect on her puppies. D.A.P. is designed to have the same effect on dogs of all ages.

• **Calming Cap™.** The Calming Cap™ is a helpful tool designed by Trish King, Director of the Animal Behavior & Training Department at the Marin Humane Society in Marin County, California. It's made of translucent fabric, which filters the vision, yet allows the dog to see shapes. The cap works, in theory, similar to blinders on a horse. It limits the vision and creates a calming effect that is more conducive to learning. Acclimate the dog to the Calming Cap first with the instructions included.

• **Massage and Acupressure.** These therapies can help maintain and improve a dog's physical and mental health. They increase circulation and release endorphins, the natural chemicals that help to relieve stress. By promoting a relaxed state of mind, these hands-on therapies can improve a dog's ability to focus, which affects behavior, training, and performance. Do your homework to find a certified, reputable canine massage therapist.

• **Body Wraps.** The concept is that gentle, uniform pressure applied to the body produces a calming effect. **Create you**r own body wrap from a T-shirt (see chapter *Wish You Were Here* on separation anxiety for details), or purchase a ready-made variety from sources like the Thundershirt Company (www.thundershirt.com).

• **Acupuncture.** There are specific acupuncture points on the body that, when activated, reduce tension and anxiety. If a dog's fearful behavior has a physiological source that can be addressed with acupuncture, this therapy can be helpful. A professional must perform acupuncture. Licensing and regulations vary from state to state, so consult with your veterinarian or veterinary behaviorist to find a reputable acupuncturist.

• **Audio.** Leave music or the television playing to calm your dog. Music without a strong beat is best. Studies show that piano music alone is more soothing than a performance by an entire orchestra. The music played should be predictable, so use recorded music (radio has blaring commercials). A wonderful resource for soothing music is *Through a Dog's Ear*. This music has been clinically researched and shown to provide practical solutions for canine anxiety issues. It is downloadable at the website: http://throughadogsear.com/

• **Pharmaceuticals.** Consult with your veterinarian or veterinary behaviorist to determine if pharmacological intervention is an option for your dog.

Commitment and Compliance

Therapy for the fearful dog takes commitment. Consider your options thoroughly before embarking on a treatment plan. Treatment can be time consuming and emotionally draining for some owners, as it requires a high level of compliance to the training regimen.

If time and owner capabilities are an issue, there may be alternatives available, such as a board-and-train or day-training program. The best treatment plan for most dogs though, is one that takes place where the issues occur and in trusted company—in the dog's home environment with his owner. The level of success and time involved depends on several factors including the dog's genetics, level of socialization, and intensity of fear. Additionally, we need to consider the dog's physical and mental condition, how long he has lived with the fear, and how much exposure he has had to it.

Dogs are individuals. We must give the fearful dog space without harsh expectation. We can best serve him by creating such a space that, with our guidance, reduces his anxiety and allows him to become the best version of himself.

13

Aggressive Dogs

To say that living with an aggressive dog is stressful would be a colossal understatement. We hope for miracles. We have visions of enrolling in some sort of canine anger management program. Better yet, we could change our identity completely—become nameless by joining the Wet-Nose Protection Program. Or, we fancy a magic pill or potion.

Someone once asked me, "Do you mean he'll still act like this after he's had his distemperment shot?"

Walking the reactive or aggressive dog can be terrifying. At the mere sight of another dog, we tighten the leash, put our seat backs in the upright position, and brace for impact. After a while, we wonder where the problem really lies. Who's more reactive, me or my dog? The sheer thought of meeting another dog on a walk launches us into orbit.

Our dogs would probably say, "See, I can't take Mom around other dogs because she freaks out!"

Our worst nightmare is the off-leash, adolescent Labradoodle that comes bounding up, followed by the distant owner waving and yelling, "Don't worry, he's friendly!" Now, we're really worried.

We might ask, "Isn't some aggression in dogs is a good thing?" After all, guard dogs and protection dogs need to show a little aggression to be effective, right? Even the nervous, trembling, teacup Chihuahua should bark to announce Freddy Kruger's presence at the front door.

Territorial aggression might seem like a good thing unless the dog, like my Mr. MoJo, falsely believes himself to be the mayor of his fine city. This self-appointed position affords him the right to be a control freak and master of his domain—at least in his own mind. Alas, the neighbors and passers by do not share his view. Good training has convinced him that he can step down and leave the politics to the politicians. They can bark all they want.

Protective aggression might seem like a good thing, unless it's carried to the extreme. The indiscriminate, protective dog that does not let one's spouse within a five-mile radius is probably overdoing it a bit.

For me, the difference between what humans and dogs value is most evident on trash pick up day. Before he learned otherwise, Mr. MoJo would put the errant trash truck on notice by running the fence line barking, "They're stealing our trash! They're stealing our trash!"

While no one worries about the aggressive teacup poodle, even the one with tattoos and a bad attitude, aggression is not a behavior to be taken lightly. We'll delve into the subject in the following pages to learn about why dogs aggress and what we can do to live more peacefully without entering the Wet-Nose Protection Program.

Peace cannot be kept by force; it can only be achieved by understanding.
–Albert Einstein

Note: This section is intended to help the reader understand canine aggression and deal with the challenges of having an aggressive dog. Aggression is a complex and serious issue for which owners should seek help from a reputable dog trainer or behaviorist. Education enables owners to make informed decisions. Knowledgeable owners will be better equipped to participate fully in the treatment plan that the professional will establish for them.

When heard in discussions about canine behavior, the word aggression, conjures up images of Cujo or the Big Bad Wolf. This topic strikes fear in our hearts and is on everyone's mind, yet it is woefully misunderstood.

It is unrealistic to presume our dogs will never fight. Yet, we expect dogs to get along with every other dog 100 percent of the time. Would we require the same from ourselves? I think not. Most humans are able to inhibit their aggression and rarely inflict injury on others. Dogs typically do the same, albeit their clashes are loud and noisy, and because they use teeth instead of fists, altercations are frightening to witness.

What is Aggression?
Aggression is an adaptive behavior, which allows species survival. To merely say that a dog is aggressive is a vague statement. The term *aggression* essentially refers to a range of behaviors, circumstances, and motives. In this section, we will explore different types of aggression, management, and treatment.

Aggression describes an array of behaviors that typically begin with a warning and could ultimately end in an attack. The progressive series of behaviors listed below are often used individually or in combination:

- Freezing with posture forward and stiff
- Growling and/or guttural barking
- Lunging or charging forward
- Muzzle punching (the dog hits the victim with his nose)
- Baring teeth
- Snapping (no contact is made)

• Biting (bites range from a nip that leaves no mark to bites that inflict serious injury

(see bite scale at the end of this section)

• Repeated biting

• Biting and shaking

Why do dogs aggress?

Aggression is a natural part of canine evolution necessary for the preservation of the species. In the wild, aggressive behavior feeds and defends the species*. Many normal dogs present various types of aggressive behavior. It becomes problematic when the intensity and doggedness behind the aggression reaches dangerous levels.

Aggression is one behavior dogs use to achieve certain objectives. Furthermore, it can be self-reinforcing. For example, a fearful dog will use aggression to get what he wants: distance from the scary thing. In this scenario, aggression works, so the behavior will likely be repeated.

Aggressive behavior most often falls into two broad categories: offensive and defensive. Defensive displays of aggression occur when a dog is feeling threatened without the option of escape. With offensive aggression, the dog takes the initiative and is not feeling threatened or fearful. Examples of offensive aggression would be territorial and social aggression or predatory behavior.

While predation might be considered a form of aggression, it differs from other types of aggressive behaviors. The motivation and emotion behind aggression and predatory behavior are dissimilar. Predation is non-affective. There is an absence of anger, unlike other forms of aggression stemming from social conflict or fear that are rife with emotion. Predatory behavior is not motivated by social discord but rather by the need to obtain food. Predatory behavior in pet dogs is explored separately at the end of this chapter.

Dynamics that Affect Aggressive Behavior

The primary reason for the development of assertive or aggressive behavior in social animals is to ensure a successful communal lifestyle. Lack of socialization can lead to aggressive behavior when dogs have not been exposed to new and various stimuli at an age when they are most receptive. For instance, puppies that have never been exposed to people during the

developmental stage where they learn to interrelate with people
(5 and 12 weeks of age,) there is a greater risk that they will become
fearful or aggressive because appropriate dog/human interaction skills
were never learned.

Under socialization, poorly executed socialization, or complete lack thereof
can lead to fear-based aggression.

Aggression can be learned, because dogs do what works for them. This is
demonstrated in the classic example of the letter carrier. Each day the letter
carrier approaches the front door, each day the dog barks, and then the
intruder leaves. The behavior is reinforced because the dog, in his mind, has
achieved his objective.

Hormonal effects on aggression are most obvious in unneutered males,
females in heat, and females with pups. Conventionally, it has been said that
spaying and neutering has been shown to significantly reduce aggressive
behavior. There are now studies bringing that into question.

Aggression can be a symptom of stress resulting from a dog's
powerlessness to control immediate circumstances. Excessive stress in a
short period of time, or stressors endured over the long run, can lead to
aggressive behavior and an over-reactive dog.

Anxiety and stress are similar, yet they are not exactly the same. Stress is the
antecedent to anxiety. Dogs subject to long-term or undue stress are
vulnerable to becoming over-reactive, fearful, and possibly aggressive.
Trauma can contribute to a dog's ability to cope with stress, and when a
dog is unable to handle stress, aggression may be a resulting symptom.

Physiology is the chemistry that drives behavior. When unbalanced, it can
lead to aggressive behavior. It is also is a contributing factor to the level of a
dog's resiliency in dealing with stress. A two-pronged treatment approach
of pharmacological intervention coupled with behavior modification may
be the best plan if a physiological condition underlies a dog's aggressive
behavior. Consult with a veterinary behaviorist to make this determination.
Careful and thorough health screening along with a thoughtful discussion
should precede the use of medications.

Ritualized Aggression

Ritualized aggression is not full-blown, fight-to-the-death violence. Actual violence among social animals would be counterproductive to survival of the species. Therefore, ritualized aggression is used to determine who would be the true winner in an actual confrontation, without having to pay the high stakes of injury. It's also utilized in situations where there is a potential for conflict or to establish control of resources. It is a form of communication employed to minimize stress and its physiological effects, such as high levels of reactivity.

This form of aggression is more like a contest, as in a human boxing match or football game. During this non-violent communication, dogs will present either confident or compliant behaviors to convey their position at any given moment. It is a dynamic dance.

Ritualized dog fighting is loud and exhibits a lot of inefficient movement. Bites are delivered to non-vital areas of the body with no major damage done. Ritualized aggression among dogs is normal, yet disturbing to witness. Some owners are alarmed at the slightest sounds of growling during play, while others are of the mind to *let them work it out* or *he needs to be put in his place*. As much as we might hope, it is unrealistic to expect dogs never to clash–as improbable as expecting humans never to quarrel with one another. However, simply allowing dogs to *work it out* could be a dangerous bet if the behavior is excessive or injuries occur.

Aggressive Behavior Differences among Breeds

It would be a mistake to label any particular breed as aggressive. Breeding selects traits and behaviors from a constellation of genes. Different breeds have different threshold levels indicating a tendency toward certain behaviors, but it's not as simple as say, selecting a certain gene for aggression.

It is neither fair nor accurate to judge dogs by breed alone. The cause of aggression cannot be delegated strictly to either nature or nurture. The two factors are just too closely interconnected to hold either solely responsible. Fair judgment takes into consideration the environment, training, the dog's individual temperament, and his history of interaction with people and dogs.

Statistically speaking, certain breeds are reported to bite more than others. These reports can be skewed. This is because they are not made by experts and the reliability of eyewitnesses is questionable. The breed's history explains that dogs originally bred for guarding, fighting, or hunting are naturally predisposed to behaviors that might include aggression. Pet dogs of these breeds rarely get to perform the jobs that they were hardwired to do, resulting in frustration and even aggressive behavior for some.

While aggression may be more prevalent in some breeds, it would be negligent to use heritage as an excuse for the behavior. We cannot dismiss agonistic or combative behavior in a guarding dog by saying, "It's just the breed." He may be predisposed to protective behavior, but when taken to a level of excess, the dog becomes a liability. Responsibility for the dog's behavior sits squarely on the shoulders of the owner who has not socialized and properly trained him.

The best insurance against aggressive behavior is appropriate socialization (see chapter on socialization) and selecting the proper breed to fit one's lifestyle (see chapter the *Choosing a Dog.*) Failure to do so can cause stress and frustration for the dog, which could possibly lead to maladaptive behavior that can include aggressive behavior.

Understanding breed attributes can help determine what is normal and what is not. Lack of understanding can lead to labeling the dog as problematic. For instance, the herding breed that pursues children, nipping at their heels, is herding, whereas, the terrier's chase may be attributed to hunting prey. Chase behavior was selected in these breeds, but each with different objectives. The herding dog chases without harming their prey, while terriers hunt to extinguish their quarry. Guard dogs are bred to be wary of newcomers, protective, and territorial, not necessarily good qualities in a terrier.

While different breeds and individual dogs present an array of the aforementioned traits, extreme and out-of-control aggressive behavior is abnormal and dangerous. Therefore, all dogs need to be socialized and trained in order to cope in the human world without the use of inappropriate aggression.

Bite Inhibition

Assessment of an aggressive dog's bite inhibition is essential in formulating a treatment plan. Bite inhibition refers to the amount of pressure a dog uses with his jaws when biting down. Most dogs acquire bite inhibition in the formative months of puppyhood, but for various reasons, there are those who don't, such as the under socialized dog.

Puppies normally learn bite inhibition by about eighteen weeks of age, with the most critical time at five to eight weeks old. They learn this from adult dogs and littermates. If the pup bites with too much force, there will be a negative response from whoever received the bite.

Since we usually bring puppies home at around eight weeks old, it is vital to continue bite inhibition training. The objective is not to restrain or prevent the biting, but to help the pup learn boundaries and control of his mouth.

Dogs with good bite inhibition can nip and mouth during play without doing damage. They can, without harm, ward off an adversary, gently correct a disorderly puppy, or resolve differences, all with teeth that have the potential to do great bodily injury. Conversely, dogs with poor bite inhibition stand to do substantial physical harm.

Aggression in a dog that has had numerous altercations with other dogs is rightfully worrisome and inappropriate. Dogfights are frightening to witness, as they can appear to be battles to the death. However, if killing were the goal, dogs would achieve it. The truth is that with numerous opportunities to do severe injury, they do not, because these dogs have good bite inhibition.

Teaching Bite Inhibition to an Aggressive Adult Dog

It is exceedingly difficult to teach bite inhibition to an adult dog. However, dogs with low bite inhibition and low-level aggression can be helped.

It is possible to improve bite inhibition for dogs at levels 1 through 3 on the bite scale (see Dr. Ian Dunbar's Dog Bite Scale at the end of this chapter). Exercise caution and make sure each individual case is thoroughly assessed by a professional trainer to make sure that all involved in the treatment are comfortable and safe. For all intents and purposes, teaching bite inhibition to a dog at level 4 through 6 on the scale is risky, and the chances of modifying the behavior are low.

Teaching bite inhibition instills a sense of carefulness and self-control in the dog, but if the fight/flight or predatory instinct mechanisms are triggered, the trained bite inhibition will have varying degrees of success.

Bite Threshold

Bite threshold refers to the intensity and amount of stimuli or triggers needed in order for a dog to bite. Dogs with a high bite threshold will present numerous, prolonged warning signals prior to biting such as freezing, barking, growling, and snarling. Less obvious signals that might occur even before this are tongue flicks, looking away or sniffing the ground, among others (see chapter on dog body language and calming signals.)Dogs with a low bite threshold tend to give very little warning and may bite sooner rather than later in the presence of the trigger.

Some owners believe that their dog should never growl and attempt to modify or train away the behavior. This is a very dangerous prospect. A growl is a warning, and if a dog intends to bite, it's best to be forewarned. Aggression is complex and must be treated comprehensively. Simply trying to stop the outward expression of the behavior is not only ineffective, but will often exacerbate the problem.

Types of Aggression

In order to develop an effective treatment plan, we must identify the source of aggression and its specific triggers. That said, we must not limit our training solutions or excuse related behaviors by pigeonholing the dog into one category. Doing so would filter our analysis and limit our creativity, not to mention the possibility of going down the wrong treatment path altogether. Aggression in dogs is a serious and complex issue. Successful treatment plans explore and analyze all of the information presented.

Fear Aggression

Fearfulness can manifest as aggression in some dogs. Fear-based aggression is a defensive behavior (as opposed to offensive aggression, where the dog's intent is to do harm). Dogs with fear-based or defensive aggression tend to stay at a distance from the source of the anxiety and bark. Their energy moves away from the source with the weight distributed more on the back legs than the front. Fearful dogs may back away as they are barking and growling, as opposed to the offensively aggressive dog that will readily lunge directly at his target.

Other body language indicating fear-based aggression is a closed mouth bark or growl with the corners of the mouth retracted. Most often, there is no display of teeth (as opposed to offensive aggression where teeth are bared, often accompanied by a low, guttural snarl). Urination and/or defecation and discharging of the anal glands may be seen in extreme fear-based aggression.

To complicate matters, many dogs are conflicted in their response to the trigger. They may lunge and bark in an effort to put up a good front. Like the bully on the playground who picks a fight, he acts tough, but his motivation is based in insecurity. Fearful dogs may cautiously approach the source of their fear, but then become frightened in close proximity and lash out.

Defensive Aggression
Defensive aggression is fear based, but the subtle difference between defensive aggression and fear aggression is in the strategy employed. A dog using defensive aggression has determined that his best defense is a good offense and will often initiate an altercation. A defensively aggressive dog has discovered that this behavior works, because it affords him what he needs: space from the trigger. Barking and lunging makes the scary thing go away. Furthermore, the behavior has been reinforced, because it was successful, and will be repeated. A dog presenting defensive aggression displays conflicting body language showing both fearful and offensive postures.

Pain-Elicited Aggression
The pain or discomfort of illness can elicit aggression. Dogs with a high incidence of painful health issues such as ear infections or sore joints may aggress to avoid further pain.

The use of pain-inflicting training equipment or excessive force can also provoke aggressive behavior. Some dogs are stoics, and some aggress at the mere anticipation of pain. Therefore, the individual dog's threshold determines how readily pain-elicited aggression is triggered. Elderly, delicate, and otherwise vulnerable dogs may become fearfully aggressive as a defensive measure. This can occur when they are exposed to rough play or chaotic situations where they are susceptible to painful interaction. Pain elicited aggression can occur in both adult dogs and puppies.

Bullying and Play Aggression

Playtime can turn to aggression when one dog becomes over stimulated and has play skill deficits. At this point, the dog may use threatening behavior and even ignore cut-off signals (see the chapter *Conversations with Dogs*) from the others that would normally end playtime. Dogs with limited or poor social skills may find themselves in trouble, because they do not know how to communicate their intent to play.

Some dogs are bullies. Bullies target certain dogs for harassment, ignoring any cut-off or escalated threatening signals, which can culminate in a fight. Bullies are different from dogs that merely have play skill deficits, as they tend to seek out specific dogs to badger or attack. Dogs with play skill deficits are apt to begin with normal play that escalates and then tips into aggression.

Play is reinforcing for most dogs, thus if inappropriate behavior causes the other dog to stop play, they learn to use more suitable methods. On the other hand, harassment is reinforcing for the bully and stressful or traumatic to the "victim," so they should be monitored closely and separated and trained to a cued time out.

Predatory Behavior and Predatory Drift

Some consider predation to be a form aggression. Because it differs greatly from other types of aggressive behaviors, it is discussed separately at the end of this chapter.

Predatory drift begins as play, a social interaction, but then tips into predatory behavior. It can happen in play between two dogs of unequal size, with the small dog panicking, thrashing about, and vocalizing with yelps or cries. The chance of predatory drift occurring is greater the more the disparity in size. However, it can occur between dogs of equal size if play becomes too rough, or if several dogs are engaged in play and one dog panics, prompting others to gang up on him. But, this is not limited to size difference. Take, for example, a Great Dane and a terrier. The terrier would be more likely to experience drift than the Great Dane because terriers are bred to be hunters with higher prey drive.

Signs of play tipping into predatory drift are when a dog's focus intensifies, he becomes silent, and/or his body is lowered.

Predatory drift differs from play aggression because with predatory drift, the dog truly sees the victim as prey. This does not happen with play aggression where the dogs are simply over stimulated.

Social Aggression

Note: Social aggression and hierarchies can be a flash point in discussions about aggression. Research is ongoing and opinions are open to change.

Dogs are communal animals adhering to hierarchies established by social interaction. Social hierarchy is a survival method, which allows dogs to settle differences without doing harm. Hierarchy establishes which members of the group have priority access to critical resources. Altercations might occur when the social structure is unstable, if the higher-ranking individual's status is challenged, or during attempts to control a social interaction.

To live harmoniously with pet dogs and this hierarchy, it behooves us to establish a solid leadership position. This is not done through force or intimidation to reduce the dog's status, but by building a strong bond and implementing a training plan based on positive methods.

Puppies learn to interact with dogs at three to eight weeks old and with humans at five to twelve weeks old. Six to eight months is adolescence, where social boundaries and authority will be tested. Confidence increases throughout adolescence and into adulthood, and is established at about two to three years of age.

Dogs reach social maturity anywhere from eighteen months to three years old. This is the age of sorting out where they fit into the hierarchy and of testing boundaries. If social aggression appears, it will likely happen within this age range.

Socialization is an important factor in preventing social aggression, particularly during adolescence. Juveniles may trigger harassment from older dogs with their rude adolescent behavior, so providing positive social experiences for puppies and adolescent dogs is a must.

Dominance or Status-Related Aggression

This form of aggression is motivated by a challenge to a dog's rank or his control of social relations, both human and canine. Dogs and people establish similar social structures, making it easy for the two species to live in harmony. However, thinking that dogs believe themselves to be members of our pack is a bit of an over simplification.

Hierarchies are dynamic and in the moment, not rigid or clear-cut. Conflicts may occur as the high-ranking dog's status decreases due to age or infirmity and when younger dogs reach social maturity, at which point they may challenge the top-ranking dog. Adjustments in hierarchy might occur with the introduction of a new dog to the group or a reintroduction after an absence.

Fights between dogs living in the same household tend to occur more often if the dogs are near equal in rank. Hierarchal conflicts are more common among dogs of the same gender, with fights between two females typically being more ferocious.

Status-related aggression is found among all breeds, but stable hierarchies are typically more difficult to maintain among breeds that are hardwired to work independently, such as terriers or herding dogs.

Dominance aggression toward people is motivated by the dog's attempt to control situations involving humans. It is not related to territorial or possessive aggression, but it can occur in parallel with these other types of aggressive behavior.

Dogs that fall into two broad categories present dominance aggression:

1. Dogs that are confident that they are in power and use aggression to control their owners

2. Dogs that are unsure of their social status and use aggression to determine their standing

They learn their position by observing the owner's reaction to their aggressive behavior. Most dogs fall into the second category.

Dogs present dominance aggression in situations where there may be struggle for control, for instance during grooming, restraint, staring at the dog, and physical punishment.

Control-Complex Aggression

The terms dominance aggression, control-complex aggression, and control-conflict aggression are often used interchangeably. Here, the term control-complex aggression is used to specifically address extreme behavior that tips into abnormal.

Control-complex aggression is an aberrant, maladaptive behavior presented by dogs with very low thresholds for frustration and anger. They lack good canine social skills and overcompensate for this ineptitude with exaggerated reactions in social situations. This dog does not seek dominance as much as he seeks control, due to his misperception and overreaction to the circumstances. Here, he becomes excessively defensive and goes into survival mode when the situation is not life or death. This type of aggression may be aimed toward dogs or humans.

Control complex aggression is seen more in spayed females and intact males than neutered animals and develops at social maturity. It is characterized by over assertiveness and overt status-seeking behavior. Such behaviors include standing over another dog or person; blocking access to a location (doorways); staring; "back talk"; placing paws or head on shoulders, head, or back; and resource guarding.

Fighting Among Dogs in the Same Household

Conflict among resident dogs is often associated with a change in the social hierarchy. Fights may occur when a new dog is introduced into the household or one leaves the home. Clashes may occur when a dog is reintroduced after a long absence, a dog becomes ill or aged and is no longer able to maintain rank, or a young dog reaches social maturity.

Trouble does not usually start immediately after a new dog is brought into the home. If aggressive behavior crops up, it typically happens a month or two down the road.

Aggression between dogs within the same household commonly occurs when the dogs are of equal or near-equal rank and if the hierarchy is unstable, vague, or in dispute.

Dogs establish their own hierarchy through an intricate progression of behaviors. This social structure is established by their control and access to valuable resources. We need not interfere with this social interaction, as dogs will establish status regardless and independent of our preference. If the dogs are fighting frequently, ferociously, and sustaining serious injuries, we must intervene with behavior modification and a treatment plan that allows the hierarchy to stay intact.

Strict management and great care should be taken to prevent further conflict. This will avert reinforcement of the learned element of aggression. For example, if a dog has learned that aggression toward his canine roommate wins him the lion's share of the food or other resources, he will continue the behavior. Even the appearance of the other dog might prompt the aggressor to initiate a conflict. Because practice makes perfect, we need to prevent fighting to keep dogs from getting good at it.

Fights among dogs of the same sex tend to be more dangerous. Inter-male fights are apt to be more ritualized, raucous, take longer to intensify, and result in fewer serious injuries than fights between females. Fights between females often begin without fanfare or warning, are quick to intensify, and more injurious.

Altercations among dogs living in the same household may occur over resources, territory, and status with the likelihood of redirected aggression as well. Some dogs with high levels of arousal learn that fighting, as in redirected aggression (see definition below), reduces stress, thus skirmishes become a form of pressure relief.

Helpful points in the prevention and management of aggression between dogs living in the same household:

- Establish firm, fair rules through benevolent leadership
- Manage resources
- Avoid further altercations
- Identify all triggers to aggression and enforce management

• Provide adequate exercise and mental stimulation

• Know canine body language to predict and prevent fighting

• Manage household stress levels

Redirected Aggression

Frustration is the most common factor in redirected aggression and happens when the dog is in a state of over stimulation or arousal. It occurs when a dog's aggressive behavior is interrupted or prevented, with him turning his aggression toward the innocent party. This individual might be a human or another dog. For instance, if two dogs are barking at someone passing by the yard, one dog may turn and attack the other when that dog interrupts or simply gets in the way. Redirected aggression is often the reason people are injured while breaking up dog fights.

Leash Aggression

Given the choice between fighting and running away, a dog that's afraid will most often choose to run. Flight is not an option for the leashed dog. Therefore, he thinks he has but one choice—to fight. Dogs on leash can feel vulnerable and threatened when other dogs approach, especially when a hapless, unleashed dog comes bounding up. Dogs approaching on leash can appear even more threatening if allowed to drag their owner. A pulling dog's stance is stiff and his weight is placed forward on his front legs, presenting a more aggressive posture to those in his path.

It is unrealistic to expect that leashes will never tighten, so we must pay attention to what happens on the human end of the lead. For example, we might become nervous about an impending situation such as the aforementioned hapless off-leash dog. If *we* tighten the leash, we'll communicate our anxiety directly through it to the dog. Who knows? He may even be thinking, "I can't take mom around other dogs, because she freaks out every time!"

A natural (and socially acceptable) human reaction to the dog that is lunging and barking at another dog is to scold or discipline him. The use of corrections and punishment tend to increase the intensity of the dog's reactivity and can even lead to redirected aggression. Therefore, the most effective training against leash aggression uses positive reinforcement, desensitization, and counter conditioning. We can teach dogs that a tense moment is a time to pay attention to us and that we can work as a team. Proactive training can teach the dog that he has options other than fight or flight (see *Beyond the Basics*.)

Frustration Aggression and Leash Frustration

Stress, which can lower the threshold of fear or anger, may lead to aggressive behavior. Stress also causes frustration. Dogs, like humans, become frustrated when unable to get something they want or to achieve an objective. Dogs that cannot predict or control situational and certain environmental factors are vulnerable to anxiety and/or frustration.

Extreme frustration resulting in aggression is sometimes redirected toward whoever is close by when levels reach the boiling point—a dangerous side effect of leash frustration.

Leash frustration that manifests into aggression can happen with even the most affable of dogs. Here's how:

The friendly dog wants to greet other dogs or people, but, not wanting to be dragged, the owner punishes him with a leash correction. Now, the dog sees approaching dogs and/or people as a predictor of punishment and thus becomes defensive. This can mean a bite to the approaching person or dog or redirected aggression toward the owner.

Living with humans presents dogs with many sources of frustration—leashes, fences, physical restraint, to name a few. These necessary management tools need counterbalancing to alleviate undue aggravation. Proper training provides dogs with coping skills to ease and prevent frustration.

Lack of structure, exercise, and mental stimulation are further sources of frustration for dogs. Well-intentioned humans may think they are doing dogs a favor by letting them run free or rule the household. But, ambiguity does not bode well with dogs, so they need gentle guidance to successfully live in our world.

With no set rules, dogs are resigned to trial and error. Trials are simply questions dogs ask, but often we don't like the manner of inquiry. To prevent frustration, consider teaching the answers up front. For example, a dog becomes aggravated on walks and pulls on the leash because he is never allowed to sniff (a natural and important behavior that gives dogs information about the world). If harshly corrected every time he wants to sniff, his frustration may manifest as aggression. To prevent this, we can teach the dog to cope through proper leash walking skills.

Territorial, Protective, and Possessive Aggression
These types of aggression are similar, with the motivation being to protect valuable resources. Territorial aggression involves the defense of property or areas. It is a valued trait in guard dogs, but problematic if the dog is indiscriminate or overly assertive in his duties. A dog that perceives everyone entering onto his turf, including a 6-year old child or a 90-year-old houseguest, a threat does not make an appropriate guard dog.

Territorially aggressive dogs will use displays of alarm barking, offensive body posturing, and demonstrative warning barks. Often these behaviors are presented even if the intruder shows that they are not a threat. Territorial aggression may be displayed in defense of familiar or specific locations. These may be fixed areas, like yards and homes, or mobile, such as vehicles. Defended areas may be established over time (yard or home) or quickly established after marking of territory, as on a walk in the park.

Protective aggression is a defensive behavior that targets someone approaching, even if that person (or dog) is not menacing. Protective aggressive dogs display intense alerting behavior directed at the oncoming party. He's barking, lunging, and positioning himself between the advancing party and the person he's protecting. The behavior increases as the distance is decreased. We can identify the behavior as protective aggression if the dog stops aggressing when person he is protecting leaves the scene.

In the wild, dogs aggress to protect members of their own pack. Pet dogs can do the same for their domestic family members, whether canine, human, or other species. Sometimes dogs exhibit more intense protective behavior to the most vulnerable family members such as their pups (maternal aggression) or human babies. As in territorial aggression, this is a respectable canine attribute unless the dog generalizes and regards everyone as a threat.

Dogs with instinctive guarding tendencies can develop this behavior if their owners allow it and do not teach the dog that they control who approaches. Passive owners may, in the dog's mind, be giving him permission to guard or that their non-action is essentially backing him up.

Possessive Aggression (Resource Guarding)

It is common for certain dogs to guard their food bowls, chew bones, toys, beds, and people. See the chapter *Bone of Contention*.

Aggression Related to Mating

This type of aggression is relatively rare among pet dogs, most often occurring among intact males vying for a female in heat. However, some males will aggress toward other males without the presence of a female. Some sex related aggression will occur among intact females but is less likely. In the wild, this species sustaining behavior means survival of the fittest, with the strongest males more likely to gain access to the strongest females.

Idiopathic Aggression

Idiopathic means *relating to or denoting any disease or condition that arises spontaneously or for which the cause is unknown.* Aggressive behavior may appear to have come out of nowhere, but in most cases, investigation reveals that the dog did indeed have a reason and gave abundant warning signs. Unfortunately, many owners are unaware of those signs or are not paying close enough attention to notice them. (See the chapter *Conversations with Dogs.*)

Idiopathic aggression is often referred to as rage syndrome. It is identified by traits such as sudden, volatile, and extreme aggression with no explainable trigger. The dog may appear confused and have a glazed-over look in his eyes.

Treatment of idiopathic aggression is extremely challenging. Success rates are low because of the behavior's unpredictability and unknown triggers. Fortunately, the condition is not a common one. After ruling out physiological reasons for aggressive behavior, good detective work on the part of the trainer or behaviorist may uncover the fact that its true cause is behavioral. Only then can a treatment plan be made.

Learned Aggression

Canine behavior is trial and error to find out what works. Thus, as in any behavior, aggression can be learned if it has been used successfully. For example, stray dogs may have learned to guard resources because of the need to fight for food. A fearful dog learns to be aggressive if his snapping at an approaching stranger makes the stranger go away. Furthermore, learned aggression instills confidence in the fearful dog. Successful use of aggression is reinforcing, and behavior that is reinforced is strengthened and repeated.

Prevention

An ounce of prevention is always worth a pound of cure. Following are some tips to avert and curb aggressive behavior.

• **Spay and neuter.** * Aggression can be hormonally driven, thus spaying and neutering will have a mitigating effect on the behavior.

• **Breeding.** If obtaining a puppy from a breeder, make sure the breeder is reputable. A responsible breeder will begin socialization and life-enriching experiences for the puppies. Furthermore, be sure to select a breed that fits into your lifestyle, as a bad fit can cause frustration for all involved.

• **Separate puppies from the litter at the proper age.** Pups should not be sent to their new homes until they are at least seven weeks of age. Smaller breeds may be kept longer (eight to twelve weeks) if the breeder is providing life-enhancing experiences.

• **Socialization.** It's more than meeting new dogs and people and the most important thing that can be done to foil the onset of aggression. See the chapter on socialization.

• **Sharing.** Teaching puppies and dogs about sharing is a good resource-guarding preventative. See the chapter *Bone of Contention.*

• **Impulse control and frustration tolerance**. To prevent frustration aggression, teach dogs that patience and polite behavior is what gets them what they want.

• **Handling.** Dogs that are taught to accept gentle restraint and handling will not need to resort to aggression. They learn not be fearful when being groomed, at vet visits, etc.

• **Mental stimulation.** Dogs trained in even the basic skills and are less prone to frustration. Enhance the dog's environment with interactive food-stuffed or puzzle toys.

• **Management.** Management eases potential frustration aggression and learned aggression among canine housemates and visitors. Use baby gates, crates, and dog-proof rooms. Separate dogs if necessary during mealtime, playtime, or when chew bones or favorite toys are present.

• **Equipment.** No-pull harnesses and head collars can help to minimize frustration (on both ends of the *leash*) and when used properly, make handling safe and manageable. Along with positive training techniques, good equipment is a viable tool in preventing some aggressive behaviors.

• **Plenty of exercise.** The axiom of *a tired dog is a good dog* holds true and can help in the prevention of frustration aggression. Each individual dog's personality, age, and breed determine what is appropriate and adequate exercise. Dog parks and daycares are great for some dogs, but not for all, as various dogs find dog parks and daycare overwhelming and frightening.

Conventional beliefs about spay and neuter state that it reduces aggression. Currently there is ongoing, open dialogue that presents another viewpoint. If an intact dog displays aggressive behavior, neutering should be considered as an adjunct to behavior modification and training. However, neutering cannot be expected to reduce aggression in all dogs, nor will it necessarily eliminate aggressive behavior altogether.

Reading Canine Body Language

Aggressive behavior that comes with no warning would be a rare case indeed. The dog almost certainly gave indications, but it's probable the signs happened so quickly or subtly that they went unnoticed by humans. If not familiar with canine body language, one may be clueless about these signals altogether. Dogs speak to us. Speaking to dogs is important, but listening to them is imperative.

Deciding Whether to Work with an Aggressive Dog

Whether or not to work with an aggressive dog is a serious decision. It requires careful thought to the probability of treatment success and safety. Situations vary vastly. Thus, trainers and owners alike should ask pertinent questions with regard to everyone's welfare.

Safety: Make sure that all family members, neighbors, and other pets are safe. Adopt a strict management plan, which limits the dog's exposure to aggression-eliciting stimuli. Management can (and often will) fail. It's not a permanent solution due to safety and liability reasons. Therefore, one must thoroughly assess the capacity to manage risk.

Health: Make sure the dog has been given a clean bill of health and it has been determined that the aggressive behavior is not physiological in nature.

The severity of the aggression is an important factor in deciding whether or not to work with the dog. Consider the following:

Bite history: What is the severity of the bites? (See dog bite scale at the end of this chapter.) How long has the dog been presenting aggressive behavior? In other words, how long has it been reinforced? Where on the body are bites delivered? Are the bites intentionally placed, or are they delivered to the nearest available body part?

Motivation: Is the dog easily motivated by food, toys, etc.? If the dog is highly motivated by these things, behavior modification will be easier.

Behavior modification for an aggressive dog can be prolonged and expensive. Therefore, consider carefully the ability and willingness to commit time and finances. Furthermore, bear in mind one's physical abilities and the feasibility of environmental management. Sometimes the best answer is re-homing or, in severe cases, euthanasia.

Treatment

A successful treatment plan first identifies the type of aggression and its triggers.

In order to determine type, we must first ascertain aggression's function. We can do this by asking the following questions:

- What benefit does the dog receive from the behavior?
- At whom was the aggression directed?
- When and where does the behavior occur?
- What environmental factors are affecting the behavior?
- What happened just before the reaction?
- What happened immediately after the reaction?
- Was there a perceived threat?
- What stopped the reaction?

Once the type and intensity of aggression is established, a treatment plan can be made. Seek the help of a reputable trainer or behaviorist.

Proper On-Leash Meet-and-Greets

Teaching dogs polite on-leash greetings is a good preventative for leash aggression. It can curb the behavior for reactive and mildly leash-aggressive dogs. See the special section *Beyond the Basics* for detailed descriptions of behavior modification techniques.

How to Break Up a Dog Fight

Human nature has us screaming and howling when a dog fight breaks out. We might jump into the storm and attempt to physically separate the dogs. Bad idea. This is often the cause of injury to humans and may even escalate the conflict.

If available, throw a blanket or water over the fighting dogs. If a hose is handy, spray the dogs directly with a strong stream of water.

Loud noises (not screaming) can be effective. Daycare facilities often use air horns to interrupt altercations. In our classes for aggressive dogs, we keep a cookie sheet and metal spoon to bang together in case a fight breaks out.

There are some products on the market, such as citronella sprays, that are designed to break up dog fights. These come in small spray cans with a belt clip and are handy to have along on walks where stray dogs are a problem. A downside to these sprays is that one needs to stand upwind when using them, which is hard to do in the heat of the moment.

Another technique to ward off approaching dogs is to carry a small umbrella. Pop it open suddenly at the advancing unleashed dog. Before employing this method, acclimate your own dog to the umbrella popping open.

Place an object between dogs, such as a baby gate, chair, or any solid object readily accessible. Never place your body or appendages between two fighting dogs.

If you must make physical contact with the dogs and there is another person available, use the following methods:

- If dogs are on leash: Each person should calmly take a leash and walk the dogs away. Do not grab collars.

- If the dogs are not on leashes: Each person should grab one of the dogs by the hind legs (above the knees to avoid injury). Lift the hind legs off the ground like holding a wheelbarrow. Make sure to hold the legs high enough so that the dog is unable to turn and redirect. Then, each person walks backward. Once the dogs are at a safe distance, leash them and remove them from each other's sight. This technique must be done firmly but carefully to prevent injury.

- Do not pick up a small dog if an altercation is happening or one is about to. While it is a natural and reflexive action to protect the small dog, it can end badly. Scooping the dog up can trigger prey behavior in the other dogs when the small dog suddenly moves away and upward. Furthermore, if the small dog is yelping the problem is compounded and can escalate further. Picking up a small dog in this situation heightens the risk of being jumped on, knocked down, or bitten.

Levels of Aggression
Determining the cause and intensity of aggression is helpful in formulating a treatment plan or deciding whether to work with the dog at all. Aggression ranges from a warning signal to retreat to an attack and varies in passion and purpose.

On the low end of the aggression scale are the warnings, which may include growling, raised hackles, bared teeth, and air snaps. Even before these warnings, we are likely to see the dog showing signs of stress (see the chapter *Conversations with Dogs.*) At this level, the dog is trying to avert rather than employ aggression.

Moving up the continuum, a more aggressive dog will make contact with his teeth. Fearful or unconfident dogs may deliver non-severe bites. They move in, nip hesitantly, and then quickly retreat.

On the high end of the spectrum are the severely aggressive dogs that do a great deal of damage or worse. If these cases are workable at all, they should be taken very seriously and handled only by reputable, experienced professionals.

"I know he'll never bite," is the most frightening statement a trainer can hear from a client. The truth is that any dog with teeth that is feeling threatened enough, will bite. If we are well versed in canine body language and able to read the warning signs, we can prevent a dog from using his final form of communication—a bite.

Below is Dr. Ian Dunbar's dog bite scale written for trainers. This useful resource standardizes the language for trainers in determining the intensity of aggression and is a valuable tool for establishing a treatment plan.

Dr. Ian Dunbar's Dog Bite Scale (Official Authorized Version)

An assessment of the severity of biting problems based on an objective evaluation of wound pathology

Level 1. Obnoxious or aggressive behavior but no skin-contact by teeth.

Level 2. Skin-contact by teeth but no skin-puncture. However, may be skin nicks (less than one tenth of an inch deep) and slight bleeding caused by forward or lateral movement of teeth against skin, but no vertical punctures.

Level 3. One to four punctures from a single bite with no puncture deeper than half the length of the dog's canine teeth. Maybe lacerations in a single direction, caused by victim pulling hand away, owner pulling dog away, or gravity (little dog jumps, bites and drops to floor).

Level 4. One to four punctures from a single bite with at least one puncture deeper than half the length of the dog's canine teeth. May also have deep bruising around the wound (dog held on for N seconds and bore down) or lacerations in both directions (dog held on and shook its head from side to side).

Level 5. Multiple-bite incident with at least two Level 4 bites or multiple-attack incident with at least one Level 4 bite in each.

Level 6. Victim dead.

The above list concerns unpleasant behavior and so, to add perspective:

Levels 1 and 2: Comprise well over 99% of dog incidents. The dog is certainly not dangerous and more likely to be fearful, rambunctious, or out of control. Wonderful prognosis. Quickly resolve the problem with basic training (control) — especially oodles of Classical Conditioning, numerous repetitive Retreat n' Treat, Come/Sit/Food Reward and Back-up/Approach/Food Reward sequences, progressive desensitization handling exercises, plus numerous bite-inhibition exercises and games. Hand feed only until resolved; do NOT waste potential food rewards by feeding from a bowl.

Level 3: Prognosis is fair to good, provided that you have owner compliance. However, treatment is both time-consuming and not without danger. Rigorous bite-inhibition exercises are essential.

Levels 4: The dog has insufficient bite inhibition and is very dangerous. Prognosis is poor because of the difficulty and danger of trying to teach bite inhibition to an adult hard-biting dog and because absolute owner-compliance is rare. Only work with the dog in exceptional circumstances, e.g., the owner is a dog professional and has sworn 100% compliance. Make sure the owner signs a form in triplicate stating that they understand and take full responsibility that: 1. The dog is a Level 4 biter and is likely to cause an equivalent amount of damage WHEN it bites again (which it most probably will) and should therefore, be confined to the home at all times and only allowed contact with adult owners. 2. Whenever, children or guests visit the house, the dog should be confined to a single locked-room or roofed, chain-link run with the only keys kept on a chain around the neck of each adult owner (to prevent children or guests entering the dog's confinement area.) 3. The dog is muzzled before leaving the house and only leaves the house for visits to a veterinary clinic. 4. The incidents have all been reported to the relevant authorities — animal control or police. Give the owners one copy, keep one copy for your files and give one copy to the dog's veterinarian.

Level 5 and 6: The dog is extremely dangerous and mutilates. The dog is simply not safe around people. I recommend euthanasia because the quality of life is so poor for dogs that have to live out their lives in solitary confinement.

The Hunter or the Hunted?

On daily walks, I know we're entering the bunny zone when my dog, MoJo slows his pace, lowers his head, and silently scans the tree line. At this point, I interrupt him with my best Elmer Fudd impression and whisper, "Be verwy, verwy quiet. We're hunting wabbits!"

Like Elmer, MoJo never actually catches that wascally wabbit (mostly because city code and I require that he be leashed). But nature dictates the matter be given his most passionate effort, and I realize that trying to thwart a dog's instincts is as futile as trying to nail Jell-O to a tree.

This was plainly illustrated early one February morning. We appreciate the abundant wildlife populating the wetland area where we walk—me for its beauty and serenity; my dogs for sniffing poop and the fantasy of off-leash chase. A lovely pair of coyotes resides here. These city coyotes, habituated to people and dogs, watch us from what's mutually considered a safe distance. Except for this day.

I'd been marveling at the sound of the coyote's call from over the ridge when I saw him crest the hill. I assumed he'd give us the usual wide berth and cross the bridge. From there, I figured he'd continue on to Starbuck's for coffee and a scone before heading to work (or whatever coyotes usually do at that early hour). I realized how wrong I was as I watched the beast move toward us with an unsettling focus. His head was dropped as he advanced stealthily in our direction. I swear his eyes glowed red. I imagined a certain, painful death by wild canine teeth awaited us!

By that point my dogs had noticed the coyote, and I could see that Penny shared my concern. The look on her big, brave, German shepherd dog face said, "The best plan would be to quietly and cautiously evacuate the premises." MoJo, on the other hand, was busy putting up his defenses. He objected to my suggestion that we return to the car. When MoJo disagreed with me, he went into his civil disobedience act, which meant he lay down and became dead weight. Meanwhile, the coyote was pressing forward, looking quite hungry.

I tried to reason with MoJo, asking that he reconsider his choice, but he continued his protest. In the meantime, the coyote was advancing, looking hungrier. At this point, my adrenaline levels were high enough to pick up my eighty-pound dog and carry him under one arm the 143 yards to my car.

Always the dog trainer, I thought briefly of turning the event into a training opportunity to work on MoJo's reactivity to other dogs. I quickly recognized my lapse of reason but then dove deeper into insanity. I considered running away.

I had another, equally dumb idea. I thought of using a trick that worked to distract stray dogs: throw a handful of treats in the coyote's face.

Thankfully, I regained my good sense and decided to act on neither plan. Running would have incited the coyote to give chase, and throwing treats would have made me a human vending machine in the coyote's mind. I imagined him lying in wait on our next walk, visualizing me as a giant Pez dispenser.

Recouping my reason, a shred of composure, and MoJo's compliance, we slowly moved toward the car with a watchful eye on our stalker.

I had just witnessed real life, wild canid predation. I was acutely aware that the wily coyote was the predator, and I was the wascally wabbit.

Predatory Behavior

Note: The term prey drive is often heard in discussions about predation. The language currently preferred among trainers and behaviorists is predatory behavior. Predatory behavior is the terminology that will be used here for the phrase commonly known as prey drive.

Dog owners often ask if predatory behavior in their dogs is aggression and whether it's cause for concern. Predatory behavior is natural, a hard-wired survival mechanism, and not aggression in the strict sense of the word. While some consider predation to be a form aggression, it differs vastly from other types of agonistic or combative behaviors.

The motivation and emotion behind aggression and predatory behavior are different. In predation, there is an absence of anger, unlike other forms of aggression stemming from social conflict or fear. Drs. Suzanne Hetts and Daniel Q. Estep of Animal Behavior Associates, define aggression as *a social behavior that occurs when animals engage in some sort of conflict over territory, space, or other resources.* Predatory behavior is not motivated by social conflict but rather by the need to obtain food.

Roger Abrantes, Ph.D. goes into further detail by delineating between the terms *aggression* and *aggressiveness* in his book *The Evolution of Canine Social Behavior.* Abrantes defines aggression as: *the initiation of unprovoked hostilities, the launching of attacks, and hostile behavior.* He defines aggressiveness as: *tending toward or exhibiting aggression, marked by combative readiness, marked by driving forceful energy or initiative.*

Abrantes says about predatory behavior, "Predatory aggression towards prey, as the name indicates, aims at obtaining food, which is not compatible with the definition of aggression nor the goal of aggressiveness. It does not make any sense to speak of aggression towards a source of energy—food."

Dog sport (i.e. flyball) enthusiasts talk of prey drive versus chase drive as it relates to a dog's performance in competition. It's worth mentioning here how it relates to the topic of predatory behavior. To differentiate the concepts of *prey drive* and *chase drive* the term *drive* is simply defined as a strong impulse or an urge. Prey drive (predatory behavior) has the dog intensely focused on the target with an absolute drive to gain access to it. Chase drive has the dog pursuing the target with less intensity, a more playful manner, and perhaps not following through with the catch. What we most often see in canine play is chase drive.

Elements of predatory behavior exist in canine play. They are instinctual and programmed into the dog as a survival mechanism. Nonviolent play can escalate and then cross a line to where predatory instincts take over. This is known as predatory drift. Events that trigger predatory behavior and predatory drift include over arousal, yelping, fast movement, and limping or jerky movement.

Predation is a sequence of behaviors that, in the wild, would result in killing another animal for food. This sequence of behaviors includes staring, stalking, chasing, pouncing, nipping, and shaking. Domestic dogs naturally present variations of these behaviors during play.

Certain dog breeds demonstrate variant predatory behaviors as a product of selective breeding. The behaviors have been subdued or amplified through the breeding process. For instance, a herding dog will show a strong desire to chase, yet the predatory biting behavior has been inhibited.

Some dog owners get nervous when they see their dogs showing fangs. An overly simplistic view of aggression would have us believe that death awaits anyone on the receiving end of those canine daggers. However, dogs have the capacity to use their teeth with remarkable force or amazing gracefulness. This ability is supplemented by an elaborate and subtle system of communication. Appreciation of this canine communication system is elusive at best to many humans. Consequently, we become nervous witnessing interactions we don't fully grasp. I suspect that if dogs were not fluent in their native body language, the species might have self-destructed long ago.

So how do we determine whether a dog is presenting predatory behavior or aggression? A basic characterization is that predation is silent, where aggression is noisy. Hunting predators do not announce their presence to their quarry, whereas aggression is likely heralded with barking and snarling.

Is it predatory behavior when a dog chases a skateboarder or a jogger? To specifically answer this question, we'll look at the behavior's motivation and the results. While the quick and unusual movement of the person might trigger a dog's chase drive, we could say that he does not actually see that person as prey. This is because the intention is not to eat the skateboarder. The chase will stop if the skateboard does. (Although, stress hormone levels take time to subside, so excitement levels will remain high for some time, maybe even hours.)

Predation crosses the line from natural, normal behavior to a serious problem when a dog is untrained, out of control, and unmanageable. He's in dangerous territory if he is unable to distinguish appropriate prey (the fox hound hunting the fox) from inappropriate prey (the dog stalking the toddler) and unable to control his behavior.

While predation is innate, it should by not dismissed or accepted if its intensity crosses the line into perilous behavior. It's our responsibility as their guardians to ensure that our dogs' instincts do not endanger themselves or others.

Management
Managing predation, like any undesirable canine behavior, first requires prevention. Disallow dogs to practice the behavior on their own accord. For example, if the dog spends his day home alone barking at the front window with the sight of every neighborhood squirrel, he needs to be denied access to the show. This behavior may not technically be prey behavior, but simple over arousal, but should be managed even so. Gate, crate, or create a visual barrier, and provide other entertainment such as a stuffed Kong® or interactive toys.

Supervision
Never leave a dog with strong predatory tendencies unsupervised in the yard, where passersby and urban wildlife can trigger his instincts. There are many reasons not to tether a dog and leave him unattended, but for a dog with a strong predatory nature, tie-outs are a sure recipe for disaster. Restraint and exposure to perceived prey may well cause him to boil over with frustration that could lead to redirected aggression or obsessive, compulsive behaviors.

Sturdy fencing is a must, even when the dog is supervised. Fencing should be solid so that the dog does not see perceived prey moving quickly by. Electronic, invisible fencing will not keep potential prey or children from entering the yard, nor will it keep the dog from crossing it if the motivation to chase is strong.

Always keep dogs with a penchant for predatory behavior leashed when on walks and hiking trails. Check equipment before each outing to ensure that it is well fitted and in good condition. Dogs should be proficient at walking on a loose lead. This will reduce the risk of injury on both ends of the leash if they should lunge toward prey.

Retractable leashes are a risky choice of equipment. They are cumbersome and allow the dog to wander too far away, making it difficult for him to pay attention. We take a gamble with a dog that is sixteen feet afield, where he may flush out prey and give chase, endangering himself and the holder of the leash.

Effective management means preventing the behavior from occurring. This is not to be confused with suppressing it (with the use of punishment, for example.) Suppression will only result in frustration. This frustration may cause some dogs to develop obsessive, compulsive disorders such as excessive licking or tail chasing. Furthermore, frustration can lead to such things as increased aggression, lower threshold for prey, and lower frustration tolerance.

Training

It's unreasonable to expect to train away or completely extinguish a dog's natural instincts. Genetics set the window for what we can realistically expect in behavior modification. Thus, we'd be hard pressed to teach a Beagle not to sniff or a Border Collie not to herd. Nevertheless, we can modify behavior within that window set by nature. We can formulate a successful training plan by determining the motivation for the behavior. Is it prey drive or chase drive? (Remember that prey drive is motivated by the intent to gain access, while chase drive is playful and not necessarily followed through with the catch.) Successful training may mean adjusting our expectations dependant on the level of intensity and the extent of the behavior in each individual dog.

Dogs that are hard-wired to chase are best served when given an acceptable outlet for the behavior. If we cannot provide the Border Collie with a herd of sheep, then it's beneficial to direct his energy and instincts into an appropriate sport, such as flyball, Trieball, or agility. Channel a dog's instincts into activities that his DNA has programmed him for. Water dogs leap at the chance to go dock diving, scent hounds inhale nose work, and terriers dig earth dog competitions.

In addition to redirecting a dog's instincts, we need to teach them alternative, incompatible behaviors for times when the chase impulse arises in the real world. Teach an emergency recall, an emergency down, and to calm on cue (see *The How-To of Training* and *Beyond the Basics*). The combination of management and training is the key to success. Trumping the desire to chase is a tall order but can be managed and modified with the right training and motivation.

14

Kids and Dogs
One Big, Happy Family

I have no bipedal kids. However, I have worked with some brilliantly fun children in my dog-training career. As I am not a parent of anyone without fur, I feel like I'm about to preach that which I do not practice. Nonetheless, as I consider my dogs to be experts in canine behavior, I consider the kids to be experts in the field of child behavior. As they say, "From the mouths of babes oft times come gems." I defer to their wisdom.

Children are superbly creative thinkers. Their unfettered minds yield simple and original solutions to the world's problems. When asked how to teach a dog to roll over, a bright 8-year-old boy responded, "Show him something dead!"

On one occasion, I had a 7-year-old girl assisting as we taught the family goldendoodle his basic manners. The child was quite skillful, so I asked her if she wanted to be a dog trainer when she grew up. A very determined, yet disappointed look came over her face as she replied, "But I was going to be President!" Follow your dreams, little girl!

6-year-old boys seem to have boundless energy. So do Australian shepherds. Put the two together and one would think that playtime would never end. As it turns out, it may be only Australian shepherds, which possess limitless stamina. I witnessed one boy and his Aussie, both adolescents, playing a rousing, prolonged game of fetch. After a time, the wearied boy approached his mother and asked, "Doesn't she ever get tired?"

The synthesis of kids and dogs is a delight to behold. They can teach us so much, if we first teach them how to coexist safely and respectfully. Their creativity and zest for life is an inspiration. I can't wait to see the President romping with her dog in the White House rose garden.

The only creatures that are evolved enough to convey pure love are dogs and infants. –**Johnny Depp**

Sitting down to write this chapter, I felt a wave of resistance. This was the voice of Marcia (the dark cheerleader of doom who lives in my head. You remember her from an earlier chapter.) Marcia called me a hypocrite because I happen to have no biological offspring. That wave of resistance subsided though, when I dove straight in to writing. I put my hands on my keyboard, began researching what the experts have to say, and added my findings to my own experience. While I can't speak from personal experience on the kid part of kids and dogs, I can share my anecdotal evidence and defer to the seasoned voices of experienced parents.

The bond between a child and a dog can hold many benefits. For everyone's well being, children should be taught about safe treatment and interaction with dogs. Teaching a child to properly relate to a dog promotes responsibility, compassion, empathy, and humane handling.

Dogs as teachers
Pets can be beneficial in child development. Companionship with a pet can enhance a child's social, cognitive, and emotional development. Children who have a positive bond with a companion animal often show more maturity, higher self-esteem, and self-confidence. While any pet cultivates learning about how to take responsibility, a dog is a strong motivator for action. Dogs are an inspiration for kids to step away from the video games and go for a romp in the park—more so than a goldfish or a hamster.

Children who love animals learn respect for their need to live a life free of pain and oppression. These compassionate traits are carried into adulthood and into interactions with all species. Observing dogs can help children learn right from wrong and how to get along with others. Dogs can teach a child about love, companionship, and the virtues of being nonjudgmental. Children who learn compassion and responsibility in caring for an animal are also learning those same valuable skills for interacting with people. Pets are social facilitators as children are naturally interested in animals. Therefore, they are more likely to interact with other children in the presence of an animal. Often, animals are a bridge for children that are less socially active, prompting the child's participation in group activities.

Animals accept us for who we are, thus helping children learn trust and acceptance. Because pets are nonjudgmental, children are willing to trust them and take comfort from them. Caring for pets fosters a sense of compassion, empathy, and nurturing. Furthermore, it can help in developing non-verbal communication. Pets provide comfort contact.

Pets set the stage for a child's cognitive development because children are curious about animals. Living with a dog provides a connection with nature, a respect for other living beings, and life lessons on survival, health, birth, and death. Parents can encourage the child to learn more about the health care by having the child accompany their pet to vet visits. Children can participate in the dog's care by helping with feeding and brushing. They can learn about how dogs think and learn by participating in obedience classes with their dog.

Before getting a dog, the child can help in researching what breed would be the best for the family (see the chapter *Choosing a Dog*) and where to acquire the dog. Proper planning and open discussion will help make life with dogs and kids a positive experience for everyone.

Kids and Responsibility

Children can be quite persistent in petitioning parents for a dog. If you are considering the matter, be sure that *you* want a dog as well. Even though kids of elementary school age can be quite helpful in the care and feeding of Scooby, ultimately the responsibility falls on the shoulders of the parents.

Children under 12 are not equipped for walking dogs without parental supervision. They are not mentally or necessarily physically equipped to deal with the real-life situations that can arise, such as frightening noises, squirrels, other dogs passing by, and strangers wanting to pet the dog. However, they can learn about leash walking and participate by having Scooby wear two leashes. The child can hold one leash while mom or dad holds the other.

Similarities between parenting kids and parenting dogs

Many of a dog's needs are roughly equivalent to the needs and behaviors of preschool children. These basic needs of feeding, grooming, and security are things for which children eventually assume responsibility. Dogs, of course, do not. Therefore, the responsibilities of basic care will remain the same throughout the dog's life.

Many disciplines work similarly for both dogs and children. Yet, this is not to say that dogs are anthropomorphized substitutes for children. There is more than the number of legs differentiating the two. Accepting dogs for the wonderful beings that they are and knowing that they are not fuzzy little humans will serve everyone well.

Discipline, defined as guidance, not punishment is a sound philosophy for raising both children and dogs. Furthermore, it models appropriate dog/human interactions for children. Puppies, like children are taught boundaries and kept safe. We hold a toddler's hand when out on a walk, as a puppy is walked on a leash. Handholding and leashes are not about control. They are about safety. Boundaries, education, and management are also about safety. One would not leave a toddler home alone with the run of the house any more than one should leave a puppy to the same circumstance.

Children and puppies learn by observation. Both are intensely curious, needing to fulfill their desire for exploring the world. Babies and puppies do this with their mouths…everything goes in. Here again, management and education keep youngsters of both species safe.

Children and dogs understand the difference between approval and disapproval, each seeking the former. As parents and leaders, we are duty bound to set them up for success and reward those successes. We need to supply feedback as a compass that leads dogs and kids in the right direction.

A time-out is a disciplinary measure that works for both young children and dogs. Children might have the naughty chair as a place to contemplate the error of their ways; we do not expect the same from the dog. For the dog, it's an intervention to diffuse the situation and to know that the behavior neither garners your approval nor does it get him what he wants.

Important keys to successful parenting of dogs and children are consistency, fairness, and love.

Before you get a dog

The gift that keeps on living: Dogs as gifts

Granting the wish of a child who's been relentlessly lobbying for a puppy is an alluring notion. Parents may entertain the idea of giving a dog as a birthday or holiday gift. It elicits visions of the happy recipient unwrapping their bundle of furry joy and welcoming puppy kisses. However, this well-intentioned gift could go terribly wrong–for the dog.

Giving a dog as a gift can create the attitude that a dog is a possession and not thought of as a family member. It says that animals are nothing more than disposable playthings.

Buying or adopting a pet is certainly more complicated than purchasing a toy. Pets cannot be tossed into the closet and forgotten along with the electronic gadgets after the warranty and novelty have expired.

Holidays may be the worst occasion to give a pet as a gift. Life is busy and chaotic for most people with time and patience in short supply. This is no time for new dog, who needs close supervision and a quiet routine while adjusting to his new home.

Instead of giving a pet as a gift, ask if your local shelter offers the option of gift cards. This alternative makes it possible for recipients to select the pet of their choice when the time is right. Wrap up a "new dog starter kit." Fill a box with dog essentials such as a collar, leash, chew toys, instructional books or videos, a gift certificate for training and a solid pledge to help find the perfect new friend when life returns to normal after the holidays. Remember that quality time spent with your children and new dog is the best gift of all.

Whose dog is it anyway?

Getting a dog and designating him to just one child in the family could be a setup for familial conflict. Like giving a dog as a gift, designating one child as the owner conveys the attitude that dogs are possessions, not family members.

When the dog comes home, the focus will be on him and family dynamics will change. Children can, and should have one-on-one time with the dog in order to satisfy the need to bond and develop their own unique relationship. Children learn that there is enough love to go around and that they each have a piece of Sparky's heart and in turn, he a piece of each of theirs.

Assess before you progress

We hold an idyllic vision of a child and their dog. In a moment of weakness, we might give in to the child's incessant hounding to get a dog. If after careful thought, you've made the decision to get a dog, there are some questions to be asked–questions about the compatibility of the child and dog.

Evaluating the child

Is the child highly social, active, confident, and does she enjoy outdoor activities? If so, you might choose a high-energy dog that enjoys and is able to participate in dog sports such as agility or fly ball. These sports promote teamwork and showcase the talents of both dog and child together.

A child that is more reserved might do well with a dog bred for companionship; one that will enjoy learning tricks and participating in backyard games.

How responsible is the child? Does the child have varied interests? Does she or he finish what they start? Does the child follow instructions and willingly comply with requests? How tolerant is the child? What is the child's level of compassion and empathy?

The answers to these questions will determine whether the decision to get a dog is the right one for you, the dog, and the kids.

Evaluating the dog

Children are unpredictable. Children are prone to running, screaming, and roughhousing. For many dogs, these things happen at eye level. For small dogs, this chaos occurs above their heads. What a very frightening prospect!

The chapter on choosing a dog covers, in detail, the process of selecting the right dog. Here are a few more things to note specifically for choosing a family dog:

- What is the dog's energy level?

- Does he jump up, paw, mouth?

- Does the dog guard resources?

- Is the dog anxious?

- How does the dog react to infants, toddlers, adolescents, teenagers?

- How does the dog react to chaos?

Size: small dogs are inappropriate for toddlers and young children, as they are too fragile and apt to feel more vulnerable, which could result in biting.

There are no guarantees in life, but careful consideration and doing your homework will help to make this life decision a good one.

The Everyday Basics of Life with Dogs and Kids

Teach Children How to Meet and Greet Dogs
Children are naturally interested in dogs and some find it difficult to contain their enthusiasm. This childish exuberance can be seen as a threat by a dog that is inexperienced or fearful around children. Teaching both children and dogs how to interact appropriately is necessary for everyone's safety.

Teach children how to pet dogs appropriately
First, teach children why they should never rush up to dogs, explaining why it might frighten him. Next, teach them to ask the owner if they may pet the dog. Tell children that sometimes the owner will say no and that's ok.

Now, have the children ask the dog. Teach children about dog body language, so that they know whether the dog is safe to pet. Have them extend their hand slowly in a fist with the palm down. This approach minimizes the risk of a nipped finger. Allow the dog to sniff. Does he say yes or no to being petted? (See the chapter *Conversations with Dogs.*)

If the owner and the dog say yes to petting, then proceed. Teach children to pet dogs on the side of the neck or the back or chest. It is natural for humans to pet dogs on top of their heads. However, dogs can't see where your hand is going. When you reach over his head, he will tilt his head up, putting the hand is right near the teeth. Make sure the child lets the dog see her hand as she's reaching toward him.

Kids, Dogs, and Crates

Young children are drawn to dog crates. They're ready-made forts right? Furthermore, crates are particularly attractive if they are deemed off limits. It is neither cute nor safe for kids crawl into the crate with the dog. Children allowed in a dog's personal area are not learning to respect the dog's space.

To help them understand respect for their dog's space, ask kids if they like little brother or sister coming into their room. Their answer would probably explain why we see so many "Keep Out" signs targeted at younger siblings posted on bedroom doors.

Failure to teach children respect for a dog's space and possessions sets an unsafe scene for kids and is unfair to the dog. Children sometimes get upset when the dog steals their toys. This can be an opportunity to teach children that the dog needs the same privileges.

Children who post "No Trespassing" signs on their bedroom doors, would have fun making one for Scooby's crate. Scooby can sign it with his paw print using non-toxic paint or a bit of moist dirt from the yard.

Have the kids build their own fort. If Scooby wants to join them, so be it. The kids' fort can be a place where everyone can be cozy, but here, it's always up to Scooby as to whether he wants to participate.

When a Child is Afraid

Children are prone to running and screaming when they are afraid. This, we know can incite the dog to come closer or to chase. Some may reason that a child having a bit of "healthy" fear is beneficial. However, having children observe dogs and teaching proper interactions with them is a much safer plan than letting them remain afraid.

What we don't understand frightens us. If we teach children about dog body language, they will better understand the dog's intent and fears will be assuaged.

A fun resource for teaching children about dog body language is the Doggone Crazy!™ board game. Doggone Crazy!™ is a family oriented game that teaches kids and adults how to read dog communication and be safe around dogs. Players race around the board collecting bones, which are earned by demonstrating safe behaviors, answering questions, and interpreting photographs of dogs.

Allow the fearful child to watch dogs from a distance and identify dogs that look friendly or frightened, happy or angry, old or young, well-mannered or out of control.

Those that are frightened must be allowed to go at their own pace, not going too far out of their comfort level.

Introduce children to calm, older dogs that you know and trust. Kids may be less afraid if they know the dog's name. Ask the child questions about how they feel and how they think the dog feels. Have the child ask the owner about the dog. What does he like to do? What is his favorite toy?

With the owner assisting with the dog's compliance, let the child issue some cues to the dog. This interaction will help the child to feel more confident and to understand the dog and that the dog understands her. Work with this one dog until the child feels safe, then she can meet more dogs when she's ready.

Progress to puppies and more active dogs once the child is comfortable with calm, adult dogs. Start at the beginning as she did with the first dog, at a distance and progress through the interactive process. Talk about how each new dog is similar and how they are different from the other she's met.

Isn't that cute?

As a trainer, it's easy for me to slip into self-righteousness about all of the online photos of children and dogs that I see. These photos of kids draped around dogs are captioned with anthropomorphized sentiments like "The world's best babysitter" or "Hugging the dog makes everything all right."

There are many opinions about what is safe for kids with dogs. A snapshot is just that. We don't know what happened right before or right after the photo was taken. Videos give us more information than a still shot, but there are yet many unknowns. We do not know the child, the parent, the context, or the dog and his normal body language. We do not know if the dog knows the child. We do not know what other factors might be influencing the dog's behavior, nor do we know the child's normal behavior.

All that said I am still compelled and obliged to state that these photos are not necessarily cute. I say it in order to prevent bites.

I'm sure that the parents' intent is not a deliberate act to put the child in danger. It's more likely that they are taken up in the "Awww" of the moment. They may be unaware of or misreading the dog's cues.

The most impactful things a parent can do to keep children safe are:

- Learn canine body language
- Be aware of the signals that show a dog is stressed
- Be a positive role model for canine/human interaction
- Train the dog and the child in appropriate interactions
- Supervise
- Use good management and common sense

Parental supervision is no guarantee. However, education and common sense are the best protection against dog bites to children.

Any Dog Can Bite: Bite Prevention

Nothing rattles my nerves more than to hear someone say, "I know he would never bite." The reality is that any dog possessing teeth *can* and *will* bite in the right (or wrong) circumstance.

Reasons Dogs Bite:

Resource guarding: A dog may bite to protect a possession, food, water, or puppies. They may bite to protect a person or a location such as his bed or crate, or when a child has tried to take something from the dog.

Territorialism: A dog may bite when he is protecting his owner or property.

Medical conditions/pain: A dog may bite when he is sick or in pain, protecting himself from further pain or discomfort.

Elderly: A dog may bite because he is old and intolerant of children's actions.

Anxiety: A dog may bite when he is afraid of the child or her actions. A dog may bite when the child has done something to provoke or frighten him. For example, the child has come into the dog's space, poked, pulled ears or tail, or hugged him. A dog may bite when the child has startled or stepped on him.

Aggression: A dog may bite when the child has tried to use force and/or intimidation with the dog. Note: The child may be mimicking what she has seen an adult do.

Bite Inhibition: A dog may bite if he has not learned proper bite inhibition and bites too hard when the child offers him food or a toy.

Over stimulation: A dog may bite when the dog and child are roughhousing and the dog becomes overly excited.

Chase drive: A dog may bite when children are running and screaming, which can incite chase drive in the dog. Herding dogs may nip while trying to herd children.

Family Life Stages

We've looked at having a dog as the new addition to the family. But, what about a new addition that takes human form, when the dog is already a member of said family? Family dynamics change drastically in either scenario. Preparation and education are vital to successful transitions.

Preparing dogs for baby's arrival

You have a few months before baby's arrival...plenty of time, right? Those months of busy preparation will fly by making it easy to forget about Sparky during the distraction. Once baby makes her entry, parents will be sleep deprived, adjusting to a new schedule, and dealing with the moment-to-moment care of the newborn. It's a very confusing time.

Think about how your new schedule will play out after the baby comes home. Will Sparky's feeding or walk time be shifted? Are wakeup and bedtime schedules going to change? If so, gradually start Sparky on the new timetable beforehand.

If making the time to walk Sparky is going to be a problem, employ the help of a dog walker or trusted friend. Dog daycare or play dates with a friend's dog can give him an outlet for his energy.

Slowly acclimate him to having less of your attention. Have Sparky spend some alone time in his crate or his designated space in the home. Do this on the anticipated schedule; say when you will be busy feeding, bathing, or rocking baby to sleep. Teach Sparky that mugging for attention is not acceptable. Teach him the word "Enough" along with a gentle, but firm pat on the head means go away and settle down. Teach him how to "Go To Place" (see below) instead of being under foot.

Make sure Sparky's leash walking skills are up to snuff. When they are, acclimate him to walking beside an empty baby stroller, practicing in the driveway or back yard. It's a risky proposition to pack up baby and Sparky, and then head out on the trail for the first time without practice.

Acclimate Sparky to the baby's arrival with a lifelike doll that makes realistic baby sounds. When the doll makes sounds, reward the dog for calm reactions. There are CDs of baby sounds, which can be used to desensitize dogs to these new noises.

Set up the nursery and let Sparky see the new apparatus, particularly that with sound and/or motion, such as a baby swing. Other considerations to prepare for baby's arrival include disallowing dogs to drink from the toilet, removing food bowls from the floor, training dogs not to jump up, and managing protective or herding instincts.

With a plan in place and the preparations made, it's time for baby to take her place in the family.

Teach "Go to place"

Note: Before teaching, "Go to place" the dog must first know how to lie down on cue and be able to do a long down stay.

Designate a specific place like a rug or his dog bed for the dog to go to. It should be nearby where the dog can see you and the baby so that he feels included. Stand next to the bed and toss a treat on it. As the dog steps on the bed to retrieve the treat say, "Place." Next, ask the dog for a down and reward him when he does so. Practice this until the dog knows what the word "place" means. Using the same hand motion you used to toss the treat on to the bed (the tossing motion has now become your hand signal) ask the dog to go to place without tossing the treat. Ask for a down and reward the dog when he does so. Progressively work up to having the dog hold his down stay while you go sit in the place where you'll be feeding or rocking the baby. You can help him by tossing a treat his direction every so often.

Gradually increase the distance you are able to stand from the bed and cue the dog to go to his place. Eventually, you will be able to cue the dog to go to place while sitting in the place where you'll be with baby.

Teach "Enough"

If the dog is prone to mugging you for attention, it's helpful to teach him, "Enough" means to go away and settle down.

When the dog seeks attention, you can give him some pets but then tell him that petting time is over. Do so by giving him a gentle, but firm pat on the head and say, "Enough." Now, turn away from him and ignore him. Do not look at him, touch him, or talk to him. He will lose interest and go away. When he has learned what the cue means, you can say, "Enough." Then, you can cue the dog to "Go to place."

Dog and baby

When introducing him to the new baby, allow the dog some supervised sniffing. However, do not force interaction if the dog seems uninterested. On the other hand, do not isolate and exclude the dog from experiencing life with baby. Common sense should prevail. Close the nursery door or use crates, gates, or tethers for safe inclusions.

Sparky may need a refresher in his basic obedience. Life has changed immensely for the whole family, including the dog. Big changes can cause confusion and regression in a dog's behavior.

When Baby Learns To Crawl

You did everything right when you brought baby home. All went well with acclimating Sparky to the new arrival. However, things change when baby inevitably begins to crawl and then to walk. Baby is now capable of moving into Sparky's space under her own power.

This new mobility can be scary for some dogs. Observe the dog carefully to understand how he is feeling about this new phase in family life. Now is the time to tighten management with the use of baby gates and dog crates. Keep dog and baby separate while the child explores, as the dog may be uncomfortable with baby crawling on his bed or investigating his toys.

Teach baby to touch Sparky gently. If Sparky is comfortable with this, help baby by taking her hand and gently petting the dog on the back or side, avoiding ears and eyes.

Dogs are quite perceptive and accepting, but if Sparky is uncomfortable with baby's approach, do not force it. Holding a dog and telling him it's okay is not comforting. It will make him more afraid and more evasive of the child.

Sometimes baby takes so much time and attention, Sparky only gets noticed when baby is asleep. For Sparky, the only fun happens when baby is absent. Help him make a positive association with baby by having fun things happen in her presence. Sparky's favorite toys are at hand when baby is present. His favorite chew toy or stuffed Kong® is there in baby's presence (baby and dog are separated and supervised when chew toys are present.) Orchestrate all interactions as positive ones.

Dog and toddler

Adult dogs recognize babies of other species and are often more tolerant of them if they've been properly socialized with children. Therefore, socialization, positive introductions, and interaction with children are a must.

Toddlers are in constant, unpredictable motion. They screech and squeal (in a dog's mind) like prey. Toddlers move like little sumo wrestlers; clumsy and often falling on anything in their way. Tots don't know the boundaries of ear and tail pulling. They will eat dog food and put anything that fits into their mouths. Toddlers can be frightening.

Explain to youngsters that dogs are different from their human playmates in that they don't have hands, thus they use their teeth during play and to pick things up. Even very young children can understand this concept.

Children of preschool age are manipulative and prone to testing boundaries. Fluffy is the only one under them in the social hierarchy, presenting the perfect opportunity for little ones to learn about sharing, and respect for others' feelings and needs. They learn about the give-and-take of friendship.

Instructing children about safe and respectful relationships with dogs begins with the parents and it begins early. Parents can take advantage of a child's natural desire to imitate by modeling healthy dog/human relationships to their children:

> • Explain how to meet a dog safely (see below on how to meet and greet a dog)

> • Teach children not to tease the dog. Children will often demonstrate their "power" over the dog by offering a toy or food, and then snatch it away. Often, the dog is corrected, so explain to the child why not to tease. Correct the teaser, not the teased.

> • Discourage the child from playing with the dog's mouth with their hands.

> • Young children should not play tug with the dog. Kids need to be old enough to understand the discipline of the game.

Dog and adolescent
Living with a dog can engender dependability, nurturing, and caring for children when they are given the chance to be responsible for someone. However, parents must realize children's limitations and be willing to take up the slack and carefully guide children placed in charge.

Dogs make dependable companions to adolescents, as they can be tireless playmates, they don't argue or tattle, and are very reliable secret keepers (although I'm not advocating for children keeping secrets.)

Adolescents are of an age where they can take satisfaction in their role of responsibility. Adolescents can be included in certain decisions made on Scruffy's behalf. Kids are prideful in what they can teach their dog, building a bond that improves their self-esteem and confidence.

"When your children are teenagers, it's important to have a dog so that someone in the house is happy to see you." –**Nora Ephron**

Dog and teenager

Teenage drama is difficult for everyone, including the dog. Many dogs think that human teens should be avoided at all cost, especially when they are traveling in packs and riding skateboards. Some of us humans might feel the same.

Teenagers lead busy lives. Unless they are highly involved and bonded with the dog, Scruffy may take a back seat to the teen's social and scholastic activities. Here is where high-energy dogs and teens may not be a good mix. High-energy dogs such as pointers and terriers need lots of exercise and mental stimulation. Without these things, they often take to chewing, digging, and barking when left alone. Likewise, puppies take more time, energy, and training, things some teens may not be equipped to provide. On the other side of the coin, a dog can help to keep teens focused and provide structure by participating in activities that include Scruffy.

Matching size, age, and energy levels is important for any dog/owner complement. Keeping these things in mind will enhance the happy home. For example, a small 14-year-old may find it challenging to walk an exuberant St. Bernard, a spirited Labrador puppy, or a determined, independent-thinking basset hound.

Activities for Kids and Dogs

Children love to play games with their dogs and teach them tricks. Dogs love to learn and be a part of the fun. Following are some family friendly activities that everyone will enjoy.

Note To Parents: Use lots of healthy dog treats. Make these activities fun for the dog as well as for the children. Never let the games become too physical, allowing children to push or pull the dog to get him to do something. If things are getting too raucous, it's a good time to play the Red Light/Green Light game, then settle down for some quiet time. If the dog seems confused or frustrated, find a way to make the game easier for him. If you see signs of frustration in either the dog or the children be ready to step in to help. Make sure the dog is physically able to do the trick or game. Once the dog has learned the trick or game, fade out treats.

Games:

Treat Hunt: This activity is one that even the youngest kids can enjoy. Have them create a trail of treats for the dog to find. One person keeps the dog with them while the children place treats every two to four feet apart. When the trail is complete, have the children come back to the dog, ask him for a sit, and then release him to follow the trail. This game could be made more difficult by placing the treats farther apart or playing it in the back yard. But, remember not to make the game too difficult, so that everyone stays interested and has fun.

Red Light/Green Light: This game is designed to help dogs and kids with impulse control. They learn that they can be energetic, but then to calm down quickly and on cue. First, have the children draw stop and go signs for this trick. Start with a designated child holding up the stop sign. Then, that child holds up the go sign and says, "Go." This is the cue for everyone to start acting silly. After a minute, the designated child holds up the stop sign calling out, "Stop." This is the cue for everyone to be calm. Have the one child closest to the dog ask him for a sit.

Hide and Seek: This game helps with the dog's recall skills, as well as paying attention to his human. It also strengthens the dog's stay. One person holds the dog's leash, or the dog is in a stay if he's capable. Have the children go hide. Then one by one, the children call the dog. When he finds them, the dog is rewarded with a treat or toy. Start by hiding in obvious places. Then, gradually make the game more interesting by hiding in more difficult locations.

Child Reads To Dog: This activity teaches dogs and kids that they can enjoy quiet times together. Have the child read their favorite story to the dog. Dogs are great listeners and kids can practice their reading skills. This is a good bedtime activity to end the day on a quiet note.

Dog Reads To Child: Kids can amaze their friends with this easy-to-teach trick. Make a sign that reads, "Wag Your Tail." Have the dog stand in front of the child holding the sign. Now, using a very happy voice, the child asks the dog to read the sign. The dog will hear the happy voice and wag his tail. It appears that he is reading the sign and following directions!

Musical Bones: This game is the canine version of musical chairs. It teaches kids and dogs to work as a team with leash walking skills. Have the children draw pictures of dog bones on paper. Cut them out and place the paper bones on the floor in a circular pattern or a trail throughout the house. Next, a designated DJ will start to play music. Whenever the DJ stops the music, the child and dog move to the nearest bone. The child then asks the dog to sit.

Dog Bowling: This game helps teach dogs to come when called. In a hallway, place empty 2-liter plastic bottles in a triangular formation. At one end of the hallway, have someone hold the dog on leash or put him in a stay if he is capable. Then, with the kids at the other end of the hallway, have them call the dog for a treat. Whoever gets the dog to knock over the most bottles wins.

Recall Races: This game teaches the dog to come to the child when called. This is a fun neighborhood activity for children and their dogs or for a multi-dog household. Have someone hold the dog on leash a short distance from the children. Then, have the children call dogs to see who has the fastest recall. Set dogs and children up for success by starting with a short distance, but as everyone becomes more accomplished, the distance can be increased. This is also a good game to teach dogs a solid stay. Instead of someone holding the leash, place the dogs in a stay, then have the children call the dogs to them. For success, have the dogs do their stay at a reasonable distance apart. As they become stronger with their stay, they can gradually move closer together.

Tricks:

Spin: With the dog standing in front of you, hold out a treat. Slowly move your hand in a circle away from you and toward the dog's tail. Let the dog follow it. After the dogs is doing this reliably, you can start using the word "spin" as the dog follows your hand. Next, fade out the treat and have the dog following your hand only. Treats can be delivered after the spin is complete.

Jump: Teaching a dog to jump over objects is fun and helps to build his confidence. Start with a broomstick on the floor. Lure the dog with a treat to jump over the broomstick. Gradually raise the broomstick so the dog jumps higher.

Seesaw: This is another confidence-building trick. It helps dogs to be comfortable walking on unfamiliar surfaces and builds trust between teacher and student. Start by laying a piece of plywood, a shelf, or a board on the floor. Have the child give the dog a treat for stepping on the board. Using treats as lures, treat the dog for every step he takes on the board. Once he his completely comfortable walking across the board, lay it across a broomstick to make a low seesaw. Repeat the above steps until the dog is walking across the seesaw. Reduce the number of treats until the dog is only rewarded for completing his walk across the seesaw.

Through the hoop: Teach dogs to jump through a hoop. Start with a hula-hoop held upright with the bottom of the hoop touching the floor. Lure the dog with a treat to jump through it. Gradually raise the hoop so the dog jumps higher.

Through the tunnel: Teach dogs go through a tunnel. Agility tunnels can be purchased, or children can fashion one out of a cardboard box (decorating the tunnel is fun too.) Homemade tunnels can also be created with chairs or low tables draped with a blanket. Lure the dog with a treat to step into the tunnel, then gradually lure him further until he goes all the way through. The dog can also be lured with a trail of treats through the tunnel.

Shake: Teach dogs to "shake hands." Start with the dog in a sit position. Hold a treat over the dog's head and off to the side a bit. Slowly move the treat upward and slightly away from the dog. When the dog leans sideways and lifts his paw, extend your cupped hand with the palm facing up and take the dog's paw. Say, "Shake" as you give him the treat. Soon, the dog will start to lift his paw on his own when you offer your hand. Next, put the behavior on cue. Say, "Shake" as the dog offers his paw. Once he knows the cue, you can hold out your hand, say, "Shake," and the dog will lift his paw.

Wave: Teach dogs to wave "bye-bye." When the dog reliably offers a paw to shake, (don't give the cue to shake, just offer your hand) don't take his paw, but pull your hand back. This allows him to miss your outstretched hand. Gradually work up to having him miss your hand two or three times. Now the dog is waving.

High Five: After the dog has learned to shake, we can easily teach him to give a "High Five." With the dog in a sit position, extend your cupped hand as you did with the "shake" trick, but higher at chest level to the dog. (Do not say, "Shake.") As the dog lifts his paw, quickly turn your hand so that your open palm is facing the dog. Touch his paw and say, "High five."

Crawl: Teach dogs to crawl on their bellies. Start with the dog in the down position. Kneel beside him and hold a treat in your hand between the dog's front paws. Hold the treat low on the ground and slowly drag it away from the dog. As the dog begins to move forward without bringing his belly off the ground, reward him with the treat. This trick can be a bit difficult. Set the dog up for success by breaking it down into baby steps. Reward even the slightest forward motion where the dog's belly remains on the floor.

Sad Dog: Teach dogs to lie down and rest their heads on their paws. With the dog in a down position, bring the treat down to the floor. When the dog's chin touches his paws or the floor, reward him. Gradually increase the time that the dog's chin is on the floor or his paws.

Puppy Push Ups: Teach dog to sit, then down, and back to a sit. First, ask the dog for a sit, then a down, and then lure him back into a sit. Reward him with a treat.

Roll Over: Teaches dog to roll over. Start with the dog in a down position. Keeping the treat low, slowly lure the dog's nose to his shoulder. Give him the treat. Continue to shape the behavior by bringing the treat slowly up and over the dog's back until the dog is rolling over completely.

Back Up: This helps build confidence for the dog, because he learns that he can move away from you. It's also a handy trick for him to know, so that he will move when he's under foot. Start in a small space, like a hallway so that the dog does not simply wander off. Have the dog in a standing position. Stand in front of him and walk gently toward him. After the dog takes a step or two backward, reward him with a treat. You can teach a hand signal such as the back of the hand held toward the dog and making a "shooing" motion. Put the behavior on cue by saying, "Back" as he moves backward.

Sit Up: This is a fun and charming trick. Some dogs sit up with their front paws curled at their chests, crossed in front of them, or raised high in the air. Start training this trick by having the dog in the sit position. Do this in a corner, so that the dog can lean against the wall to keep his balance. Stand in front of the dog and hold a treat in front of his nose. Keeping the treat close to his nose, slowly raise it up over the dog's head. He will follow the treat upward raising his front feet off the floor, balancing on his hindquarters. Immediately, when the dog is in this position say, "Sit up" and give him the treat.

Note: This trick is not appropriate for all dogs. Long-bodied dogs such as Dachshunds, or deep-chested dogs like Doberman Pinschers may have difficulty sitting up. Dogs with hip or back problems should not be asked to perform this trick.

Treat On Paw: This trick builds confidence and patience for both dog and child. First, the dog must know how to lie down and to wait (see *The How-To of Training*.) Start with having the dog lie down. Place a dog treat on the dog's paw, keeping your hand hovering over it. Cue the dog to wait. After a couple of seconds, give the dog his release word and allow him to take the treat. As the dog gets proficient at this, you do not need to keep your hand over the treat. You can also gradually increase the time the dog waits. Do not make this game torturous for the dog by having him wait *too* long.

Kids can participate in many competitive sports with their dogs. Start with obedience and have the child help with the training. A dog must be obedience trained before he's able to participate in dog sports and the dog and child must work as a team.

- Agility
- Freestyle
- Rally-O
- Flyball
- Trieball
- Frisbee
- Junior Showmanship
- AKC Canine Good Citizen
- Volunteer visiting therapy dogs

Resources: Websites

Doggone Safe: http://doggonesafe.com/

Doggone Crazy: http://www.doggonecrazy.ca/

Liam Perk Foundation: http://www.liamjperkfoundation.org/

Living With Kids and Dogs: http://www.livingwithkidsanddogs.com/

Family Paws Parent Education: Dogs & Storks, Dog & Baby Connection: http://familypaws.com/

Animal Behavior Associates: Helping Fido Welcome Your Baby: http://www.animalbehaviorassociates.com/helpingfido-baby.htm

Resources: Books, CDs and DVDs

Wag School Books: http://www.wagschoolbooks.com.au

Dogwise: http://dogwise.com/

Books for adults:

Living With Kids and Dogs…Without Losing Your Mind by Colleen Pelar

Raising Puppies and Kids Together – A guide for Parents by Pia Silvani and Lynn Eckhardt

Happy Kids, Happy Dogs: Building a Friendship Right from the Start by Barbara Shumannfang

Parenting With Pets – The Magic of Raising Children with Animals by Christine Hammer and Margaret Hevel

DVDs and CDs for adults:

Helping Fido Welcome Your Baby by Suzanne Hetts and Daniel Estep

Sounds Good Audio CD – Children by Terry Ryan

Sounds Good Audio CD – Babies by Terry Ryan

Books for children:

Good Dog! Kids Teach Kids About Dog Behavior and Training by Evelyn Pang and Hilary Louie

Don't Lick the Dog – Making Friends with Dogs by Wendy Wahman

May I Pet Your Dog? The How-To Guide for Kids Meeting Dogs by Stephanie Calmenson

Meeting Milo by Yvette Van Veen and David Perks

DVDs and CDs for children:

Dog Training for Children DVD by Ian Dunbar

15

The Art of Positive Practice and Premise

There are those who think that positive dog training methods translate to permissiveness. I've been asked if I ever say no to my dogs. My answer is yes. I've been called a weenie flinger and a praise addict, but I'm not overly permissive. I've been asked if I ever raise my voice to my dogs. My answer to this question is yes, as well. If my dog is in danger, I'll turn up the volume to level 11 if necessary to keep him safe.

I'm only human; a mere mortal who sometimes loses it (a little). I'm sure my dogs wonder what my clients and readers would think of Ms. Positive Reinforcement if they could see her during the occasional un-Zen-like episode. Like our own children, our dogs, even without the benefit of opposable thumbs, can push buttons and twist nerves. My redemption lies (usually) in the ability to catch myself, breathe deeply, take my own advice, eat an entire chocolate cake, and carry on.

I've trained dogs for more than a few years. In the beginning, I used choke chains, compulsory methods, and a militant attitude. These combative methods worked in producing a servile dog, but that's not who I am. It's not who my dog is either.

Positive training methods look more like good parenting than military training. Positive methods do not establish leadership through dominance, force, and intimidation, as the compulsory training methods do. I believe the best leaders are the ones who say the least and lead with their hearts, not their wills. Positive methods establish benevolent leadership, making me the type of leader that my dog wants to follow.

My dog Mr. MoJo has been known to be reactive and a bit of a bully toward other dogs. Thus, I used to walk him very early in the morning in a state of avoidance sprinkled with a dash of denial. At this early hour, we usually had the park to ourselves, with the exception of the occasional distant coyote. However, the arrival of springtime brought out the dog walkers en mass. I found myself tightening the leash, wondering what these people were doing in "our" park, and where I could find a good dog trainer to help change MoJo's behavior.

I thunked myself on the forehead and remembered that I did know a good dog trainer (me). I called her out of her state of denial and got to work. We went from avoidance to awesome through awareness, positive and effective training methods, and patience. This turned our walks from frustration to fun. Now, instead of conflict, we have composure on both ends of the leash.

There is no end to education. It is not that you read a book, pass an examination, and finish with education. The whole of life, from the moment you are born to the moment you die, is a process of learning.
—**Jiddu Krishnamurti**

How Dogs Learn

Dogs come equipped with certain innate knowledge—instincts designed for survival, such as breeding and hunting. Beyond this preordained knowledge, dogs must learn the rest of what they need to know about life. We are their teachers of how to live life in the human world.

Dogs learn from environment and experience, as humans do. At birth, puppies begin to absorb information from their littermates, parents, other dogs, and humans. They can learn by imitating the behavior of other dogs, and they will experiment to find out what behaviors work. Early on, puppies learn to read signals, the body language of other dogs. They learn bite inhibition and consequences to their behavior.

Effective training takes these things into consideration and channels them into learning through open lines of communication and understanding.

Believe nothing, no matter where you read it or who said it, not even if I have said it, unless it agrees with your own reason and your own common sense. —**Buddha**

Training From the Heart and Mind

Successful training comes from the heart as well as the mind and contributes to the wellbeing of both teacher and student. This was vividly illustrated to me in a consultation I did with a family that had adopted a five-year-old Shih-poo mill dog. The dog was showing fear aggression by barking and nipping at friends and family members, especially the nine-year-old daughter. The family had been advised to put their hands on their hips, get "big," and march past the dog when he displayed this "naughtiness." They were told that doing this would prove to the dog that they were dominant and in charge.

When I explained that we would no longer be doing that (and why), the little girl let out a sigh of relief and said, "Oh, good!" She knew that what they had been doing was not what was in her heart. By the end of the session, we had the dog voluntarily approaching the girl and touching her hand. It was something everyone felt good about–a touching experience.

This chapter discusses learning theory, methodology, and scientific principles as applied to dog training. It's valuable information. However, experiments are done in sterile, consistent laboratories with animals (usually rats or pigeons, not dogs) given limited options for their behavior and monitored by unfailingly accurate, data-spewing computers. That is just not the same as training a dog to do a down stay while you accept a package delivery during your four-year-old's birthday party.

We are inconsistent humans training dogs in an environment with many distracting elements. We need to know and understand the science of the laboratory *and* how to apply it intuitively to life with Fido. Remember that Fido did not read the research and analyze the data. This chapter is intended to build a bridge between the real laboratory and real life.

It is what we know already that often prevents us from learning
–Claude Bernard

Positive Training –General Theory and Principle

Positive: Both positive and compulsory training methods work. However, there is a difference between simply acquiring a behavior and having the dog learn. Furthermore, a positive approach is the only method that does not damage the relationship between owner and dog. In fact, it strengthens it. Positive methods respect the individuality and spirit of dogs. They just feel right. I'm positive of it.

Timing: Because dogs don't understand our lectures and explanations, they must rely on the association between a behavior and the ensuing consequence (reward or correction). In order for them to do so, the consequence must immediately follow the behavior, as in one second. Timing is paramount for learning, and it teaches the dog to respond immediately.

Consistency: Lack of consistency engenders confusion and anxiety for dogs. Everyone who is involved in the dog's life should be on the same page, including sitters, walkers, and frequent visitors. If we are consistent with rules, boundaries, and communication, dogs will generalize their behavior among humans, realizing that all humans know the same tricks.

Motivation (Rewards): A dog must be motivated to do a behavior. Rewards are motivation, a paycheck in human terms. My German shepherd will serve me coffee in bed for a baby carrot. Food is a motivator for most dogs and easy to use. However, let's not overlook toys, play, exercise, praise, and affection as inspiration for dogs.

Rewards are anything the dog likes. Choose what most motivates the dog, and make it special by limiting it to training and good behavior (not just for being wonderful and cute). Vary the rewards by making a trail mix of treats. This makes it more interesting because the dog does not know what high-value reward he's going to get next.

At times, you will need to increase the motivation by increasing the value of the reward. While lower value rewards work well at home where distractions are low, situations that are more difficult require a higher-value prize. However, if the dog refuses rewards, he may be too distracted or stressed, and we need to adjust the environment accordingly.

Corrections: Corrections are not punishment, but feedback. They are verbal cues used to interrupt the dog from the behavior and redirect him. Time outs can also serve as corrections by giving the dog a short (30-seconds) break, so that you can both regroup.

A teacher who is attempting to teach without inspiring the pupil with a desire to learn is hammering on cold iron. –**Horace Mann**

Training Principles and Application

Instead of teaching the dog, let's allow him to learn. There is a subtle but very important difference between this concept and that of compulsory, dominance-based obedience training. The best we can do for dogs is to present the opportunity for them to learn and to be successful instead of putting them through boot camp.

First, we'll start with the science, the immutable facts of how dogs learn, and then we'll enter the realm of that which cannot be taught in a book or a classroom. Happy training combines scientific method and mindfulness, communication and common sense, ethology and ethics.

Operant Conditioning

Dogs are avaricious animals, and we have good stuff that they want. Dogs learn to work the environment with their behavior to get those things that they want from us.

The difference between classical conditioning and operant conditioning is that in operant conditioning the subject *operates* on the environment with behavior.

Operant conditioning is founded on the theory that future behavior is based on consequences. Behavior that produces a pleasant consequence will be repeated, and behavior that produces an unpleasant consequence will decrease.

In dog training, we capitalize on this theory by manipulating the consequences with reinforcement in order to shape future behavior. This principle is usually associated with Edward Thorndike, who said that if an association is followed by a "satisfying state of affairs," it would be strengthened; and if it is followed by an "annoying state of affairs," it will be weakened.

Thorndike found this in experiments with hungry cats. A cat was placed in a box that could be opened if the animal pressed a lever or pulled a loop. Thorndike noted the amount of time it took the cat to free itself in successive trials. He discovered that during the first few trials the cat would respond in ineffective ways. Then, through trial and error, would finally free itself. With each successive trial, it took the cat less and less time to escape. This experiment showed that the correct response was reinforced by its consequence, release from the box.

Classical Conditioning

Like humans, dogs learn by association. Ivan Pavlov demonstrated this in his famous study of dogs salivating in response to being fed.

His findings showed that two stimuli become associated when repeatedly presented closely together and will elicit a reflexive response. Pavlov noticed that his dogs began to salivate whenever he entered the room, even when he was not bringing them food. This reflex was innate—an unconditioned response that required no learning. Food was an unconditioned stimulus. Salivation was an unconditioned response.

Pavlov discovered that any object or event that the dogs learned to associate with food (such as the lab assistant) would trigger the same response. This must have been learned, because they had not previously done it. Their behavior had changed. The behavioral change must have been the result of learning.

The lab assistant was originally a neutral stimulus (a neutral stimulus produces no response). What happened was the neutral stimulus became associated with an unconditioned stimulus, which was the food.

In his experiment, Pavlov used a bell as a neutral stimulus. Whenever he gave food to his dogs, he also rang a bell. After a number of repetitions, he rang the bell without giving the dogs food. The bell on its own caused an increase in salivation. The dogs had learned an association between the bell and the food, and a new behavior resulted. Because this response was learned (or conditioned), it was called a conditioned response. The neutral stimulus became a conditioned stimulus.

In summary, classical conditioning involves learning to associate an unconditioned stimulus that already elicits a particular reflex response with a new, conditioned stimulus, so that the new stimulus elicits the same response. The unconditioned stimulus is the thing or experience that originally produces the reflexive, innate response. The response to this is called the unconditioned response. The neutral stimulus is a new stimulus that does not produce a response. When the neutral stimulus becomes associated with the unconditioned stimulus, it becomes a conditioned stimulus. The conditioned response is the response to the conditioned stimulus.

We see examples of classical conditioning happening every day when a dog gets excited as the leash is brought out or when the car keys are picked up. The dog anticipates these things with joy. The other side of the classical conditioning coin is the dog cowering when the brush appears, if he is not comfortable being groomed.

Speaking of the other side of the classical conditioning coin, I wonder if the dogs in Pavlov's experiments learned that when they salivated, Pavlov's conditioned response was to write in his notebook.

Counter Conditioning

Counter conditioning and operant conditioning are easily confused. To be clear, classical conditioning deals with reflexive, automatic responses. They are involuntary behaviors, not those that are learned or offered voluntarily. Salivation is an automatic reflexive response. Sitting is voluntary, learned behavior.

Counter conditioning works with the reflexive or emotional responses. It is the method used to replace a previously classical-conditioned response with a new classical-conditioned response. This happens when the dog learns an association between two stimuli, as described in the definition of classical conditioning above. Counter conditioning generates changes that occur in the dog's emotional state on a reflexive level.

In reality, observable behavior sequences include both operant and classical conditioning.

The two components are also present in emotions, with most responses being a combination of emotional and physiological effects. A dog in a stressful situation might experience the physiological event of increased heart rate and the release of stress hormones. There can also be an automatic emotional response such as fear.

Physiological reactions are strongly connected to emotions, and it's virtually impossible to separate them. We cannot live even a short distance from our bodies, no matter how much we might want to. Dogs do not. In training dogs, we must remember that emotions are the link between body and mind.

Reactions to reflexive emotions can be learned. Therefore, we can teach dogs a valuable coping skill, which is to take a voluntary action when an emotion is felt. Counter conditioning changes the way dogs perceive and *feel*, which consequently changes how he *acts* in life situations. Counter conditioning changes the physiological state (production of stress hormones), thus creating a psychological state conducive to learning.

We must be careful with the use of counter conditioning, especially when working with aggression. Rewards must truly build a new, positive association with the stimulus. Food is a strong and effective motivator, yet we must know the difference between using it as a motivator and using it as a distraction. Food used as a distraction can merely suppress the behavior, not change it. Rewards must reinforce the desired behavior (calm or nonreactive in the presence of the stimulus) and cause change on an emotional and reflexive level.

Reinforcement makes a behavior stronger. Distraction can mask the behavior or override it instead of modifying it. For example, if an aggressive dog is more motivated by treats than the need to aggress, he will be nonreactive in the presence of the stimulus only when the treats are present. The behavior hasn't been changed and will be presented when the food is not available.

Leadership and learning are indispensable to each other.

–John F. Kennedy

Basic Principles of Canine Learning

Good news here for the analytical, mathematical readers among you. Learning follows a pattern or formula, which is A-B-C. This is the only part of training that a computer could do.

A=antecedent   B=behavior   C=consequence

Any variation in this formula means that learning will be impeded or inhibited. Behaviors are learned when an antecedent is associated with a consequence. Consequence always drives behavior, even though sometimes it seems like the antecedent is at the wheel. For example, it appears that the starting gun (antecedent) makes the track star run (behavior), but the consequence, the gold, the medal, the fame, the endorsements (consequence) is what actually drives the behavior.

The rule: consequence drives behavior. Successful manipulation of consequences, along with good communication and timing, make for a solid learning environment.

Antecedents
An antecedent is an event that takes place before a behavior occurs.
- Cues
- Commands
- Prompts
- Targets
- Lures

Consequences
Consequences are events that either reinforce (strengthen behavior) or punish (weaken behavior.)

Consequences are controlled by:
- Adding something desirable, such as a food treat (positive reinforcement)
- Subtracting something desirable, such as a food treat (negative punishment)
- Adding something undesirable, such as putting pressure on the choke collar (positive punishment)
- Subtracting something undesirable, such as pressure on the choke collar (negative reinforcement)

Rewards
Rewards do not equal reinforcement. Behaviors are reinforced. People (dogs) are rewarded.

Rewards are often determined from the trainer's perspective, but in reality, only the dog can determine what is rewarding. I'd rather get twenty dollars than a liver snack any day. My dog, not so much.

Positive and Negative Markers
Positive and negative markers are feedback for the dog. They let him know if the behavior he's offering is the correct one. Many trainers use "yes" and "no." A word of caution: these are emotionally charged words. A negative marker such as "oh, oh" or "try again" are less likely to elicit our emotions, thus we're able to deliver them with a neutral, non-judgmental tone. This fact makes clickers an excellent choice for markers. Markers are used simply to deliver information, to let the dog know whether he's offering the desired behavior or not.

You may wonder why we don't use praise as a marker. We talk to our dogs all day long and tell them they are good just for being the cute and wonderful beings that they are. A positive marker gives the dog feedback by telling him he's *doing* the right thing and is a harbinger of the forthcoming reward. Praise can be the reward, but not the marker.

Verbal and Visual Cues

It seems that some dogs understand every word of our lectures and stream of consciousness. I'm reminded of Gary Larson's Far Side cartoon that illuminates the point. The cartoon is divided into two illustrations with the first captioned, "What We Say to Dogs" and the second "What They Hear." What we say to dogs is, "OK, Ginger! I've had it! You stay out of the garbage! Understand, Ginger? Stay out of the garbage, or else!" What dogs hear is, "Blah blah GINGER blah blah blah blah blah blah blah blah GINGER blah blah blah blah blah…."

Dogs learn by association. We've taught them that the word sit means to put his bum on the floor. We will confuse him if we sometimes say "sit down" or "park it." We'll mystify him if we repeat "sit, sit, sit" or ask a question, "Would you please sit?" Short and simple is key.

Tone of voice should be consistent and clear, yet upbeat, with cues delivered firmly. Markers should be given with an assertive, even, and gentle tone. Some dogs are more sensitive than others and cower if markers and cues are too forceful. Others may become over stimulated if cues and markers are given with too much exuberance.

Hand signals need also be clear. Pointing to the floor for a sit and pointing to the floor a bit lower for a down are not clear to the dog, especially when you consider how this would look from the dog's point of view. It is difficult for humans to keep their gestures consistent, but gestures are easier for dogs to read. Be sure that hands and mouth are saying the same thing.

A teacher affects eternity; he can never tell where his influence stops.
—**Henry Adams**

Principles of Operant Conditioning

Operant conditioning techniques and procedures were first studied by E. L. Thorndike and later expanded by B. F. Skinner. These studies showed that with classical conditioning, new emotional and reflexive reactions developed in response to previously neutral environmental stimuli. Operant conditioning explains how a behavior develops that operates on the environment to elicit behavioral consequences.

Operant conditioning is a method of learning that occurs through rewards and punishments, where an association is made between a behavior and a consequence for that behavior.

Behaviorist B.F. Skinner coined the term operant conditioning. Skinner used the term *operant* to refer to any "active behavior that operates upon the environment to generate consequences."

Skinner expanded on the earlier work of both Pavlov and Thorndike and developed the principles of operant conditioning. He defined the concept of "reward" as that which has "positive reinforcement" effects (increased likelihood of a behavior occurring).

Even painful consequences can increase the likelihood of behaviors that eliminate or avoid such consequences. Thus, Skinner described their function as "negative reinforcements." According to Skinner, reinforcement, whether positive or negative, is the process of increasing behavioral probabilities. When followed by a reinforcer, behaviors will increase in frequency.

Skinner also defined punishment as behavioral probabilities may be decreased by consequences. Any behavior that is followed by punishment decreases in frequency.

Examples of operant conditioning are evident in everyday life. Children eat their broccoli in order to earn dessert or video game time as a reward. Here, the promise of reward causes an increase in behavior. Operant conditioning can also be used to decrease or prevent a behavior with the removal of an undesirable outcome or the use of punishment. A child may be told she will lose video privileges for taunting her little sister. This prospective punishment may lead to a decrease in the disorderly behavior.

Reinforcement

Reinforcement is any event that strengthens or increases the behavior it follows.

Conventional definitions characterize positive as good and negative as bad. Punishment is defined as infliction of a penalty; reinforcement as the process of strengthening. These terms are described a bit differently in the context of behavior modification and training.

To behaviorists and trainers the term punishment is something that *decreases* the likelihood of a behavior being repeated. Reinforcement is that which *increases* the likelihood that the behavior will be repeated.

Eyebrows are raised and confusion sets in with the phrase "positive punishment." In the context of training, positive simply means that something has been added, with no bearing on whether the thing is "good" (a toy or treat) or "bad" (a verbal or physical correction).

The term negative refers to something being taken away or subtracted. Again, it does not matter whether the thing that's removed is "good" (toy or treat) or "bad" (leash correction, shock or choke collar).

Punishment and Reinforcement

There are two types of reinforcement and two types of punishment:

Positive Reinforcement

Positive reinforcement means that favorable events or outcomes happen after the behavior is presented. A response or behavior is strengthened by the addition of something that is considered pleasant, such as praise or a direct reward.

Negative Reinforcement

Negative reinforcement involves the removal of unfavorable events or outcomes after a behavior is presented. A response or behavior is strengthened by the removal of something considered unpleasant, such as pressure on a choke collar or the shock of an electronic collar*.

Positive Punishment

Positive punishment means that unfavorable events or outcomes happen after the behavior is presented. A response or behavior is weakened by the addition of something that is considered unpleasant, such as a leash correction or shock of an electronic collar.

Negative Punishment

Negative punishment involves the removal of favorable events or outcomes after a behavior is presented. A response or behavior is weakened by the removal of something considered pleasant, such as praise or a direct reward.

*Note: Shock collars and leash corrections are not techniques recommended by this author. Technically, these coercive methods work to elicit or prevent behaviors, but they are harmful to both the physical and psychological wellbeing of the dog and will destroy his trust in your relationship.

The Adverse Effects of Positive Punishment and Negative Reinforcement

Frequent use of negative reinforcement will lead to escape and/or avoidance behavior. For example, if the floor of an operant conditioning chamber delivers a mild electrical shock, and a rat presses a bar, which turns off the shock, then the behavior of pressing the bar is negatively reinforced. The rat will always experience the shock, but through negative reinforcement, the rat learns to escape the unpleasant event by pressing the lever that terminates the shock.

Avoidance behavior also develops because of negative reinforcement and typically appears following learned escape behavior. If a rat learns to press a lever to avoid a brief shock, and if pressing delays the next onset of shock, eventually that rat begins to press the lever even before the shock is delivered. In this case, the rat may never experience the shock, but it will continue to press the bar, because it has been negatively reinforced.

We can see how the use of shock collars and leash corrections as negative reinforcement work to elicit or prevent behaviors in dogs. However, like the rat in the laboratory, dogs learn escape and/or avoidance behaviors, and whom they learn to escape and avoid is us.

Punishment

By and large, punishment is not an effective means of behavior control.

However, it is valuable to know the definition and dynamics of punishment in order to understand why it's not advocated.

In his studies of operant conditioning, Skinner described punishment as well as reinforcement. Positive punishment decreases the probability of a behavior through the addition of an aversive stimulus as a behavioral consequence. Negative punishment involves the removal of a pleasant stimulus as a behavioral consequence. The stimulus that is presented in positive punishment is usually a painful or otherwise aversive stimulus, while those stimuli that are removed in negative punishment are desirable ones.

According to Skinner, a stimulus cannot be considered a punisher if its presentation (positive punishment) or removal (negative punishment) does not decrease the likelihood of a behavior. For instance, it may seem that shaking a can filled with coins would be a good punishment for a barking dog. If, however, the dog continues to bark with the same frequency, then shaking the can is not a punisher, and the dog has not been punished. However, there are factors that will modify its effectiveness.

Skinner observed that every behavior serves some purpose for the organism, and if the likelihood of a behavior is decreased, it will reappear unless a new behavior has been shaped that serves the same purpose for the organism. Punishment doesn't extinguish behaviors; rather, it simply reduces the likelihood that they will appear.

As mentioned above, another problem with punishment is what happens to the relationship between the punisher and the punished. A dog may come to find the person who continually punishes him as the aversive, and he will attempt to escape or avoid the individual, because he associates him or her with punishment.

In order for punishment to be effective, it must occur immediately after the behavior. It must be firm, but not overpowering, and it must consistently follow every occurrence of the behavior to be reduced. Delayed punishment is ineffective in that it negates future punishment as random or nonexistent. It's like the empty threat of "just wait until your father comes home." In order for punishment to decrease the occurrence of a behavior, it must occur immediately after the inappropriate behavior.

Premack

My Border collie will do my taxes for a liver snack. This is the tenet of the Premack Principle, derived by Professor David Premack, from a study of Cebus monkeys. In human behavior modification, Premack's Principle suggests that if a person wants to perform a given activity, they will perform a less desirable activity to get the more desirable one.

Relying on this rule is one way to positively reinforce behavior by using activities as reinforcers. According to the Premack Principle, a typically higher frequency behavior can be used to positively reinforce a desired behavior that is normally lower in frequency. If high-probability behaviors (more desirable behaviors) are made contingent upon lower-probability behaviors (less desirable behaviors), then the lower-probability behaviors are more likely to occur.

More simply put: The dog will learn that if he does the behavior that we want him to do, he'll get what he wants.

Example: The dog wants to go for a walk. We've already taught him how to sit, so if he sits quietly while we snap on the leash, we will then open the door, and he gets to go on his walk.

Reinforcers

A consequential stimulus is not a reinforcer if it's presentation (positive reinforcement) or removal (negative reinforcement) does not increase the likelihood that the behavior will occur. For instance, it may seem that a food reward would reinforce a dog for coming when called. However, if the behavior (coming when called) does not increase in frequency when he's given food for doing so, then food is not a reinforcer.

Two types of stimuli positively reinforce behaviors. These are described as primary reinforcers and secondary (conditioned) reinforcers. According to Skinner, reinforcement (an increase in the probability of a behavior) is much better at controlling behavior than punishment (a decrease in the probability of a behavior).

Primary Reinforcers

A primary reinforcer is something that a dog needs for survival and is common to all members of the species: air, water, food, sex, social interaction, and sleep. Primary reinforcers are often used in operant conditioning because of their powerful and direct impact in modifying behavior. This power is due to their innate biological value.

Secondary Reinforcers

A secondary reinforcer is something that the dog wants but does not need for survival, and it is not common to all members of the species: toys, praise, or petting. Dogs must be taught that secondary reinforcers are important by connecting them to something that the dog wants. A secondary or conditioned reinforcer is that which increases the probability of behavior because of its consistent association with primary reinforcers. This is classical conditioning (think Pavlov) at work.

For most humans, money is a powerful secondary reinforcer. Even though money, in and of itself, has no real use, it is a reinforcer because it can buy the things that meet essential needs for survival, such as food and shelter. This is an example of classical conditioning with money as the secondary (conditioned or learned) reinforcer and food, etc. as the primary (unconditioned, not learned) reinforcer. Because money has been associated with these primary reinforcers, it has acquired the power to increase the probability of behavior all on its own.

Reinforcement Schedules

It is worth mentioning that a variety of reinforcement schedules have been developed in laboratory studies. Real life training has shown that most of these are ineffective and/or impossible to put into practice. The exceptions are that of variable ratio and differential reinforcement. Here, we'll have a brief look at various reinforcement schedules, why they work or don't work, and their effect on the art of happy training.

Continuous Reinforcement (CR)

A continuous reinforcement schedule means that the dog is rewarded after every correct response. For example, the dog is rewarded after every sit.

Continuous reinforcement is problematic, because the dog often receives too many rewards. CR temporarily increases the frequency of behavior but fails at maintaining regularity. Furthermore, it does not improve the quality of behavior. If a dog is rewarded for every correct response, this means he's been rewarded for all responses, be they excellent, average, or inferior.

Consequently, the quality of the behavior will decline, because the dog expects all responses to be rewarded. Slackers show up for work every day, because they're paid every Friday whether or not they performed their jobs well.

Additionally, CR makes fading out food rewards difficult. Both trainer and dog become dependent on the presence food. I call this a "Show Me the Money Dog," which means the dog will only comply when he sees what's in it for him. You have become a human Pez dispenser, and the dog will only work for you when he feels like having a treat. The first time you fail to deliver, he'll cease to comply.

Fixed Duration Reinforcement (FD)
A fixed duration reinforcement schedule means that the dog is rewarded after a specific time; for example, after every five seconds of sit-stay.

FD will not improve performance or consistency in the quality of behavior.

Typically, behavior quality improves as the dog anticipates the reward but then decreases immediately after the he's rewarded. This is because he anticipates the next reward.

Fixed Ratio Reinforcement (FR)
A fixed ratio reinforcement schedule means that the dog is rewarded after a specific number of responses; for example, after every third sit.

FR might initially increase the frequency of the behavior, but the dog may hurry through the repetitions in anticipation of the next reward, thus decreasing the quality of the behavior. Furthermore, the dog may become frustrated or quit entirely if too many responses are required for a single reward.

Fixed schedules do not reliably increase the frequency, quality, or duration of behavior, nor do they reinforce the dog for improvement of behavior, because they fail to provide feedback.

Slackers happily show up for work on Fridays because they expect a paycheck, but they drag themselves in on Monday mornings (FD.) Paying workers by piece rate (FR) may increase production, but often quality will take a back seat. If the quota is too high, workers will simply go on strike.

Variable Duration Reinforcement (VD)

A variable duration reinforcement schedule means that the dog is rewarded after random length periods. For example, the dog is rewarded after varying durations of sit-stay. On a variable duration reinforcement schedule of 5, the duration of an average sit-stay is 5 seconds.

Variable duration reinforcement works well for getting dogs to perform for increasing lengths of time and for phasing out rewards. Since the time between rewards is random, the behavior does not decrease immediately after each reward, as it can in FD. This is because the dog anticipates that the next reward could be delivered at any second.

Variable duration reinforcement in the laboratory would hold to a strict schedule and have us doing mathematical calculations in our heads. A variable duration reinforcement of 5-second sit stays would have us reward the dog after 5, 1, 7, 2, 6, 5, 9, 3, 4, and 8 seconds. I say save it for the lab (as in laboratory, not Labrador). Don't worry about exact timing. We can instead use a Random Duration Reinforcement schedule, which rewards the dog after random lengths of sit-stay and progressively increases the average duration. This will increase the duration of the sit-stays and phase out rewards, but it will not improve the quality of the behavior.

Variable Ratio Reinforcement (VR)

A variable ratio reinforcement schedule means that the dog is rewarded after an unpredictable number of responses. A variable ratio reinforcement schedule of 5, means that the dog is rewarded after varying numbers of sits averaging five sits per reward.

VR reinforcement maintains high frequencies of behavior, increases duration, and facilitates phasing out food rewards. Variable ratio reinforcement has the dog working for an increasing number of repetitions without reward.

Variable Ratio Reinforcement is what's at work when we humans play a slot machine. We keep pulling that lever, because the machine randomly reinforces the behavior. Sometimes we win; sometimes we win big; and we're convinced that the next try will win the reward.

Here again, the laboratory would have us doing the math in our heads. Instead, we can use a Random Ratio Reinforcement schedule, which doesn't strain our brains. Reward sits at random, and the dog will enthusiastically present sits at a high frequency. He's a sitting machine.

Variable ratio reinforcement will increase the frequency of the behavior, but not the quality, as you are reinforcing all sits, whether they are above or below average.

Differential Reinforcement (DR)

A differential reinforcement schedule means that the dog is reinforced for specific chosen behaviors. Additionally DR can be used to raise the criteria of behaviors by giving rewards of varied value according to the quality of the performance (higher pay for higher quality).

Differential reinforcement increases the probability that a dog will choose a specific behavior by varying and manipulating what is reinforced. Following are some examples of DR:

• Reinforce alternative behaviors, which give the dog a new focus (changing the subject, if you will). For example, the dog comes away from the window when called and stops barking. Here, we've already taught the dog to come when called, so we can have him refocus and interrupt the barking with a recall. From this point, we could also train the dog to shush on cue.

• Reinforce any alternative behavior other than the undesirable one. For example, if the dog is whining for attention, we could reinforce any moment that the whining stops, such as chewing on a toy or looking away at something that has distracted him. (It should be noted that in this example we want to *capture* the moment of quiet behavior. Distracting the dog with a treat while he's whining will reinforce the behavior of whining.)

• Reinforce behaviors that are incompatible with the undesirable one. For example, reinforce the dog for sitting instead of jumping up.

• Raise the bar on the current behavior by reinforcing only higher levels of compliance or skill. For example, the dog is reinforced only for quick and snappy recalls. By rewarding only the above-average responses, the quality of the behavior improves.

Differential reinforcement teaches the dog to choose the new, desired behavior over the old, undesirable behavior. This is because we've made the new behavior more appealing than the former one, even though the surrounding circumstances haven't changed. For example, the dog still sees the mail carrier approach the house every day, but now he chooses to come away from the window and sit quietly beside you.

Always remember that we can choose what to reinforce.

Where you tend a rose, my lad, a thistle cannot grow.
                                                    –Frances Hodgson Burnett

Capturing and Shaping (Behaviors Offered)

Simple behaviors can be taught easily and quickly by capturing them. When a dog offers a behavior, such as sit (which they often do), one can simply mark and reward.

Shaping: Shaping is a process that uses operant conditioning to develop a new behavior by reinforcing successive approximations until the desired or *target* behavior is achieved. The method uses small and gradual steps toward the desired form of behavior.

Begin the shaping process by reinforcing what the dog already knows (i.e. sit on cue). Then, gradually reinforce only selective variations of behaviors that lead to the target behavior.

Shaping is often used to teach behaviors that are more complex or those that take precise timing to capture. To shape a behavior means to break it down into small steps and then mark and reward each step until the dog learns the entire behavior.

A down could be shaped either by capturing, luring, or a combination of both. Let's say that the dog is standing up from a sitting position whenever you attempt to lure him into a down (having the dog follow a treat with his nose to the floor). Break the behavior down into smaller steps by luring the dog into just looking down at the floor while remaining in a sit. Mark and reward this step. Gradually lure the dog's nose closer to the floor, marking and rewarding as you go. Next, draw the treat away from the dog and then mark and reward any indication that the dog is going to lie down, such as moving a paw forward. Gradually raise the criteria by only marking and rewarding behavior that is closer to the goal. Finally, you will only mark and reward the behavior of lying down.

A down could also be taught by capturing (very effective when teaching a dog to relax–see Zen Down). First, capture a sit. Next, capture the dog looking at the floor. Then, capture a paw moving forward, and finally capture the down.

Shaping by capturing is very effective because it has the dog thinking. It's his idea. He's not just following a treat.

Modeling, Luring, Molding (Elicited Behaviors)

Evoking behaviors and then marking and rewarding them, can teach a dog new behavior.

Modeling: We primates are experts at learning by imitating the behavior of others. Dogs are not prone to imitating human behavior, but they do learn by emulating other dogs. If you have a dog already trained to come when called, you can capture the behavior when your new puppy follows him when you call.

Luring: Behaviors can be taught by luring dogs with treats into the desired behavior. For example: to teach sit, hold the treat directly in front of the dog's nose and slowly bring the treat up and over his head. As the dog's nose follows the treat, he will naturally put his bum on the floor. Mark (with a click or a verbal marker) and reward the sit (deliver the treat).

There are some caveats to luring. Lures must be faded and eliminated as quickly as possible, or both trainer and dog can become dependent on them. As described earlier, a continuous reinforcement schedule often causes a decline in the quality and frequency of a behavior, because the dog expects that he will always be rewarded. Additionally, continuous luring will create and even reinforce passivity, because the dog does not have to think about his behavior or the consequences. He merely has to follow the treat like a magnet with his nose.

There is another problem with luring. We want to avoid luring a dog after he's refused or not complied with a cue. If we lure a dog to get him unstuck, we simply teach him that we'll help him to get unstuck. He'll wait for the lure instead of offering the behavior. For example, if I produce a treat for my dog *after* his refusal to come when called, I've just taught him not to come on the first call, but to wait for the lure.

A final word of warning about using lures: never lure a dog into a fearful situation. Doing so will make you and the lure (food) untrustworthy.

Molding: Physically assisting a dog into a behavior (pushing his bum down to have him sit) is not an effective training method. It's distracting for the dog and does not engender responsibility for learning. If I physically position my dog into a sit after his refusal of the cue, he'll not learn how to sit. He'll learn that I will help him if he doesn't comply.

Chaining: In shaping complex behaviors, an operant conditioning procedure known as chaining may be employed. Here, one behavior is linked to another by use of a discriminative stimulus that is always associated with the next behavior being reinforced. This process allows for a series of behaviors to happen before reinforcement occurs. Eventually, the discriminative stimuli that link each behavior to the next may be phased out, creating a sequence where one behavior cues the next. Reinforcement only occurs at the end of the chain of behaviors.

Let's say I want to teach a dog to sit, take a toy, go to his bed, lie down, and then drop the toy. The dog already knows how to sit and lie down on cue. To create the behavior chain, I would first teach the dog to go to his bed on cue. The cue could be something like "bedtime." * Once he's reliably going to his bed, I would teach him to drop the toy on cue. (This toy should be specific to this behavior chain.)

Finally, I would present the toy (a second discriminative stimulus), have the dog sit, take the toy, go to his bed (when the cue "bedtime" is given), lie down, and then drop the toy. The dog is only reinforced after he drops the toy, completing the entire behavioral sequence.

The dog learns that sitting brings about the toy, which signals that going to bed, lying down, and dropping the toy will be reinforced.

"Bedtime" is a handy behavior to have when guests arrive. Instead of running to the door and jumping on guests, the dog can get his specific toy, go to bed, drop the toy, and wait for the guest to come greet him. This could be paired with the sound of the doorbell ringing. Whenever the doorbell rings, I'll say "bedtime," and the dog will go wait with his toy on his bed. Eventually, if done consistently, the behavior will happen without the verbal cue, and the doorbell will become the cue.

Superstitious Learning: Although managed during operant conditioning, reinforcement can occur by chance naturally within the environment. Superstitious learning can happen when reinforcement occurs independently of a specific behavior.

Humans demonstrate superstitious learning when we think that knocking on wood, finding a four-leaf clover, or wearing one's lucky underwear will bring good luck. If Brian happened to wear his new boxers to the game on the day that his team won a playoff spot, you can bet he'll wear that "lucky" underwear to every game thereafter. Brian's behavior (wearing of choice undergarment) had nothing to do with the reinforcement (his team winning). Yet, it has increased the likelihood of him repeating the behavior. Superstitious learning can occur with punishment as well. If Brian's team had lost (punishment), it would result in a decreased likelihood of him repeating the behavior (wearing of the boxers).

Extinction

Reinforcement, whether intentional (in training) or unintentional (from the environment), means that behavior will be repeated.

Extinction is an operant conditioning process as well as a one of classical conditioning. It occurs when a reliable reinforcement or punishment is no longer a consequence for a given behavior. Since the behavior no longer produces a reinforcing result, it is rarely offered and usually disappears altogether. We commonly see a determined burst of the behavior when a behavior is first put on extinction. This is called an extinction burst and often occurs along with new, interrelated behaviors. Because the expected consequence is no longer happening, the dog offers the known behavior more diligently, frenetically, or furiously. He may even try another new behavior to elicit the expected consequence.

Extinction may not be permanent, as spontaneous recovery can occur. Behaviors can be reacquired if reinforcement is a reestablished consequence for behavior.

Desensitization

Desensitization slowly and systematically changes the dog's internal emotional state through controlled, gradual exposure to stimuli that the dog finds unnerving. The goal is to change how the dog feels when presented with the stimulus that triggers the negative emotion (like fear). This is accomplished by coupling the stimulus with a positive event such as treats or playtime.

The key to successful desensitization is to control the environment during treatment. In an ideal world, the dog would never be exposed to stimuli that sent him over the edge during the desensitization process. If this happens, it puts us back to the beginning. For example, the dog that is afraid of unfamiliar people has been desensitized to the point of staying calm when he sees a person across the street. If suddenly a friendly stranger comes around the corner and reaches to pet the dog, he will be startled, react, and learn that people are, in fact, untrustworthy.

It is paramount to work within a controlled stimulus gradient that raises the criteria but keeps the dog just under threshold. If the dog is too far below threshold or over it, desensitization and learning do not take place.

Successful desensitization will have the dog contextually habituate to the stimuli, (i.e. he is comfortable with an unfamiliar person approaching when out on a walk as well as when he encounters one while shopping or at the groomer).

In the beginner's mind, there are many possibilities; in the expert's mind, there are few. —Suzuki Roshi

Mixing Art and Science for Happy Training

This chapter has presented immutable scientific fact and formula, along with ideas that cannot be learned in the classroom or laboratory. If we fill our heads with facts, we must also make room in our hearts for truth. The palette of dog training holds many colors from which to choose. We can create new hues by mixing the lessons of the laboratory and real life, of experimentation and intuition.

The Art of Happy Training Requires Choosing the Right Medium

A friend once gave me a book called Home How To. *It was a do-it-yourself manual on home repair. She practically threw it at me saying, "Take this book! It's gotten me into so much trouble!"*

"If you want something done right, do it yourself" is the old maxim, which holds true for many things. For example, I have another friend who always says that she has more time than money. She dug up her main water line and repaired it herself. That turned out just fine.

Whatever the project or problem, we need to make a choice. We must choose whether to do it ourselves or to hire a professional. I've hired professionals to do everything from remodeling my kitchen to coloring my hair. I've attempted doing some of these things myself–all with varying degrees of success.

I've had "professionals" install the brakes on my van...backwards. There was the "professional" lawn mowing service that let my dogs out of yard and then denied responsibility. On the other hand, the contractors that remodeled my kitchen and rebuilt my front porch did beautiful work. I've successfully colored my own hair and quite unsuccessfully wallpapered my office (which ultimately required a professional to fix the damage I'd done.)

We need to carefully consider the choices available in the training of our canine friends. I would not attempt to teach my child trigonometry (because I don't even know what trigonometry is or why one would need to learn it) any more than I would give myself an appendectomy. And there are some things that I just don't want to do. My friend who repaired her own main water line still tries to talk me into doing my own oil changes. She may be talking a very long time.

We've all gotten unsolicited advice on topics ranging from gardening to proper rules of etiquette for meeting the queen. Dog training may be second only to parenting on the list of freely given counsel. Add in the unlimited, easily accessed information on the Internet, and confusion reaches critical mass.

Everyone on this blue planet knows how to train a dog, and the only apparent credential required is that of dog ownership. If that's the case, then I could give free advice on how to install a new transmission, because I own a car. I do own a car, and I can make it take me where I want to go, but I need an expert's help when something goes wrong or I want things to continue to run smoothly.

There are infinite variations among dog owners, dogs, behavior problems, and trainers. Dog owners will do well to find a trustworthy, reliable trainer to help them achieve their training goals. Dog trainers will do well to find a good fit between client goals and workable training solutions.

Owners care about their dogs and want a positive training experience. Trainers care about their dogs and clients and want them to have a positive experience, as well. Owners wonder whether to choose a group class, private in-home training, send Fido away to boot camp, or buy a book or DVD and go it alone.

Making that decision will depend on the owner's individual needs, so it's important to ask some pertinent questions:

Does a weekly group class fit into your schedule?

- Can you and your dog handle the distraction of a group class?

- Do weekly coaching sessions fit into your schedule?

- What are your specific training goals?

- How involved do you want to be in your dog's training?

- Would you rather leave the training to the experts?

- Is your dog aggressive toward people or other dogs?

- Which type of training best fits your budget?

- Does your dog have issues that are specific to your home environment?

- Do you or your dog have special physical requirements or limitations?

- What is your learning style?

- What equipment and methods are you most comfortable with?

- What training method is in alignment with your philosophies?

Answering these questions will help owners make an informed decision as to what type of training will be the most beneficial.

Private In-Home Training

Private in-home training provides a personal experience. The trainer is able to focus completely on the owner and their dog, tailoring a flexible program unique to their individual needs. Solutions are built around and within the environment where the issues occur.

Private in-home training is commonly offered as coaching or day training sessions. Coaching sessions are designed to teach owners to train their dog. These training services are typically offered in weekly, one-hour sessions. Day training leaves the training to the expert, and the owner need not be present. Day training is commonly done in several one-hour sessions per week with just the trainer and dog, followed by a handover session. The handover session provides the owner with information and techniques to maintain the new behaviors that the dog has learned.

Group Classes

While group classes cannot offer the same personal attention as coaching, they do provide an economical, hands-on, social experience. People and dogs learn to perform under distraction, which strengthens relationships and opens the lines of communication between them. Group classes are easier to fit into the budget, but they can be trickier to fit into the schedule.

Going It Alone

Reading books and watching DVDs or TV shows on the subject can achieve successful basic dog training. However, if one gets stuck, it's difficult to ask the TV or book how to get unstuck. Furthermore, when dealing with serious issues, such as aggression or fearfulness, one should procure the services of a professional trainer and/or behaviorist.

Choosing a Trainer

Whichever type of training agenda is chosen, the most important part of the picture is the trainer.

A good trainer will:

- Connect with the client and their dog and encourage dialogue
- Make training fun for both owner and dog
- Be courteous to both species
- Be up to date and informed on current training equipment and techniques
- Be vetted and readily offer references
- Have both dog training skills and instructor skills

Guarantees

Consider the amount of variables in owner commitment, personality, lifestyle, and experience, along with differences in dog breeds and temperaments. With this in mind, it would be foolish for trainers to offer guarantees. However, trainers should ensure customer satisfaction with their services and back up their methods with scientific theory and anecdotal experience.

A good place to find a Certified Professional Dog Trainer is the website for the Association of Professional Dog Trainers: http://apdt.com/. See resources for a listing of books.

Dog owners seeking a trainer should look for a professional with reputable credentials, do the homework, ask for references, and trust their instincts. Your dog will thank you!

16

The How-To of Training
Teaching the Basics

To use shock as an effective dog training method you will need:
A thorough understanding of canine behavior.
A thorough understanding of learning theory.
Impeccable timing.
And if you have those three things, you don't need a shock collar.

–Dr. Ian Dunbar

Positive and Negative Verbal Markers

Positive and negative markers are feedback used simply to deliver information, to let the dog know whether he's offering the desired behavior or not. Many people use the words "Yes" and "No."

Immediately upon the dog's performance of the desired behavior, say, "yes" and reward him. "Yes" is one, short, sharp word that tells the dog he is offering the desired behavior and has earned a reward. Using a marker is like taking a snapshot of the behavior. Negative markers are used when the dog presents the "wrong" behavior. "No" or "uh-oh" are common negative markers.

You may wonder why we don't use praise as a marker. We talk to our dogs all day long and tell them they are good just for being the cute and wonderful beings that they are. The positive marker is a harbinger of the forthcoming reward. Praise can be the reward, but not the marker.

Verbal and Visual Cues

Hand signals and tone of voice should be consistent and clear. Markers should be given with a confident, even, and gentle tone. Sensitive or timid dogs may shy away if markers and cues are delivered forcefully. Other dogs may become over stimulated if cues and markers are given with too much enthusiasm.

Treats:

Use small, soft treats in training so that the dog does not get full (or fat) during training. Small treats are best for timing. Ideally, a dog should receive his payment within one second of performing the behavior.

Fading out the treats:

It is important to fade out treats as continuous reinforcement. Continuous reinforcement means that the dog is rewarded after every correct response, such as being rewarded after every sit.

Continuous reinforcement temporarily increases the frequency of behavior but fails at maintaining regularity. Furthermore, it does not improve the quality of behavior. If a dog is rewarded for every correct response, this means he's been rewarded for all responses, be they excellent, average, or inferior. Consequently, the quality of the behavior will decline because the dog expects all responses to be rewarded. Furthermore, continuous reinforcement will have both trainer and dog become dependent on the presence food.

Therefore, we want to implement a Variable ratio reinforcement schedule, which means that the dog is rewarded after an unpredictable number of responses. Variable ratio reinforcement maintains high frequencies of behavior, increases duration, and facilitates phasing out food rewards.

Variable ratio reinforcement is what's at work when we humans play a slot machine. We keep pulling that lever, because the machine randomly reinforces the behavior. Sometimes we win. Sometimes we win big, and we're convinced that the next try will win the jackpot. It works the same for dogs. Randomly reward his sits and the dog will enthusiastically present them at a high frequency.

Variable ratio reinforcement will increase the frequency of the behavior, but not the quality, as you are reinforcing all sits, whether they are above or below average. If we want to improve the quality of a behavior, we can implement a differential reinforcement schedule.

A differential reinforcement schedule means that the dog is reinforced for specific chosen behaviors. It can be used to raise the criteria of behaviors by giving rewards of varied value according to the quality of the performance (higher pay for higher quality.)

Differential reinforcement increases the probability that a dog will choose a specific behavior by varying and manipulating what is reinforced. Following are some examples of differential reinforcement:

Reinforce alternative behaviors to the undesirable one. This gives the dog a new focus, changes the subject, if you will. For example, the dog comes away from the window when called and stops barking. Here, we've already taught the dog to come when called, so we can have him refocus and interrupt the barking with a recall, then reinforce the recall and sitting quietly.

Reinforce behaviors that are incompatible to the undesirable one. For example, reinforce the dog for sitting instead of jumping up.

Raise the bar on the current behavior by reinforcing only higher levels of compliance or skill. For example, the dog is reinforced only for quick and snappy recalls. By rewarding only the above-average responses, the quality of the behavior improves.

Differential reinforcement teaches the dog to choose the new, desired behavior over the old, undesirable one. This works because we've made the new behavior more reinforcing than the former one, even though the surrounding circumstances haven't changed. For example, the dog still sees the mail carrier approach the house, but now he chooses to come away from the window and sit quietly beside you.

Getting Down To Basics: Training The Behaviors

Body Blocks: Body blocks allow us to move dogs around and direct their behavior without using a leash or touching them. It allows us to manage the space around them. Dependency on leashes and touching means that we have no control in unexpected circumstances or emergencies. If my dog escapes or if I drop the leash, I've got no recourse. Some dogs are perfectly behaved on the leash, but if the leash is off, so are all bets. Therefore, I want to train my dog for paying attention and compliance, no matter what he's wearing.

Dogs exercise control over other dogs and influence their behavior without the use of leashes or grabbing them and moving them where they want them. They use their bodies instead of leashes or their paws. Dogs take charge of the space around them by putting their body between the other dog and the space where he does not want him to go. He leaves an open path to the way he does want the dog to go.

I suggest we take a page from the book of dog, and not use hands to push them away. Instead, use your shoulder, hip, and torso to lean into the dog and block him from moving into your space. Occupy the space before the dog does and allow an open path to where you want him to go.

Example: If the dog breaks his stay, simply step into his path. When he stops, lean back slightly to take the pressure off. Be ready to execute another block if he attempts another break. Body blocks take the form of stepping into the dog's intended path, shuffling toward him, or leaning into the space that he intends to occupy.

Teach a Release Word

Dogs need to learn a release word in order for them to know when an exercise is over; that it has a beginning and an end. For example, if we put a dog in a stay and let him get up whenever he wants, he's not doing a stay. Stay means to sit, stand, or lie down and remain stationary until hearing a release word.

The release word should be said with a happy, animated, singsong, tone accompanied by a hand signal. Many people use the word, "Okay" as their release word, but beware, as "Okay" is a word used frequently in everyday conversation. If using "Okay" be sure to be very animated and use that hand signal.

(Note: If you have more than one dog, it is necessary to have the dogs' names be their individual release word. This is helpful for releasing dogs individually from a group wait. When used as a release word, the name is said in the same happy, animated voice as general release word.)

Attaching Hand Signals To Behaviors

Hand signals are easily taught by incorporating them into the luring method for teaching a behavior. By consistently holding the treat in the same manner, the motion of the hand becomes the hand signal after the treats are faded out.

Attaching the Cue To Behaviors

Dogs learn words by association as humans do. We want to have the dog doing the behavior reliably before we begin to attach the cue. For example, we have taught the dog to sit using the luring method (see below). When he is consistently offering sits, begin to say, "Sit" the moment the dog's bottom hits the floor. He will begin to make the association between the word and the behavior. Once he does, you will be able to say the cue and the dog will understand what it is that you want him to do.

To better illustrate this, think about it in human terms: Imagine that I don't understand English. If every time I sit down, you say, "Sit" and give me twenty dollars, I would very soon learn what the word "Sit" means.

Equipment

The most important piece of training equipment is patience. In the real world we need to use collars, harnesses, and leashes. We can and must use them with compassion.

When asked what the main function of the leash is, most people answer, "Control." As human beings, we inherently *use* a leash when it's in our hands. A leash need only be used to keep the dog safe, not to *make* him go where we want him to go.

Collars are only for tags. When we attach the leash to the collar, we set the dog up for failure. We set him up for choking and possible injury, not to mention a psychological and physiological disconnect. The more a dog chokes, the less he can think. If the leash attached to the collar tightens, the dog is pulled off balance with more of his weight distributed on his hind legs. His only option to regain balance is to pull. Thus, successful leash training begins off leash. This has the dog doing the work and the thinking. Then, when the leash is needed, all we need to do is pick it up. The dog already knows how to walk nicely beside you.

Watch:

Watch is a foundation behavior on which other exercises depend. Use it any time you want to gain the dog's attention or have him refocus.

First, swipe the treat in front of the dog's nose and bring it up to your eyes. When the dog makes eye contact say, "Watch" and give him the treat.

A more advanced "Watch" can be taught next. The advanced "Watch" should have a beginning and an end, meaning the dog should hold eye contact until released. Swipe the treat in front of the dog's nose and bring the treat up to your eyes. Keep the dog's eye contact by talking and making movements with your hand. Give the treat, and then say, "Okay" to release the dog. This behavior is handy for keeping the dog engaged and refocused during distracting situations.

For more difficult dogs or situations:
Getting attention: Hold the leash, stand still, and allow the dog to become mildly distracted. Without saying anything, simply wait for the dog to turn toward you or look at you. When he does, reward him. This teaches the dog that even though he's distracted, it is worth his while to "check in" with you.

Sit:

A sit is easily taught using the luring method: Hold the treat between your thumb and index finger with the palm upward directly in front of the dog's nose. Slowly bring the treat up and over his head. As the dog follows the treat, he will naturally put his bottom on the floor. As he does this, say, "Yes" and give him the treat. Be careful that all four feet and his bottom are on the floor as he receives his reward.

(Lie) Down:

A down can be taught using the luring method. Hold the treat between your thumb and index finger with the palm facing down. Slowly bring the treat straight down to the floor (nose to toes.) Think of drawing an "L" with the treat. After you bring it straight to the floor, slowly draw the treat away from the dog. The dog will follow the treat and lie down. As he does this, say, "yes" and reward him.

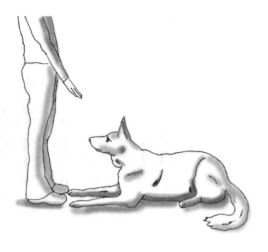

Some dogs will do better if you push the treat toward them instead of pulling it away. They will fold back into the down position. If during the process, the dog stands up instead of lying down, quickly take the treat away and say your negative marker (for example, "Uh-oh").

Wait a few seconds and try again.

If the dog is having trouble, break the behavior into small steps using shaping as described above.

Sit Stay:

Ask the dog to sit. Hold your hand out toward the dog with palm flat. Wait two or three seconds and treat the dog. When he is successful in holding the stay, repeat the above step. Now, add one slow step backward away from the dog. Return to him, mark the behavior with, "Yes," (or click) and deliver the treat. While teaching stay, always return to the dog to reward him for holding the stay. If you call the dog out of the stay and treat him, you are rewarding him for coming, not for staying.

If the dog breaks the stay, say, "No" and step towards the dog. Do a body block to get him back to his original position and have him sit again.

A down stay is taught using the same technique with the dog in a down.

Stay with duration and distraction:

Put the dog into a sit stay. Take a few steps backward and drop a treat behind you. If the dog breaks the stay say, "No" and do a body block to get him back to his original sitting position.

When he is successful in holding the stay, return to him, mark the behavior with, "Yes," (or click) and deliver a treat. Next, release him to get the treat on the floor. Gradually increase the time the dog stays before releasing him. If the dog is having problems holding his stay, help him to be successful by putting more space between him and the treat dropped on the floor.

Leash walking: Depend on your relationship, not on your leash.
Many dogs pull so hard on the leash that they choke themselves. This is because when we pull on the leash in one direction, we elicit an opposition reflex from the dog. This means that he will naturally pull in the opposite direction.

The opposition reflex has to do with the biomechanics of tight leashes. A typical collar or harness has the leash attach behind the dog's shoulders giving the dog license to pull with his entire body (as a horse in a harness.) The biomechanics at work here will have the dog pulling because a tight leash sets him off balance— more of his weight is distributed on his hind legs. The dog will pull in an attempt to regain his balance—to get his weight evenly distributed between his front legs and hind legs.

If you put a leash in a human's hands, we tend to use it. We want to pull, drag, and correct the dog by jerking on the leash. Leashes should be used only to keep dogs safe, not to control them.

Dominance based training methods declare that in order for me to be alpha, my dog must walk beside or behind me. I don't care where my dog walks. However, I do have two requirements of my dogs when we are walking: The first requirement is that they don't choke themselves and/or wrest my arm from its socket by pulling on the leash. The second is that they pay attention when I ask them to.

Even small dogs need to walk nicely on leash, to prevent choking themselves (unless a harness is used.) There is some good, safe no-pull equipment on the market, which serve as useful tools to prevent pulling. However, this equipment does not serve as effective leash training. If we're not training the dog, we are not addressing the real problem; a dog that pulls constantly is a dog that will be gone, if the leash is accidently dropped, or equipment fails.

Off-Leash Training:
It is not natural for dogs to walk beside us at our glacial human pace, so we

must teach them to do so. It may seem counterintuitive, but to teach a dog to walk nicely on the leash, we will start by training him off-leash (in a safe environment.) Before off-leash training begins, we will have taught the dog the basics of sit, down, and stay. Then we will establish a *psychic leash*–a desire from the dog to follow, remain close, and pay attention to the other end of the leash.

Pay Attention

First, we will develop a hand signal that indicates to the dog that he should pay attention. Hold a few food treats in your fist and tap your hip. When

the dog looks at you, you will mark and reward the behavior. Small dogs may jump up to get the treat, so tap lower at nose level on your leg. (You can gradually work your way up to tapping your hip, so that you don't have to walk stooped over.)

With young puppies or dogs that are easily over stimulated, simply stand still and wait for the dog to look at you without prompting. When he does so, mark and reward the behavior. Once, he realizes there is someone on the other end of the leash, introduce the hip tap.

Off-leash Heel

Next, start to walk while tapping your hip. Distribute treats from your hip-tapping hand as the dog follows along. Engage the dog by talking happily, making silly noises, singing, and/or whistling. Put a bounce in your step.

When the dog is responding reliably to the hip tap, add a cue word. As you tap your hip and the dog looks at you, say, "Heel," or whatever cue word you wish. Continue to distribute treats as the dog follows.

If the dog forges ahead, slow down or turn about. If the dog lags behind, speed up. If he turns left, go right and vice versa. Keep the dog engaged and following you. You are leading and he is following.

This exercise should begin at a low level of distraction, and then gradually worked to a higher level of distraction. Begin indoors and then move to the back yard, etc.

Sit, Down, Stay

Following off-leash takes a lot of concentration for both dog and trainer; it's easy to let the dog and your thoughts drift away. Adding some sits and downs to the exercise will help keep everyone focused. Cue the dog to sit every ten yards or so as he follows along. Have the dog sit for only be a couple of seconds, just to be sure that he is paying attention, then continue to walk.

To practice calm and control, ask for an occasional down stay, then just relax with your dog and watch the world go by.

On-Leash Training

Sit and Walk In The Heel Position
It is helpful for dogs to know how sit and walk in the heel position in order to stay close and wait. This is a handy behavior to have before crossing the street.

With the dog standing in front of you, hold a food treat in your left hand at the dog's nose. Move the treat in a circular motion to your left, while taking a step back. As the dog moves to your left, bring the treat slightly behind you, and then take a step forward. Now, the dog should be at your left side*. Ask the dog to sit.

Practice by having the dog follow off-leash in the heel position, as described above.

*The heel position is traditionally on the left, but you can train your dog to walk on whichever side you favor. Simply choose which side you prefer and be consistent.

Stand Before Walking
Before learning to walk nicely on leash, we will teach the dog to stand still

336

nicely. Hold the leash firmly. If the dog strains at the leash, stand still and do not budge until he slackens the leash. This takes patience, as it may take the dog a while to give you some slack.

Eventually the dog will loosen the leash and sit. Immediately, mark and reward the behavior, then take one giant step forward. Stand still. The dog will likely lunge forward, pulling on the leash. Once again, stand firm and wait for the dog to loosen the leash and sit.

By allowing the dog to pull on the leash, we're inadvertently reinforcing the behavior. This is because the dog gets to go where he wants to. He's taking the lead (in more ways than one.) Repeat the sequence of 1) take one step 2) stop 3) wait for the dog to slacken the leash and sit. Do this until the dog is walking nicely without lunging to the end of the leash. With this technique, the dog learns that pulling on the leash is like putting on the brakes–every time he pulls, you stop.

When the dog is able to advance on a loose leash with a single step, begin taking two steps at a time in the above sequence. Proceed by increasing the number of steps you take with the dog walking nicely beside you on a loose leash. Now, here's a bonus–every time you stop, the dog will automatically sit.

To keep the dog engaged, alternate heeling and walking on-leash. Let the dog roam and sniff. Then, have him come back to the heel position and sit. Do this every few yards.

Fast and Slow
It is helpful to have a dog know how to change pace on cue. For instance, when crossing a busy street, we want him to hustle and heel. When a dog is pulling, and the leash is tight, we want him to slow down. Cueing the dog to slow down has him loosening the leash without having him heel.

To teach the dog to speed up, simply and enthusiastically say, "Hurry" (or whatever cue word you wish) as you jog or walk quickly with the dog following beside you. Next, say, "Easy" right before you slow down. Reward the dog with a food treat, when he slows down to match your pace.

With enthusiastic dogs, it is helpful to cue them to slow down as you approach a wall or other visual physical barrier.

Leash Walking Part II

Now the dog is walking nicely on leash—most of the time—except when he smells something that he MUST investigate further. This is when he suddenly veers off the path, dragging you with him and by surprise. This happens for different reasons: we are caught off guard, we cannot physically hold the dog, or we simply acquiesce. When this happens, the dog learns that if he wants something bad enough and he pulls hard enough, he gets it.

Let's apply a bit of psychology here. Anything that the dog wants can be employed as a reinforcer. The dog wants to sniff the tree, so let's use that to our advantage. Let him sniff it as a reward for walking nicely on a slack leash. In other words, the dog gets what he wants (to sniff the tree) if he gives you what you want (a slack leash.)

When the dog begins to strain on the leash, hold the leash firmly and stand still. You've already taught the dog to slacken the leash on cue, so say, "Easy." Do not budge until the dog slackens the leash. When he does so, allow him to proceed to sniff the tree. Repeat this step if the dog forges again.

Let's walk

Dogs need to sniff and explore on walks. They need the mental stimulation that it provides. However, there are times when we need to cue the dog to move along. For example, we don't want the dog to stop to sniff while crossing the street.

When the dog shows intent to stop and sniff, or has been sniffing and you want to move along, tap your hip, cue the dog by saying, "Let's walk," or whatever word you wish. Treat the dog for coming along.

This cue can easily become tainted—a signal to the dog that he won't get what he wants or that the fun is over. Therefore, we want to mix it up—sometimes we stop, sometimes we don't, sometimes I change my mind.

As described above, when the dog shows intent to stop and sniff, tap your hip, cue the dog by saying, "Let's walk." When the dog comes along with you, you can then change your mind and release the dog to go sniff. Here again, you are using what the dog wants as a reinforcer. You also prevent the cue from becoming tainted, because sometimes "Let's walk" means we're moving on, and sometimes it doesn't.

Drop and Stop

A handy behavior to teach a dog is that he should stop whenever the leash is dropped. This helps to keep the dog close and will have him checking in with you whenever off leash.

Walk with the dog in the heel position. Stop and drop the leash. Say, "Wait" as the dog stops. Treat the dog for stopping. If he doesn't stop, step on the leash and say, "Wait" as the leash stops him. If you have worked through the off-leash follow-along, your dog should be automatically stopping when you do. At this point, all you should need to do is add the cue word "Wait" when the leash is dropped.

Next, practice dropping the leash as the dog is walking a bit ahead of you. Be prepared to step on the leash if necessary.

Next, practice having the dog stop in the heel position and you continue to walk. As the dog is walking beside you, stop and say, "Wait." Then, continue to walk ahead one step while the dog sits and waits. Return to the dog a treat him. If the dog breaks, do a body block and have him return to the original sitting position. Gradually increase the distance you can walk ahead of the dog while he sits and waits.

Pass Bys

Dogs can be taught to pass by other dogs without straining on the leash.

Start with two dogs at a distance where they are aware of the other dog's presence, but still able to focus on you. Engage your dog by talking to him and cueing him to "heel." Begin walking the dogs parallel to each other, then gradually decrease the distance between the dogs.

When the dogs are successfully walking parallel to each other, you can progress to doing pass-bys. Position the dogs at a distance where your dog is able to focus on you. Engage the dog by talking to him and cueing him to "heel." Keep his focus on you by talking and/or holding a treat up by your eyes as you pass by the approaching dog.

Meeting & Greeting People:

We can teach dogs to sit politely by our side while greeting friends.

First, cue the dog to sit in the heel position. Next, cue him to "stay." Have a friend approach, shake hands, and exchange pleasantries. Then release the dog from his stay and move on. If the dog breaks his stay, reposition him and try again. Make sure you set the dog up for success by having your friend approach slowly and calmly. Later, you can progress toward more animated greetings.

Proper Dog-To-Dog On-Leash Greetings:
Dogs approaching each other on leash often pull forward in their excitement to meet. There are some problems with allowing this behavior. A dog straining on his leash is standing forward and often stiff, which presents a more aggressive posture to the approaching dog. This could land him in some trouble, if the approaching dog feels threatened.

Additionally, allowing a dog to pull and strain as they approach another dog teaches him that pulling and straining gets him what he wants. Proper dog-to-dog greetings teaches the dog that polite behavior gets him what he wants—to greet another dog.

Teach your dog to do a sit-stay as in the "meeting and greeting people" exercise above. Hold him in a sit-stay as a friend approaches with her dog on leash. Next, the friend will put her dog in a sit stay. Release your dog from the sit stay and allow him to approach the other dog. Keep the leash loose. If he strains on the leash, return him to his sit stay and start again.

Leave It/Drop It
Teach dogs to drop an object on cue or to avoid an object when asked to do so.

Drop It:
Allow the dog to pick up a desired object such as a toy. Make an exchange with something of equal or higher value to the dog, e.g. another toy or a treat. As the dog lets go of the object, say, "Drop It."

Practice "Drop It" with various items, some of which you will give back to the dog (i.e. toys) and some that will not be returned (i.e. shoes.) This is important. If we always take things away from dogs without returning them, then "Drop It" becomes tainted; a cue that means the fun is over.

Refrain from chasing the dog is he's stolen something. Dogs love to be chased and to play keep-away. To avoid these games, be proactive about teaching your dog to drop objects. If we attempt training only when the dog has stolen something, he may learn to steal things so that you'll tell him to drop it, and then give him a treat.

Sometimes dogs will steal things simply to get attention. If the dog has an object that is not valuable (to you) and is not harmful to the dog, then ignore him and he'll probably lose interest.

Leave It:
Start by holding a treat in each hand. Offer one of the treats to the dog with closed fist. When the dog naturally diverts his attention say, "Leave it." Now give him the treat from the other hand. It is very important that the dog never receives the treat that you've told him to leave alone*. Next, place the treat on the floor and cover it with your hand. Tell the dog to "Leave it" and when he looks away, present him with a treat from your other hand. Practice this behavior with a variety of objects.

To generalize the behavior outdoors: When the dog is sniffing the ground (nothing in particular) wait for him to naturally divert his attention, and as he does say, "Leave it." Treat the dog. Gradually work up to "Leave It" with more interesting and enticing things.

*We do not want the dog to learn that "Leave It" means simply to look away, get a treat, and then come back to what he's been told to leave alone. If we've told the dog "Leave It" with a puddle of antifreeze, we don't want him coming back to it.

Recall (Come When Called):
This is the most important behavior we can teach our dogs, as it can surely save their lives. We must instill in our dogs a desire to come to us; making it worth his while to come when called.

Set the dog up for success by starting inside with little distraction. Begin in a hallway or a stairwell, where the dog has no choice but to come straight to you. Say the dog's name to get his attention and show him that you have a treat by placing it in front of his nose. Lure him toward you by taking a few quick steps backward. As he follows you, move the treat toward your chest and say, "Come." Reward him with treat.

When the dog is reliable with the above steps, slowly begin to add distraction and distance. Also, practice in different locations. Help him to generalize. A behavior taught in the kitchen may not be remembered in the yard.

Never chase the dog if he doesn't respond to the your call. Know that moving toward a dog will have him move away from you. This is because dogs love to be chased. Also, know that because dogs love to chase, moving away from him will have him move toward you.

If the dog isn't performing a reliable recall, set him up for success. Do so by reducing distractions, being more animated, increasing the value of the treat, and/or reducing the distance between you.

Important points to remember about recall:

Always make recall a pleasant experience. Never call the dog to scold him or to do anything he doesn't like. For instance, if he does not like to have a bath, do not call him to come and then put him in the tub.

Recall should not become a tainted cue; a word that means the fun is over. For instance, if we only call the dog to come when we are crating him and leaving for work, he will not want to come because he associates the behavior with being left home alone.

Always use a happy voice when calling the dog to come and likewise, excited and happy when he arrives.

Emergency Recall:
This is the "911" of recall. The emergency recall teaches the dog to return in an emergency, i.e. his collar breaks and he bolts towards a busy street. All dogs can learn two recalls: The normal recall, which means to come in a reasonable amount of time and the emergency recall, which means to come here right NOW.

The techniques for teaching the emergency recall are similar to the regular recall with some key differences:

> • Use a different word from the regular recall. Perhaps, you would use something like, "Back" or "Now" for emergencies. Choose a word that will come out of your mouth naturally in an emergency; something easy to remember.

> • Use a treat that is very special to the dog; something he will not get any other time than when practicing the emergency recall.

> • Give the dog a jackpot. Praise and feed the very special treats, one at a time for a full 30 seconds (20 seconds for small dogs.) This makes a huge impact on the dog. It conditions him to come without a second thought upon hearing this special word.

To train the behavior, have someone hold the dog on leash. Let the dog smell the very special treat, then run a few yards away while he watches. Turn and say the dog's name to get his attention. Next, say your special word. The person holding the dog should drop the leash and let the dog come to you.

When the dog gets to you, praise abundantly and feed the very special treats—one at a time for a full 30 seconds.

After the first trial, you can remain a few yards away to call the dog. You will not need to let him sniff the treat because he already knows you have something wonderful for him.

Do not practice this training procedure more than 3 times in any given day. We want to keep this special and fun.

As in training any new behavior, we want to set the dog up for success.

Start the training with little or no distraction.

Note: Voice inflection is an important factor in training the emergency recall. In a real emergency, your voice will have a sense of urgency, so practice the recall using an urgent tone to your voice. Additionally, your voice will be happy and full of praise when your dog returns to you in a real emergency. Practice your happy, praising voice inflection while jackpotting your dog when he does his emergency recall.

Jumping up:

Turn away
Jumping up is a natural, attention seeking canine greeting. We often respond by pushing dogs down and verbally reprimanding them. This response can actually reinforce the behavior by giving the dog the attention he seeks (even though the attention is negative, it is still better to the dog than no attention at all.)

To discourage the behavior, simply turn away from the dog when he jumps up. Do not speak to, look at, or touch the dog. Wait until he gets down and then turn to him. Next, ask for a sit (or he may offer one) treat him if you like, and then give him the attention he seeks. Consistency and persistency are key elements in extinguishing jumping.

On Leash
Tether the dog or have someone hold the leash and remain stationary. Approach the dog. If the dog jumps up, simply back away from him, out of reach of the leash. Ask the dog for a sit or wait for him to offer one. As soon as he does, approach him again. If he remains in a sit, treat and/or pet him. If he jumps, move away again. Repeat the exercise until the dog is offering sits. This exercise teaches the dog that jumping up makes you go away and sitting makes you approach.

Dogs often learn the pattern of jump, sit, and get a treat. To avoid this, wait a few seconds while the dog is sitting before approaching him. Capture only the sits that are not preceded by jumping.

Time outs

Some dogs will jump on your back when you turn away from them or persistently circle you and continue to jump. In this case, give the dog a time out. Time outs for dogs are similar to time outs for children except they are very short–only 30 to 60 seconds.

A time out means to simply leave the room and close the door when the dog jumps up. Wait 30 seconds and re-enter the room. If the dog jumps again, leave again. Repeat this until the dog learns that his jumping up makes you leave.

Some dogs, especially puppies, can get into trouble in the 30 seconds you are absent. To prevent this, have the puppy on leash. When you leave the room, keep hold of the leash, and close the door on it so that the puppy cannot wander off.

Controlling Space

Movement in space is very important to a dog. That is his, yours, or the movement of other dogs. Remember how body blocks allow us to direct a dog's behavior without using a leash or touching them. It allows us to manage the space around him. As dogs do, we can take charge of the space around us by putting our bodies between the dog and the space where we do not want him to go. Apply this knowledge to turning away from a jumping dog. Think about how you are turning. Which way is your body's energy flowing? Is your body moving forward toward the dog or away him? If you are turning away from the dog and giving up space to him, he will most likely continue to move toward you and jump. If you are turning into him and moving toward him, the dog is more likely to stop jumping.

Wait At The Door:

Teaching a dog to wait at the door keeps him safe. It teaches him that not every open door or gate as an opportunity to bolt through it.

Start by placing your body between the dog and the door so that you can use a body block if necessary. Have the dog on leash for safety, but keep it loose. In other words, the dog needs to be holding the wait himself. You can tether him or have someone hold the leash.

Have the dog sit a few feet from the door. Slowly open it. If the dog moves toward the door, do a body block or quickly close the door (be careful not to slam the dog in the door.) Move the dog back to his original position by shuffling toward him using a body block. Repeat the step above until the dog is able to wait with the door open, then release him to go through it.

If you use a treat, be sure to reinforce the wait by treating the dog inside before releasing him. Actually, a food treat is not necessary in training this behavior because the real treat is getting to go through the door.

Some dogs will break their wait the moment you touch the doorknob. If this happens, simply reach for the doorknob, and then treat the dog with a food treat before he breaks. Get him solid on holding his wait while seeing you touch the doorknob before moving on to the next step of opening the door.

Be sure to practice this by standing to the side of the door, not always between the dog and the door. He needs to respond to the cue and not be dependant on a body block.

Once the dog is holding himself reliably in a wait, attach the cue. As he is sitting say, "Wait" and then open the door. Use your release word to give the dog permission to go through the door.

Note: You may hear that in order to be alpha, you must always go through doors first. I believe that until dogs grow opposable thumbs and can open the door themselves, I'm in charge. Waiting at the door is about the polite behavior that gets a dog what he wants.

Wait For Food

Start with the dog in a sit and stand two or three feet in front of him, holding a treat in the palm of your hand. Slowly lower the treat to the level of the dog's nose. If he breaks his sit and moves toward the food, mark the behavior with a negative marker ("Uh-uh") and quickly move the treat away. Repeat until the dog learns to hold his sit. Release the dog to come and take the treat. Do not hand the treat to the dog, but allow him to approach and take it upon hearing the release word.

Wait for the food bowl:

Teaching a dog to wait patiently for his food bowl to be put down, eliminates chaos at mealtime. Too often, we allow dogs to bark, do the happy food dance, and back flips during meal preparation. We then reinforce the behavior by presenting the dog with a bowl of food. For quieter mealtimes, teach the dog to wait politely for food.

Start with the dog in a sit two or three feet from his feeding spot. Slowly bend over and lower the bowl toward the floor. If the dog breaks his sit and moves toward the food, mark the behavior with a negative marker ("Uh-uh") and quickly stand back up, moving the bowl away. Repeat until the dog learns to hold his sit. Release the dog to come and to the bowl. Do not hand the food to the dog, but allow him to approach the bowl upon hearing the release word.

Be sure to place the bowl on the floor and stand back upright before saying the release word. If you say the release word as the bowl hits the floor, the dog will take his cue from the action of the bowl hitting the floor, and not your release word.

Note: You may hear that in order to be alpha, you must always eat first. You do not need to eat before your dog. Learning to wait for food shows your dog that polite behavior gets him what he wants and who is in charge of the critical resources.

Food on the floor

Dropped or found food on the ground is much more tempting than food you hold in your hand, so the next step is to teach "Wait" with food on the ground.

Say, "Wait" and drop a small treat on the ground behind you or on your other side. If the dog moves toward the food, do a body block to prevent him from taking it. When he pauses, even for an instant, use your release word and allow him to take the food. Be sure to practice this by standing to the side of the food, not always between the dog and the food. Food doesn't always fall between you and the dog, so he needs to respond to the cue and not be dependant on the body block. He's learning to control his impulse to grab for the food.

Additional Thoughts

The greatest leader is the one who says the least and listens the most. This is true of leaders of dogs or humans. Think of authority figures that bellow commands constantly in order to gain control. Ultimately, their subordinates learn to ignore and avoid them. Now, think of a soft-spoken authority figure. If on the rare occasion he or she raises their voice, they are more likely to be met with compliance and respect.

Effective trainers open the lines of communication by becoming astute observers. A dog's first language is body language, so it's essential to become fluent in this subtle form of canine communication. Let's begin to hear what dogs are saying. Instead of merely correcting dogs for undesirable behavior, we must hear them, and then show them what is acceptable instead. If we don't, we leave our dogs out of the loop, failing to give them feedback and acknowledgment.

The best leaders don't actually lead anyone; they guide them. Furthermore, followers retain their dignity and feel they are respected. There is a sense of participation as opposed to domination. This concept is valid in our relationships with dogs as well is humans.

Make dog training a two-way street. Replace ownership mentality with an attitude of cooperation. Doing this diffuses many frustrations that come with expectations of complete control. Trust yourself and your dog. When you do not trust your dog, he will not trust you.

Set your dog up for success. Effective and fun training means setting dogs up for success and helping them to act responsibly.

There is a time for restraint and a time for letting go. It is possible to afford dogs freedom within the margins of safety and the law. We can manage and train them so they remain safe, happy, and active. We can be gentle compasses to guide our dogs while loosening the lead enough to let them be dogs.

Troubleshooting

For learning to take place, we must first get the behavior before it can be reinforced. If you are not getting the desired behavior from the dog, ask yourself the following questions:

Q: Is the dog too distracted?

A: If distraction is a problem, adjust the environment accordingly.

Q: Is the dog motivated enough?

A: Remember that the dog chooses the reinforcer. The reward must be something that he wants.

Q: Have you thoroughly taught the dog what you are asking him to do?

A: Be sure that you are not asking the dog for too much too soon. We often get ahead of ourselves and think that the dog knows the behavior when he does not.

Q: Is the dog frightened?

A: Fear prevents learning. If it is something in the environment that is frightening the dog, adjust accordingly. Dogs that are more fearful may need to be worked through their fears before training can begin.

Q: Is the dog confused?

A: Be sure that you are being clear and concise with your cues.

Q: Is the dog frustrated?

A: Be sure that you are not confusing the dog, asking for too much, or not reinforcing him enough.

The key to effective training is to set the dog up for success.

17

Solving Common Problems with Common Sense

Insanity: doing the same thing over and over again and expecting different results. —**Albert Einstein**

When it comes to solving common canine problems, common sense can be easily abandoned and frustration will reign. We keep trying the same things that *should* work, and then wonder which end of the leash has a problem.

This brings to mind a comment made by a man walking his dog on a choke chain. Sadly, the dog was strangling himself as he doggedly pulled on the leash. The man remarked, "I've been using this thing for three years. You'd think he'd learn!"

Commonsense solutions to common problems involve baby steps. We'll break the training down into small steps and train each step solidly before moving on to the next. Oftentimes, this means starting from the end. For instance, if we're trying to change the behavior of a dog with CGD (Canine Greeting Disorder– aka jumping on guests) we won't start by inviting guests to our home and then expect to teach the dog to sit quietly when the doorbell rings. Instead, we'll teach the dog to sit quietly for greetings with people already in the house and work backwards from there.

In this chapter, we'll take a fresh look at some common problems and make a plan for commonsense solutions.

Speaking of Barking

For nine years, I lived with my dog, Bob Barker. He taught me everything there is to know about excessive barking. He barked at me. He barked at squirrels. He jumped up on the roof of the doghouse and evangelized to his brothers. Before training, Bob was noise with fur whose disproportionate barking was an acoustic blight on the neighborhood.

I define excessive barking as that which bothers me, bothers my neighbors, or the dog won't cease on request.

When my dogs are barking, I must first put any frustration in check and resist the temptation to yell, "Quiet!" I must not dismiss their alert to perceived danger because after all, they are doing their duty. There might actually be a sleeper cell of terrorists in the alley—or a squirrel.

All dogs bark. It's an essential part of communication and it would be absurd to expect them to live in silence. Dogs bark in response to other dogs barking. Dogs bark as an alert to danger, to seek attention, announce their presence to other dogs, claim their territory, and to protect their resources.

Barking can become habit. For example, a dog that always barks from excitement in the car when riding to the dog park will make it routine unless taught otherwise. Dogs may become habitual barkers if they regularly bark at passersby or guests entering house because either the environment or we have reinforced it.

Some dogs are more vocal than others. High energy, exuberant dogs are often quite talkative. Various herding breeds and some terriers tend to be more vocal. Certain breeds bark by design. Dachshunds, for instance, were bred to hunt badgers—to go down the badger hole and bark when they found their quarry. However, breed and personality traits are no excuse for enduring canine cacophony. Despite genetics and individuality, dogs can be trained to be quiet on cue.

A barking dog can be especially annoying; even a liability. Dogs bark for different reasons and there are different solutions for each reason. Understanding why barking occurs, training, and management will help us reach a peaceful resolution.

Basic Needs: Dogs will bark if their basic needs such as food, water, or shelter are not being met. Dogs may also bark if they are in pain. The obvious solution here is to provide life's necessities.

Fear: Dogs may bark because they are fearful of loud noises such as thunder or unfamiliar sounds like those from construction. Many dogs are afraid to be alone and will vocalize their fear and loneliness. Dogs left outside are more likely to bark because there are more stimuli present.

Fearful dogs should be kept indoors in a quiet, inside room with ambient noise such as a fan or radio turned on to muffle outside noises. Interactive toys stuffed with food can also help ease mild anxiety. A reputable trainer and/or veterinary behaviorist should be consulted for dogs with severe separation anxiety.

Boredom: If a dog has nothing else to do, he may choose to bark. Boredom can also lead to digging, escape, and destructive chewing, so we must be sure our dogs are getting enough exercise and mental stimulation. Interactive chew toys like a Kong® can remedy boredom. Stuff one or several of these toys with the dog's moistened food and freeze it overnight. Rover will spend a good amount of time working for his food instead of being bored. Furthermore, he's lying down quietly while eating his meal instead of wolfing it from a bowl in under 30 seconds, leaving him more time to bark.

A dog left unattended outside is a recipe for excessive barking and angry neighbors. Dogs are exposed to more stimuli outdoors, which could be cause for alert barking, gossiping, (joining in with other barking dogs) or vocalizing fear. Create a comfortable place for your dog to stay while you're away. This should be an inside room away from the both visual and auditory distractions outside. An inside room is also recommended for those living in apartments so the dog and the neighbors are insulated from environmental sounds. Turn on a fan, TV, or radio to mask outside sounds.

Attention Seeking Barking: Some dogs will bark simply for attention. This type of barking must absolutely be ignored. If we look at the dog, even tell him to be quiet; we are giving him exactly what he wants–attention. Even though the attention he receives is negative, to him, it's better than none at all.

At first, when the behavior is ignored, you may notice the attention seeking barking escalate. This is called an extinction burst, and happens because the barking has worked for the dog previously. Now that he's being ignored, he tries barking longer and louder to garner attention. Do not give in at this time, or you will inadvertently teach your dog that he must be more obnoxious to get noticed. Parents with small children know not to give in to their child's tantrum for the same reason.

Alert Barking:
Dogs bark to alert "the pack" to perceived danger. When my dog barks to alert me, I first thank him for the report. Saying "thank you" reminds me that he is doing his job and diffuses any frustration on my part.
I do not yell at my barking dog. To him, yelling is the equivalent of me joining in the excitement. I also remember that my neighbors don't want to hear me "barking" either. Instead of shouting, I call my dog to me and tell him to "Shush."

Shush on Cue
Most people want a dog that will bark when someone is at the door or has entered the property. Some are concerned that teaching a dog to control his barking means that he will never bark again, not even to alert them to danger. No worries. Dogs will still bark to announce perceived peril, protect their turf, or herald the arrival of a welcome friend. Personally, there is no need for an alarm system or even a doorbell in my home. My dogs are much more efficient than any bell and an extremely persuasive security system.

The goal is to train the dog to be quiet on cue after he's made his announcement. Teaching shush on cue, as with any behavior, should not be attempted in the heat of the moment. Episodes of uncontrollable barking are not teachable moments. The dog simply cannot learn to shush on cue while he is barking hysterically. Worse yet, we may end up reinforcing it. Here's why. Say we try to get the dog to stop barking by offering up a treat. If we deliver the treat immediately after he stops barking, we've reinforced him for barking, not for being quiet. The dog may learn to bark so that he'll be told to be quiet, and then rewarded. This is why timing and sequence are important, where the subtle difference between bribery and rewards need to be understood, and we must have the dog in the right state of mind.

To teach the dog to be quiet on cue we'll first train him to bark on cue. That way we can teach him to stop when he is calm and cognitive, not barking frantically.

To teach him to bark on cue, do something that you know will cause the dog to bark. The doorbell usually does the trick, but anything that consistently triggers barking will do.

Step 1: Station a friend outside the door. Say, "Speak" (or whatever cue word you'd like.) The word "Speak" is also the signal for your friend to ring the doorbell.

Step 2: When the dog barks, praise him abundantly. Be animated and happily excited.

Step 3: After the dog has barked a few times, hold your finger to your lips and say, "Sshhhh" or "Shush." "Sshhhh" makes a good cue because you can't yell it. Holding the finger to the lips is a hand signal, handy for when you are on the phone and do not want to interrupt your conversation (and dogs, like children, will always "talk" when you are on the phone.)

Step 4: As you say, "Sshhhh" wave a treat directly in front of the dog's nose. He will stop barking in order to sniff the treat because it is physically impossible for a dog to sniff and bark at the same time. Praise the dog for being quiet and then give him the treat. Praise should be calm and quiet, as excited, animated praise may incite more barking.

Step 5: Repeat steps 1 through 3 until the dog anticipates the doorbell ringing whenever you say "Speak." He has learned to bark on cue when he hears "Speak" and barks before the doorbell rings. He has also learned to anticipate a treat and stop barking when hears "Sshhhh."

Step 6: Progressively increase the length of time between saying "Sshhhh" and the dog receiving the treat. Alternating between "Speak" and "Sshhhh" has the dog earning rewards for barking on request and then quieting on request. Lengthening the time between "Sshhhh" and the reward ensures that the treat is a reward and not a bribe. Once the dog is reliable with quieting on cue, the treats can be faded out.

Step 7: Put the "Speak" and "Sshhhh" into practice in the real world and help your dog to generalize the behavior. If your dog barks at passers by, employ a friend to walk back and forth in front of your house. Ask the dog to "Sshhhh" while the person passes by. Repeat until the dog can watch in the passerby in silence. Next, have the person walk to the front door. Ask the dog to "Speak" and then to "Sshhhh" and sit quietly while the visitor enters. Now, the dog has learned to watch passers by silently, but to bark when someone enters the property, and to stop on request.

A Word on Bark Collars

Bark collars are a quick fix. Ah, don't we humans always want a quick fix–a pill, a button we can push? Bark collars control barking through punishment. They do not change the behavior. Bark collars are stressful for dogs, not only because they deliver physical punishment, but they also suppress a natural behavior. Just as we humans are stressed if held to silence, so are dogs. Training will change the behavior, not simply suppress it– a more peaceful, humane solution resulting in a happier dog.

Controlling Canine Chaos At The Front Door

Whenever I visit my childhood friend back home, Gary receives me by charging the front door, delivering a giant bear hug, and then proceeds to cover my face with slobbery kisses. My friend has somewhat better manners than that...Gary is the resident Labrador retriever.

Let's face it. Even the greatest dog lover in the world, which is arguably me, doesn't care to be welcomed by a furry freight train with kibble breath.

Jumping up is a canine greeting. However, slobbery salutations are not widely accepted in human society. A profusion of advice exists on how to remedy the problem. Suggestions include shoving the dog down, stepping on back toes or putting a knee to the dog's chest. These methods do not get my endorsement as each employs physical punishment. They could result in injury to the dog, not to mention the fact that a trusting relationship will be destroyed.

You cannot teach a dog what *not* to do. You can only teach him what *to* do instead. If door greetings have always been a train wreck in the past, let's teach the dog that the sound of the doorbell means to go to place or go get a toy and wait. He will learn the routine at the front door involves calm and quiet, not chaos.

Start from the end, not from the bell. We think that to eliminate front door chaos, we should simply invite people over, have them ring the bell, and then try to get the dog to stay while we ask our guests in. Insanity ensues. This routine is what we've always done, and now we're expecting different results.

Before the Lesson:

Master the Basics

We must have a strong foundation and reliability on the basic skills before we can expect a dog to hold it together for door greetings. See the chapter *The How-To of Training* for instructions on jumping up and holding a stay with distractions. The dog must be a master at these skills before moving forward with door greetings.

Impulse Control

Impulse control is the foundation for polite greetings. Practice the following exercises to alleviate the compulsion for chaos.

- Red Light/Green Light (see the chapter *Kids and Dogs*)

- Wait (see the chapter *Teaching the Basics*)

- Learning to be alone (see the puppy section in the chapter *In It For Life*)

Ignore

It's easy to get caught up in the chaos and excitement of door greetings, which only makes matters worse. No matter how happy we are to see that wagging tail when we come through the door, we must remain calm, even ignore the dog. Doing so interrupts the old pattern of canine calamity and the dog learns that people entering the home will ignore him if he's overzealous. He'll learn that a calm dog gets the attention. Change the routine by ignoring the dog while you come in, set down your things, hang up your coat, even change your clothes. Then, when you're ready, cue the dog to come greet you calmly. If you'd like to have some exuberant playtime, put it on cue and make it by invitation only. Now greetings are on your terms.

Go to Place

Designate an area such as a rug, crate, or dog bed where the dog can see the front door, but is far enough away for him to be successful. Follow instructions for teaching dogs to "go to place" as described in the chapter *Beyond the Basics*. When the dog has learned to go to place on cue, have someone ring the doorbell. Then, ask the dog to "go to place." Repeat this exercise until the dog associates the doorbell with going to his place.

Desensitize to the Doorbell

To break the old pattern of excitement at the sound of the doorbell, it's helpful to do a bit of desensitization. With the dog on leash, have someone stand in plain sight and ring the bell. If the dog barks, ask him to "shush." Then, cue him to go to his place, escorting him on a loose leash. Repeat this exercise until the dog is able to go to his place independently and on cue.

Get a Toy and Go to Place

Dogs can learn an alternative behavior to running to the door and flattening all who enter. Upon hearing the doorbell, they can run get a special toy, then go to place with it.

Front Door Leash

Keep a leash by the door so that it can be snapped on to the dog's collar when the doorbell rings and before opening the door. This should be a separate leash from the one used for walks so that the dog does not get excited when he sees it. This sets the dog up for success and prevents him from being variably reinforced for chaotic greetings. The chapter *The Art of Positive Practice and Premise* explains variable reinforcement. We use Variable Ratio Reinforcement to our advantage in dog training by keeping the dog guessing as to when he'll receive a reward. It's what's at work when we humans play a slot machine. We keep pulling that lever, because the machine randomly reinforces the behavior. Sometimes we win; sometimes we win big; and we're convinced that the next try will win the reward.

Variable ratio reinforcement can work against us as well. If the dog sometimes gets to go to the door and jump on people and the behavior is reinforced, he will repeat it. Thus, door greetings should be done on leash so that there is no rehearsal of old behavior (see Jumping Up: On Leash, in the chapter *The How-To of Training*.)

The Lesson:

Step 1: Have the dog go to his place and put him in a stay. Walk to the door and touch the doorknob. If the dog breaks the stay, do a body block and have him return to the same spot. Set him up for success. If he can't hold the stay, then don't go all the way to the door. Go as far as you can. Return to the dog, treat, and release him.

Step 2: Cue the dog to stay on his place. Walk to the door and calmly open it. You can face the dog and remind him to stay. Close the door. Return to the dog, treat, and release him.

Step 3: Cue the dog to stay on his place. Walk to the door, turn your back to the dog, and calmly open the door. Close the door. Return to the dog, treat, and release him.

Step 4: Cue the dog to stay on his place. Walk to the door, turn your back to the dog, and calmly open the door. Pretend there is someone there and speak to the imaginary visitor in a calm voice. Close the door. Return to the dog, treat, and release him.

Step 5: Repeat the above exercises with another person present. Next, have the person go outside and stand at the front door. Have the dog on leash and put him in a stay on his place. Place yourself between the dog and the door so that you can do a body block if necessary. Have the dog hold the stay while you ask the person to calmly enter and not approach the dog. Treat the dog and then release him. Keep hold of the leash in case the dog attempts to jump.

Step 6: Have the person go outside and stand at the front door. With the dog on leash, put him in a stay. Have the dog hold the stay while the person knocks lightly on the door. Treat the dog for holding the stay, but do not release him. Ask the person to calmly enter and not approach the dog. Treat the dog and then release him.

Step 7: Have the person go outside and ring the doorbell. With the dog on leash and in a stay, ask the person to calmly enter and not approach the dog. Treat the dog for holding the stay, but do not release him. Ask the person to calmly enter and not approach the dog. Treat the dog and then release him.

On the Loose (Leash)

Walking nicely on leash can be time consuming and mentally exhausting yet, the most rewarding behavior one can teach a dog. My German shepherd, Jude was ninety pounds of exuberant, unmannered muscle when I adopted him at the age of six months. That dog could pull a dump truck up a mountain! I had visions of him pulling the bloody stump of my arm down the street! Therefore, in order to prevent dismemberment, my first objective was to teach Jude about loose leash walking.

In the end, Jude was a qualified champ at leash walking. One day, as we were doing a particularly fine job of strutting our stuff, a car slowed, the driver lowered the window and said, "Magnificent!" I smiled and responded, "Thanks! And, my dog ain't bad either!"

Polite leash walking makes for enjoyable outings with dogs. The dogs are happy, we're happy and passers by are envious. However, those green with envy are seeing the fruits of our efforts, the highlight reel, and not the behind-the-scenes footage. When people ask me about that guy on TV that takes the out-of-control psycho dog for a 10-minute walk, and then returns with "Lassie on a Leash," I say, "That's editing." In reality, good manners on both ends of the leash take time and effort.

If you put a leash in my hand, I seem to have a compulsion to use it. That's because I'm human. When it comes to leash training, perhaps we've gotten it backwards. We bring our new dog home, snap the leash on, and then wonder why there is so much pulling…on *both* ends of the leash. I propose that we depend more on our relationship with our dogs than we do on the leash. Successful leash training achieved without the use of force or leash corrections results in a dog that *wants* to be near us.

I often ask people why we put dogs on leashes. The most common response is, "To control them." I beg to differ. I believe the only reason to have a dog on leash is to keep him safe (and to comply with leash laws, of course.)

Many small dogs have abysmal leash walking skills. This may be because people think leash training for small dogs is unnecessary. After all, you can just pick them up. But, what happens if you drop the small dog's leash? He's outta there!

More large dogs are trained to walk nicely on leash because we have to—because we can't pick them up. However, we still hold the belief that the leash is for control. Think about horses. We can't pick them up, we can't drag them by force to follow us or prevent them from dragging us on lead. We must train them, not control them. It's the same with dogs.

Aversive devices such as choke chains, prong collars, and shock collars employ pain to elicit behavior. Sure, they get results, but the dog is offering behaviors only to avoid painful punishment. Without the aversive apparatus, the dog will revert to pulling on the leash. Some people say that with the collar, the dog does not pull and that they never have to jerk it. How many times have I seen people unconsciously tightening the leash? What happens when the dog sees a rabbit and instinctively tries to give chase? What happens when the dog sees a child or another dog and wants to greet them? The dog will be in pain when the leash tightens.

Any event or anything present in the environment at the time the dog feels pain can take on a negative association. He may develop a negative association with the things that excite him, like children and other dogs—even us. The use of painful punishment here is a recipe for a reactive or even aggressive dog.

Equipment
Proper equipment is a helpful tool in teaching leash walking. However, it is no substitute for humane training, relationship building, and patience.

Choke chains and prong collars are potentially harmful as they can do cumulative damage to the dog's trachea, thyroid, and spine. Additionally, they do potential damage to the dog's emotional wellbeing and most certainly our relationship with him.

Physically speaking, there is a disconnect that happens when a dog is choking. Think about trying to learn a new computer program while your coworker strangles you. Aversive devices do not teach dogs to think for themselves. Therefore, without them dogs will revert to the old behaviors.

Choke Chains
These metal chains put pressure on the dog's neck when the leash is tightened. They are used to correct the dog for misbehavior or

noncompliance by popping, jerking, or even hanging the dog (hoisting him by the neck until front feet are off the ground.) These techniques can get results, but the dog complies only to avoid pain. If he is confused, he is likely to shut down for fear of retribution by chain. Choke chains are intended as punishment. Punishment decreases the likelihood of a behavior being repeated. Dogs who continue to pull on leash with a choke chain are not being punished, nor are they being trained.

Prong Collars

Prong or pinch collars are metal collars with inward protruding prongs that put pressure on the dog's neck when the leash is tightened. They work through positive punishment and negative reinforcement. Positive punishment happens when the dog pulls on the leash and the collar delivers painful pressure, thus he stops pulling. Negative reinforcement happens when the dog stops pulling and the painful pressure is relieved. The dog is reinforced for walking on a loose leash, increasing the likelihood that he will not pull in the future.

The supposed theory behind prong collars is that they simulate the teeth of the alpha dog giving a correction or mimic the action of a mother correcting her puppy. Pinch collars can cause serious injury when the prongs dig into the skin and cause puncture wounds. Mothers do not use their teeth to inflict pain on their puppies. Dogs do not apply pressure on both sides of the neck, which is how the pinch collar works. Therefore, pinch collars do not replicate canine corrections.

Punishment, unless administered with impeccable timing and an appropriate, humane level of force, is ineffective. It can backfire with undesirable and unintended side effects. These side effects include aggression in the form of preemptive strikes toward other dogs or people, or redirected aggression toward the person on the other end of the leash.

Head Collars

Head collars are designed to handle and guide dogs by their heads just as halters and leads are tools used to handle horses. The theory is that if you can handle a 1,000-pound horse with a halter, you can handle a dog. The leash is attached to a ring under the dog's chin. Since dogs tend to go where their heads go, the system works by turning the head if the leash is tightened. The dog cannot physically pull hard if he cannot move in the direction he wants to go. The leash and collar used to gently, yet firmly guide the dog's head in the direction you lead him.

Head collars are designed for use with a flat, 6-foot or 4-foot lead. Retractable leashes defeat the purpose of the head collar in that there is no control of the dog's head if he is 15 or 20 feet away.

Head collars typically take some getting used to for dogs, but if acclimated properly these collars can be effective training tools.

Note: Acclimating a dog to a head collar is done the same as acclimating him to a muzzle. See the chapter *Aggressive Dogs* for information on acclimating dogs to muzzles. Many people think that head collars are muzzles. They are not. Properly fitted head collars allow the dog to pant, eat and drink, bark, and bite without restriction.

The use of head collars has been called into question out of concern that they could cause injury to the dog's neck. I would not suggest administering leash corrections with them, as they are not designed as such. Other worries are that if a dog, for whatever reason charges to the end of the leash and flails around, injury will ensue.

Dr. Sophia Yin, Veterinarian and Animal Behaviorist states the following in her blog dated June 4, 2012: *Now if this were a person, flailing on the end of a leash attached to an apparatus on his head, he'd surely have a neck injury. But anyone who has seen a dog that goes to town playing tug-o-war knows that a dog's neck is built differently. Because of this neck strength, few cases of injury due to head collars have been proven or medically documented (I actually haven't seen any). Not to say injury could not happen. However, veterinary documented injuries caused or exacerbated by choke chain corrections and electronic collars are easy to find. Most likely if dogs are pulling on their head collar a lot or running to the end, they may need massage or chiropractic care just the way people who work or study at a desk all day need back adjustments periodically.*

Harnesses

Regular harnesses are those that have the leash attach to a D-ring located on the top at the dog's shoulders or back. Harnesses prevent choking and putting pressure put on the dog's neck, which is the case when the leash is attached to the collar. However, because the leash attaches to the harness on the dog's back, it gives him a mechanical advantage—a license to pull with his whole body. We use harnesses with horses and Huskies when we want them to pull, so why would we use a regular harness unless we want to participate in the Iditarod?

Harnesses are rightfully popular with owners of small dogs because they relieve pressure on the dog's neck. However, they should not be used in lieu of training. Just because small dogs can't drag us down the street or tear our arms from their sockets, we still want to train them to walk nicely on leash—because if don't and we should drop the leash, the dog is gone. Make sure harnesses fit well and that the dog cannot slip out of it. Another reason to depend on training and not the equipment.

No-pull Harnesses

No-pull harnesses are designed with the leash attachment ring located on a strap running across the dog's chest. They give the handler a mechanical advantage over the dog because leading from the front provides steering. If the leash tightens, the no-pull harness turns the dog's body. This prevents evocation of the dog's natural opposition reflex (the innate impulse to pull in the opposite direction of applied pressure.) Tension on the leash from behind (as with a regular harness where the leash attaches on the back) makes the dog want to pull forward.

Dogs have a lower more stable center of gravity than humans, which makes leash walking difficult, even dangerous when dogs pull. Physics are working against us with regular harnesses having leash attachments on the shoulders or back. Attaching the leash to the front counteracts the dog's natural mechanical advantage.

Recent debate has raised the question about whether no-pull harnesses are detrimental to a dog's structure and gait, especially dogs that are athletic and very physically active, such as dogs that jog with their owners.

Remember that equipment is no substitute for training. If the equipment assists us in getting the behavior, thus the opportunity to reinforce it, we can then decide to fade out its use after the dog has been trained. No-pull harnesses are non-aversive and most likely the lowest risk for doing harm to either dog or human.

Missed Calls

Perhaps, in some parallel universe there exist dogs that feel compelled to respond without delay to their person's call–as obliged as we are to instantly answer our cell phones; anytime, anywhere. I've heard about a human experience, one of many precipitated by the Internet and social media. This phenomenon, of course, has its own acronym–FOMO.

FOMO means fear of missing out. It seems that in addition to another acronym, the Internet, has generated a new apprehension. We now worry about what photos of food we've missed on Facebook. OMG! I might miss out on seeing what my Facebook friends had for lunch! If my dogs are in the house, they never fail to notice what's on the lunch menu, but I doubt they are worrying about it if they are on squirrel patrol in the yard. When it comes to coming when called, maybe our dogs need a bit of FOMO.

It's been said that dogs come when called; cats come when they're interested. I think that dogs also need to be interested; additionally they need to feel safe.

I've often witnessed this heartbreaking scenario: A dog at large with his person chasing after, screaming angrily in an effort to get the dog to come. If the dog returns, he's then scolded or punished. We can easily fall victim to this folly because emotions run high when our dog is running loose. Furthermore, it is socially acceptable to admonish dogs for "misbehavior." That is the human outlook. From the dog's perspective, he's happily roaming free; just being a dog, when he was called to come back. Upon return, he is punished for doing the very thing he was asked to do.

Young puppies and insecure dogs are more reliable on recall. The majority of dogs, however, must be convinced that we are interesting. Certain breeds are less dependable with recall. Scent hounds tend to naturally fall into this category because they are bred to get on a scent and stay on it no matter what.

Think about it. Why *would* a dog want to come when called? After all, squirrels need to be put on notice that the yard is off limits–or there are tantalizing scents to be decoded and numerous pee-mails to be read. In other words, in a dog's world there are more appealing things do than answer our call.

There is no 100% guaranteed recall. But, with creativity, patience, understanding, and persistence, even the most independent of dogs can have a reliable recall.

For reliable recalls, we need to build a rapport that has the dog interested. He needs to know that compliance is worth his effort. It's not about controlling the dog and simply having an obligatory prompt recall. It's about a willing enthusiastic one.

Key points for a reliable recall:

Capture the behavior

Every time your dog comes to you, whether asked to or not, acknowledge and praise him. Act like the sun rises and sets with his presence. This will have your dog doing voluntary check ins. See *Attentive Dog* in the puppy training section of the chapter *In It for Life*.

Avoid becoming background noise

If we're constantly yammering on to our dogs, they will simply tune us out. This is how I react when my Cousin Mikey calls, droning on about everything and nothing. I can take the opportunity to rearrange my sock drawer, have lunch, and then come back to the conversation. Don't be Cousin Mikey with your dog.

Be ridiculously happy

Even if you're feeling scared and frustrated, use a happy, high-pitched voice to call your dog. Praise him every step of the way in order to hold his interest and keep him from taking a side trip. Take a page from the "Book of Labrador." Labrador retrievers are happy on a molecular level. They have a whole-body happiness. Use your body language to encourage your dog to come to you. Be animated, stoop down, extend open arms—be Lab Happy.

Resist the urge to chase

Running toward a dog will incite him to run away, either from fear or because it's fun. Dogs love to be chased, so don't be tempted. The up side here is that dogs love to chase. Do the counterintuitive thing and run away from your dog. Fall to the ground laughing if necessary. Don't worry about what onlookers think. I'd act as outrageous as necessary to get my dog to safety.

Generalize the behavior

Set your dog up for success. Start with little or no distraction. If a dog can't do a behavior when it's easy, he certainly can't do it when it's difficult. Avoid training recall at the dog park where your dog is susceptible to *dog park induced deafness*. Start easy, like in a hallway or stairwell, where your dog's best option is to come directly to you. Once he is reliable with his recall here, gradually progress to increasingly difficult situations.

Try doing recall in other locations inside the house then, try the back yard. In each location, start with little or no distraction, and then increase the difficulty. Do so by scattering a few of the dog's toys around so he must pass by them to get to you. Have another person present. Have another dog present. Next, you are ready to try the park on a quiet day. Do the recall on a long line (a long leash 20ft long or longer, not a retractable one) or in a safe fenced area such as a tennis court if dogs are allowed.

Avoid the Recall Pitfalls

• Avoid calling the dog, and then asking him to do something he doesn't like to do, such as get his nails trimmed or to take a pill. For these things, simply go get him. Otherwise, you lose his trust and he will be suspicious of recall.

• Avoid calling the dog and then scolding him. Again, you will lose your dog's trust in recall.

• Avoid repeating the cue. Avoid repeating the cue. Avoid repeating the cue. Repeating cues teaches your dog to ignore you.

• Avoid recall on a prayer. Calling your dog and then praying he'll come teaches the dog that your call means nothing. Until you've got a reliable recall in which your dog can come even if he's on squirrel safari, save your prayers and your breath. Go get him instead.

Know what your dog is saying to you

People often say that their dog "ignores" them when they call. Some even think that their dog can't hear them because he's unresponsive. Listen, my dogs can hear me peel a banana at 300 yards. Unless your dog has been diagnosed with a real hearing impairment, he can hear your call.

If your dog is "ignoring" you, check in with your emotions. Are you sounding angry or frustrated? Dogs use "calming" signals when they are feeling stressed or asked to do something they don't want to do. One of these calming signals is to ignore the source of anxiety by turning away or sniffing the ground. If I am the source of my dog's discomfort, he may ignore me as a peacekeeping effort.

Know the pitfalls of bribery and teach check-ins

When I hear that dogs won't come when called from the back yard or at the dog park, I always ask, "In what other situations do you call your dog?" Often the answer is, "None." If that's the case, the dog has learned that recall means the fun has ended. To avoid this consequence, I suggest doing "check-ins." Call your dog, offer a treat or play with a toy, then let him return to what he was doing. Thus, recall is worth your dog's while, yet the fun continues.

Bribery works with dogs and I'm not above using it on rare occasion. However, I don't want to become dependant on it. The caveat here is that dogs are smart and can train us to use bribes. Here's how they do it: 1) you call your dog to you 2) he doesn't come 3) you fetch a tasty bribe. Your dog has just learned that holding out will get him a treat. He's effectively trained you that bribery works.

If bribery is your only choice (for instance, you'll be late for work if your dog won't come in the house) then you can use bribery successfully, but use it thoughtfully and sparingly. Offer a treat the *first* time you call your dog. You must change the aforementioned pattern so that the dog doesn't hold out for the treat: 1) call your dog 2) offer a treat 3) your dog comes to you.

Now that you have a better understanding of the pitfalls of training recall, you're ready for the nuts and bolts of training your dog to come when called. See Recall in *The How-To of Training* chapter.

The name of the game is fun

Make recall even more reliable. Have fun by playing hide-and-seek with your dog. Offer a food reward or play his favorite game when he comes when called. Finding you, makes recall fun. Recall means being rewarded with a treat or a spontaneous game of tug, fetch, or chase.

With training, understanding, and fun your dog will have a rock-solid recall. He'll be safe and you'll be happy when you have no more missed calls.

Demolition Dogs

Many years ago when Mr. MoJo, was 6 months old, I came home after a long day at work to find him lying proudly atop a heap of trash. He had spent some quality time removing the garbage from it's rightful place in the bin, rearranging select pieces of furniture, and ripping the living room drapes from their rods and then shredding them to bits!

We commonly assume destructive behavior means the dog is suffering from separation anxiety. In Mr. MoJo's case, he was bored and the event was attributable to something more like separation fun. This was a lesson for me in how to deal with an energetic adolescent dog with an aptitude for interior design.

Destructive chewing is not only well, destructive, it's dangerous and expensive. Chewing is in a dog's nature, but they might also engage their teeth out of boredom and anxiety. Therefore, we must understand, manage, and redirect those teeth in order to keep our domain in order.

Nature

Puppies bite. It is a normal, natural, and necessary behavior. It develops bite inhibition. Puppies chew to soothe the inflammation of teething and to explore the world. It's how they determine the difference between sentient living beings and inanimate objects.

Adult dogs chew. It's normal. It's one way they investigate the environment and it's fun. Chewing is necessary to maintain healthy gums and clean teeth. Additionally, dogs chew out of boredom and some chew to relieve stress (as in the case of the dog with separation anxiety.)

Dogs chew. Therefore, it is our job to provide them with appropriate toys and teach them what is acceptable to chew on and what is not. See chapter *In it for Life* on how to establish appropriate chewing habits.

Boredom

Left alone for long periods of time with nothing to do, dogs will make their own fun. A dog's definition of fun may be to destroy furniture, books, clothing…whatever is available. There are a multitude of interactive toys on the market, which provide mentally stimulating ways for dogs to pass the time. Providing appropriate chew toys and teaching your dog appropriate chewing habits will preserve your home décor and keep your belongings in tact. See the chapter In it for Life for teaching dogs to be comfortable with alone time.

Anxiety

General anxiety can manifest itself as destructive behavior. Thunder, fireworks, construction noise, other dogs barking, unfamiliar people and schedule changes are just a few things that can trigger episodes of destruction. Adequate exercise, mental stimulation, and training good chewing habits will help with mild anxiety. See the chapter *Fearful Dogs* and *Wish You Were Here* for more information on destructive chewing due to anxiety.

Management

Until the dog learns what is appropriate to chew on, we are responsible for setting him up for success. This means managing the environment. Having a dog with a propensity for chewing makes one a better housekeeper. Keep shoes, clothing, anything you want to keep in one piece picked up. Make a dog proof room or utilize a crates and baby gates to manage Fido when you are unable to supervise him.

Build an obsession with chew toys. Remove the food bowl and have the dog eat only from chew toys. This helps him learn what items are suitable to chew. He will be rewarded for lying down quietly and chewing on an appropriate item, not reinforced for chewing the furniture because it's fun. Chew toys must be indestructible and inconsumable. Otherwise, the dog doesn't learn not to be destructive. Plush toys or plastic squeaky toys are destructible–the dog can consume them, therefore they are inappropriate for teaching good chewing habits.

A number of taste deterrents are available on the market. These products are designed to spray on objects dogs are tempted to chew such as furniture. They have varying results, are expensive, and must be applied daily. Taste deterrents may be used as short-term management while the dog learns what is appropriate to chew, but they are no substitute for training.

Management allows us to be proactive rather than reactive. Reactively punishing the dog for destructive chewing is ineffective. Effective punishment would mean absolute consistency by disciplining the pup every time he chews something inappropriate. This is simply not possible. See chapter *In it for Life* on how to establish appropriate chewing habits and proper protocol for those times when he slips up.

Exercise and Mental Stimulation

Exercise is important to prevent destructive behavior. Make sure your dog gets plenty by going for brisk walks, swimming, or playing chase or fetch games. Keep Fido active by taking him to a reputable doggie daycare or hire a responsible dog walker. Dog park time and play dates might be good outlets for Fido's energy.

The Scoop On Digging

Years ago, my friends Carol and Chuck had an Airedale named Brutus. Brutus had fine accommodations atop a hill in the back yard of the couple's lovely country home. True to his terrier nature, Brutus had a penchant for digging and there were several Airedale sized holes surrounding his doghouse to prove the fact. During the dog days of one Midwestern summer, Carol and Chuck noticed Brutus emerge from one of his self-constructed dens and disappear into the next adjacent one. Further observation revealed a pattern. As the day wore on, Brutus was moving from one den to the next, when the sun's rays entered each. From then on, Carol and Chuck could tell the time by which den Brutus inhabited. They had their own living, breathing, canine sundial!

Dogs dig. That's a fact. Dogs dig holes to bury bones and to recover them. Dogs dig when they're bored and dogs dig to escape. They dig sleeping hollows to keep cool in summer and warm in winter and they dig dens. Dogs hunt when they hear ultrasonic sounds of underground prey and dig up things to eat like worms and roots. But, the number one reason dogs dig is because it's fun!

Before your yard ends up looking like the gigantic, natural timepiece described above, let's explore some tips on how to keep your dog happy and your yard in tact.

Some breeds dig more than others–terriers, for instance. The word terrier comes from the Middle French *terre*, derived from the Latin *terra*, meaning earth. *Terrier* is also the modern French for *burrow*. Terriers vie for titles in earthdog competitions. In other words, terriers were built for digging and we're not going to stop them, but through management and training, we can peacefully coexist with dogs that dig.

A common go-to solution for digging is punishment. However, punishment will only teach a dog not to dig in our presence. While we are away, he will carry on with the excavations. It's tempting to use punishment after the crime has been committed–when we arrive home to find our prize roses have been indelicately transplanted. Alas, after-the-fact reprimands are useless because the dog does not understand that he's being punished for an act that took place hours or even a few minutes past. He will understand that you are angry at that moment, but he won't reason that if he didn't dig in the first place you won't get mad.

Even if we catch the dog in the act, reprimand him, and remove him from the hole, he will return immediately unless redirected. Thus, the dog's behavior does not improve and punishment is not working. He may even be training us. He may be bored and knows that digging will get our attention. (Note, this applies to other behaviors such as barking, counter surfing, even potty training.) If the behavior has not changed, then what we believe to be punishment is not what the dog believes to be punishment.

For instance, putting poop in the hole is questionable as an effective punishment. Feces are not offensive to most dogs. You may hear of punishing dogs for digging by putting an inflated toy balloon in the hole. This can be dangerous (the dog may ingest the balloon) as well as futile. The probable result is that the dog will simply dig somewhere else.

Redirect: Physically removing the dog from the dig site and scolding is an exercise in futility. Instead, catch him in the act, tell him no, then praise him immediately when he stops. Next, redirect him by calling him and running with him to the Treasure Trove–the appropriate digging area you've created for him (see below.)

Supervision and Management: Many dogs are relegated to the backyard because they've not been taught how to behave indoors. Train them how to conduct themselves both inside and outside. Manage the environment using baby gates, crates, dog runs, and effective fencing. Supervise during training until the dog learns proper manners. He'll never learn them if he's left alone and to his own devices.

Bring them inside: Dogs should never be tied out and left unsupervised. This could create an aggressive, fearful dog, not to mention the potential for physical harm. Dogs are social animals. Left alone in the backyard, they will become bored and lonely. The digging problem will not just go away without intervention and could certainly get worse. Boredom can generate other behavior problems such as barking, escaping, de-socializing, and hyperactivity. Teach your dog to be calm and polite indoors so that he'll be welcome there.

Provide a comfortable outdoor sleeping area: For the dog that digs sleeping hollows– a cool place for him to sleep in the summer and a warm one for cooler temps. Water filled cooling beds available on the market keep dogs comfortable by an evaporative cooling process. Elevated beds constructed of mesh fabric allow air to circulate underneath to keep Fido cool.

Exercise: A dog that gets adequate exercise is less likely to become bored and fill his time by digging. If a dog is a digging hobbyist, then provide alternative activities such as chew toys (inside and out.) Physical exercise and mental stimulation mean dogs are too busy and tired to dig.

Mental Stimulation: Provide your dog with plenty of interactive, food stuffed puzzle toys. These will involve the use of his brainpower to obtain the rewards instead of the use of his paws to obtain prizes from the garden.

Create Dog Zones: Use fencing to create areas in the yard where the dog is allowed and make it an interesting place to be. Tie stuffed chew toys to ground stakes or hang them from tree branches in dog zones to encourage the dog to spend time in those areas. This will mitigate boredom and the likelihood of the dog digging to escape. Fencing need not have the yard looking like a prison facility. It need not be dog proof, but simply act as demarcation of the no-dog zone. Accompany and supervise your dog during training to prevent him from making mistakes.

Treasure Trove: The question is not whether to dig, but where to dig. Allow the dog an area where he can dig to his heart's content. Bury a treasure like an appropriate, safe bone in the area where he'll be allowed to dig. Once he finds buried treasure, he will naturally continue to mine that area. It's common sense. After all, we don't go to the laundry room to look for a snack we go to the kitchen.

Make the digging area more inviting by leaving the soft dirt. Place rocks and sand in the bottom for proper water drainage if necessary.

If you don't want to dig up the yard, fill a child's wading pool with clean dirt or sand. Bury awesome treasures there for the dog to find. Once he discovers the cache, he'll make this area his preferred digging spot. Bury chew toys there every morning until it becomes the spot of favor.

Common canine problems need not create insanity. They can be solved with creativity and common sense, avoiding frustration for both human and canine.

18

Mannerly Mutts in the Real World
Beyond the Basics

Etiquette is the fine tuning of education.

–Nadine Daher, Etiquette and Image Consultant

To me, etiquette means that one should behave better than what is required–to outshine the rest of the crowd. At very least I don't want to draw attention to my propriety deficiencies. Etiquette will hopefully save me from embarrassing myself in front of the entire planet and keep my dogs and me in the good graces of authority and society.

Life would be more enjoyable for lovers of dogs if our furry friends could accompany us everywhere. Social decorum and public health regulations prevent the everyday dog from doing so, but there are plenty of dog-friendly venues to welcome well-behaved dogs.

The key to dogs being welcomed in public is manners–on both ends of the leash.

When it comes to dog parks, I've seen as many human arguments there as I have canine confrontations. Where it seems that common sense would make, um…sense, I've witnessed a few human dog park attendees who are apparently clueless. In the Dog Park Dos *section below, I've listed wearing appropriate clothing. Ladies, we can't run after our dogs in open toed wedges…and yes, I've seen this poor choice of footwear at the dog park. Really, I have!*

I once had a client request a training session because her Yorkshire terrier had a bad habit of climbing on the table to eat from her plate. Imagine taking that little guy to a restaurant! On the other end of the scale, I attended a dinner with seven service dogs present–you wouldn't have known any of them were there. In general, manners for dining with canines should fall closer to the service dog end of the scale than to the self-serve attitude of the Yorkie.

Dining with dogs means they have impeccable under-the-table manners. Hiking trails, open spaces, and dog parks are Doggie Disneyland. Dogs can't read. Therefore, we must read and obey posted rules. Trail manners mean reliable voice command and leash laws require that the dog not only wear a leash, but that a responsible human be holding it.

Beyond the Basics Means Enjoying More of Life with Dogs

This chapter addresses life in the real human world with dogs. We'd love to take our dogs everywhere–dining, hiking, festivals, parks, playgrounds, and the like. Far and away, the most important consideration for everyone's comfort, safety, and enjoyment of these activities is the dog's temperament.

Although our hearts may be in the right place, we must be sure that the dog's heart is there as well. As some dogs are not cut out for therapy dog work or agility trials, we must face the fact that some dogs simply would not enjoy a romp at the dog park or lying quietly during a meal at a busy bistro. We must set aside our ambitions and aspirations if the dog is not enjoying the activity. A fearful dog might find the hiking trail a terrifying place, should he encounter horses or unfamiliar people wearing backpacks and carrying walking sticks. Only the dog can make the decision as to what he enjoys, but if he enjoys dining out with you, a romp at the dog park or dog beach, or exploring the hiking trail, then by all means, have a go at it. But, manners first!

Café Canines: Dine with your canine

Dining at restaurants with dogs is not a right, but a privilege and one ill-mannered dog (or person) can spoil that privilege. It is ultimately a courtesy of the restaurant to allow dogs. Because state health regulations must be followed, owners have the final say as to whether or not dogs are allowed in their establishments' outside dining areas.

Pets are mainly banned from restaurants due to health and safety concerns. Therefore, only the best-behaved, well-groomed dogs should be ambassadors for the cause. Dogs must be masters of basic obedience behaviors. If your dog *don't know sit*, he will not be welcomed by restaurateurs and patrons. At the very least, dogs must know sit, down, and stay. But, to set a good example and remain in favor with the establishment, we'll have Fido rocking his behavior in public.

Beyond Fido's Manners: Minding our End of the Leash

- The dog should be clean and well groomed

- The dog should wear current vaccination tags

- Give the dog a potty break beforehand (a courteous distance from the dining area)

- Exercise the dog beforehand

- Always keep the dog on leash (not a retractable)

- Tether the dog to a fixed object like a railing. If a fixed object is not available, tether him to your chair, not the table.

- Choose a table on the perimeter, preferably with a quick exit plan

- Choose a table away from other dogs

- Keep the dog out of the wait staff's path

- Do not take the dog inside the restaurant, even to get to the patio

- Bring your own water bowl

- Do not allow the dog to drink or eat from restaurant dishes (health code prohibits pets from using glasses and dishes)

- Do not feed the dog from the table

- Do not allow the dog on the table or chairs

- Be prepared to pay the check and leave if the dog creates a disturbance or becomes stressed

- Leave a nice tip for your server

Fido's Manners

- No barking

- No whining

- No jumping

- No socializing unless invited

- No resource guarding (food, mats, or people)

Beyond the Basics for Dining with Fido

As with teaching any behavior, we won't be doing on-the-job training. We'll do it at home with little or no distraction, and then gradually work up to the real life situation. We must first build a firm foundation and then help the dog to generalize the behaviors. The first visit to a restaurant will be short, having a only a cup of coffee. We'll practice and generalize beforehand by going to other places where dogs are allowed, such as pet supply and home improvement stores.

Beyond Attentive Dog

For instructions on teaching dogs to pay attention, see the puppy section on attentive dog in the chapter, *In It for Life*. Also, see *The How-To of Training* for lessons in "Watch."

Once your dog is a master of these skills at home, take him to a quiet park and sit with him on leash. Let him explore and ignore him, waiting until he looks at you. Don't be concerned about how long it takes or how brief the look is. When your dog looks at you, no matter how briefly, mark the behavior and reward him. Now, let him go back to exploring and wait for him to look at you again. Every time he looks at you, mark, praise, and treat. He'll start checking in more frequently. When he does, raise the bar by gradually lengthening the time the dog is looking at you before he receives his reward.

Repeat the attentive dog exercise under progressively higher levels of distraction. Go to the park at a busier time. Sit outside of a restaurant where you'll see passersby. Here, he can get used to the sounds, smells, and sights of restaurant activity—the clatter of dishes, the aroma of food being prepared, and the bustling wait staff. Make sure to give the dog enough space to be successful and not to disturb the diners.

Dogs dining out must be able to handle the distraction of busy eateries and the surrounding environment. If your dog is reactive to bicycles, skateboards, other dogs, children, and the like, he might not be a dog that can dine with you. Reactive means barking, lunging, whining at the sight of what triggers him. If the reactivity is mild, then possibly the behavior can be eliminated by working with a reputable trainer.

Beyond Loose Leash Walking:

See the chapter on *The How-To of Training* for teaching pass bys, to meet and greet people, and proper dog-to-dog on-leash greetings. Once your dog is a pro at these skills, practice them by going to a pet supply or home improvement store where dogs are welcome. Practice leash manners by walking past outdoor dining establishments that you intend to visit with your dog. Stop within a courteous distance of diners and have your dog do an on-leash down stay. Pass by some dogs and people and stop to meet and greet others. This teaches your dog that he doesn't meet *everyone* on the path.

Beyond Stay:
In order to dine out with Fido, he must have the ability to do a prolonged down stay with distraction. See the instructions in *The How-To of Training* for sit stay and do it in a down position. Next, follow the instructions for stay with duration and distraction doing it in the down position.

Once the dog has learned a down stay at home, gradually increase the level of distraction by having him do it in the presence of other dogs and people. While learning to stay under distraction, make the down stays short and then gradually increase the duration.

I've taught my dogs to do a prolonged down stay on movie night and I've done it with popcorn. Sitting with my bowl of buttery goodness, I ask my dogs for a down stay and every few seconds, I toss them a piece of popcorn. I then, gradually increased the time between tosses. If one dog breaks his stay, I toss a piece of popcorn to the dogs that were holding theirs. The dog that broke his stay realized his breech of etiquette and resumed his down position.

Dogs must be able to do a down stay in a tight space under a restaurant table. Generalize to these specific situations. Practice at home with your dog in a down stay under your table before taking him out to lunch in public.

Settle and Chew
To help Fido know his place at a restaurant, bring his place along. Teach him to rest on a mat and "go to place" on cue. A mat will make him more comfortable and know that this is the spot for remaining calm. Additionally bring along a chew toy to help Fido occupy his time. Be sure the mat and toy are clean. We'd hate to spoil other diners' appetites with the nasty femur bone that Fido dug up from the back yard.

Go To Place
Begin at home with no distraction using the mat you will be taking along to the restaurant. Stand beside the mat and toss a treat on it. As the dog steps onto the mat to retrieve the treat, say, "Place." Repeat a few times. Now, after the dog has stepped onto the mat, ask him for a "down." Repeat several times until the dog is readily going to the mat and lying down. Next, ask the dog for a "stay."

Practice this at your table at home. Start with short down stays on the mat and progress gradually to longer stays while you have your meal. In preparation for the real life experience at the restaurant, have Fido practice down stays by having someone serve you food.

Beyond Begging

Teach dogs to drop an object on cue or to avoid an object when asked. See the instructions in *The How-To of Training* for "drop it" and "leave it." Also, see "food on the floor" in the same section. Practice these exercises while you are sitting at your table at home. Go beyond begging by having the dog chew on a chew toy while resting on his mat. Do not encourage begging by feeding the dog from the table.

Now you're ready to practice dining with canines by going for a quick cup of coffee. Go when it's not busy and make it brief. The point is to set the dog up for success. Success means that Fido will be welcomed back.

Trail Manners On and Off Leash

Hiking with well-mannered dogs is a pleasure, but unmannered dogs can be a menace to other hikers, wildlife, and the landscape. Trail etiquette is not simply about polite behavior. Good manners reduce conflict between dogs, people, and wildlife. Regulations vary, so know them before hitting the trail with your dog.

Select trails, such as some near Boulder, Colorado have instituted the Voice and Sight Dog Tag Program. This program allows registered dogs to be off leash in designated areas as long as they wear the program's tag, are within sight, under voice command, and obey the trail rules. These guidelines are a good idea for all trails, whether or not there is a formal program like this in place.

Always carry a leash, even with the best-trained dogs. You may find yourself in an area where leashes are required or you may want it as a common courtesy. Keep your dog on leash and on the path in areas where snakes are prevalent. Snakes are less likely to be found on the trail than in the bush.

Dogs on the trail need to have impeccable leash walking skills for times when they must be leashed. Allowing a dog to pull toward other dogs presents an aggressive posture, which can be threatening to another dog. This can get us into trouble because we don't know if the other dog is friendly nor do others know if our dog is.

Be sure your dog is fit enough for hiking. If there is a body of water at your destination, make sure your dog can swim and enjoys it.

Tips for Success on the Trail
- Always carry water/first-aid
- Always bring a leash
- Obey posted signs
- Do not harass wildlife
- No digging
- Clean up after your dog

• Make sure the dog is wearing current ID tags and is microchipped

• Make sure your dog can obey basic commands

• Keep your dog a safe distance from walkers/runners/bikers/horseback riders. Take your dog off the trail to let them go by.

• Acclimate the dog to horses, bicycles,

• Put your dog on leash when approaching another dog on leash

• Know the dangers of where you're hiking. Bear country? Poisonous snakes? Flea and tick season?

Trail Gear

• Collar and ID tags

• Leash

• Backpack (for longer hikes and big dogs)

• Booties or Musher's Secret (protects paws from snow, sand, etc.)

• First-aid kit

• Sunscreen (consult your veterinarian for pet safe sunscreen usage)

• Water and water bowl

• Food and treats

• Cleanup bags

The most important trail gear for your dog is that of good manners.

Acclimate to the sights, sounds, and smells, of the trail

The sights, sounds, and smells of the trail are new and exciting–a canine sensory overload. Make sure that Fido has horse sense. If he's never seen a horse before, you don't want his first encounter to be on a narrow, steep trail. The rules of the trail dictate that hikers yield to horses by moving off the path while they pass.

Make sure that the sight of people carrying backpacks and using walking sticks or ski poles doesn't alarm your dog. When it comes to wildlife scat and horse manure, or other trail distractions, he should be able to "leave it" on cue.

Expose the dog to the things that might be found on the trail beforehand by taking him to see horses grazing in a pasture. Have him at a distance where he will not disturb the animals. Let him sniff areas where the horses have been.

Hang out at a trailhead where there is plenty of space for the dog to see people with backpacks, dogs wearing backpacks, horses, and pack animals such as llamas. Know the trail usage, so you know whether to expect heavy foot traffic, horses, bicycles, motor vehicles, etc. Know what wildlife dangers to anticipate such as bears, mountain lions, and rattlesnakes.

Trail Etiquette Training

For trail etiquette training, we'll be using a long line. A long line is a leash that is 20ft. long or longer. It is NOT a retractable leash.

Beyond Attentive Dog

See the puppy section on attentive dog in the chapter, *In It for Life* for instructions on how to teach your dog to pay attention. See *The How-To of Training* for lessons in "Watch."

Beyond Meet and Greets

See the chapter on *The How-To of Training* for teaching pass bys, how to meet and greet people, and proper dog-to-dog on-leash greetings. Once your dog is a pro at these skills, practice them by going to a pet supply store where dogs are welcome or walk near the dog park entrance–anywhere you will see dogs and people walking. Pass by some dogs and people and stop to meet and greet others. This teaches your dog that we don't meet *everyone* on the trail.

Start with a long line and begin to practice trail manners. Go to a park where you will see urban wildlife. Start training in an open space area, preferably where trails are wide and visibility is good. That way, other trail users will not surprise you.

Rocking the Recall

Hiking dogs need a rock solid recall. This means you should be able to call them away from other dogs and people. You should be able to call your dog even if he's about to give chase. See the instructions in *The How-To of Training* for emergency recall.

Check-Ins at a Distance

Always keep the dog in sight when on the trail, and *pay attention*. Both of you need to know where the other is at all times.

Teach your dog to do check-ins. With the dog on a long line, allow him to walk a few paces ahead of you sniffing and exploring. Call his name. When he looks at you, praise him, and then let him continue on his way. Ask for check-ins at approximately the same distance, so that the dog begins to check in voluntarily at that point. Occasionally call the dog back to you, treat him, and then release him to go back to the trail ahead.

Fido can wander farther afield on open trails, but on narrow, curving, and wooded paths, keep him closer. Be sure that he has a rock-solid recall, just in case.

Down Stay at a Distance

Hiking dogs should be able to do a down stay in order to allow other hikers or cyclists to pass. The dog should also have the ability to do a down stay when cued from a distance. In the event a hiker, horseback rider, or cyclist suddenly appears when your dog is ahead of you, you can cue him to down, allowing people to pass without concern.

See the instructions in *The How-To of Training* for down stay. At home, gradually increase the distance you are able to cue the down stay. Start by standing next to the dog, and then take one or two steps away. Cue the dog to down. Gradually increase the distance you are able to cue your dog to down. Have a strong down stay before trying it on the trail. Repeat the training on the trail using a long line, start with cuing the dog to down beside you and then gradually increase the distance and level of distraction.

From Drop and Stop to Stop and Drop

After the dog knows to "drop and stop," (stop when you drop the leash) we can teach him to do it on the trail when off leash. See the instructions in *The How-To of Training* for drop and stop. Start with a long line and practice on the trail, preferably one with a wide path and good visibility so as not to be surprised by approaching cyclists and hikers.

With the dog dragging a long line, practice the drop and stop by walking with the dog in the heel position. Stop and say, "wait." Treat the dog for stopping. If he doesn't stop, step on the leash and say, "wait" as the leash stops him. Now, ask the dog for a down.

Repeat the exercise, letting the dog walk just a bit ahead of you (only a couple of paces.) Tell him to stop, and then ask for a down. Be prepared to step on the leash if necessary.

Allow the dog to turn to look at you before doing a down. Gradually increase the distance the dog is ahead of you.

Anti-recall (dog stops when he's moving toward you)

It's handy for hiking dogs to be able to stop when moving toward you. This maneuver prevents the dog from running into the path of oncoming traffic.

You'll need an assistant and a long line for training the anti-recall. Station yourselves several yards apart with the dog between you on the long line. Do something to attract the dog's attention, such as bouncing a ball or acting goofy. Do not call the dog, as we do not want to compromise his recall nor do we want the dog running full speed toward you. When the dog starts to move toward you, face him, step toward him, hold up your hand palm facing toward him, and say, "Stop!" "Stop" is also the cue for your assistant to step on the long line, bringing the dog to a halt (this is why we don't want the dog running full speed, so as not to strangle him.)

Repeat the exercise several times until the dog is stopping himself and there is no need to step on the long line. Once he is able to stop himself, begin asking him for a down.

Dog Park Etiquette:
Dog Fights, Strollers, and High Heels–Oh My!

Dog parks and beaches can be doggie Disneyland or doggie disasters. Which experience you have, depends on the facility and the patrons (both canine and human.) Every park or beach is different and every dog and person is different. Every moment is different, so be prepared to leave anytime you see that your dog is not having fun. Be prepared to leave if you feel the energy changing for the worse. Sometimes, you just know with the arrival of a certain dog (or person) that things are getting tense.

A dog's temperament is the most important consideration as to whether he's cut out for the dog park. Not every dog is–just because we have dogs parks, doesn't mean we must take our dogs. Some dogs are dog-park ready, some are not a good fit at all, and some just need a little help with their etiquette.

It's important to know canine body language. This allows you to determine if your dog is having fun, whether he's being bullied or being a bully. Overly stimulated dogs and rough play are the most common causes of problems at the dog park.

Watch your dog at all times to see the precursory behaviors that can lead to a fight and intervene before the fight starts.

Let your dog enjoy the park in his own way. If he prefers to sniff bushes and butts, play fetch, wrestle, or race–leave it up to him.

Dogs need rock solid recalls so we can call them out of a potentially bad situation before it happens. Dogs need a rock solid fetch if they are a toy stealer. Teach them fetch so they will return the toy to you. Then, you can return it to the rightful owner. A toy stealer with a solid fetch can play appropriately with you and not engage in thievery.

Is your dog a dog park dog?

Does your dog have the right temperament for the dog park? To answer that question, we'll ask the following questions. If the answer is yes, then your dog is a good candidate for the dog park.

- Is he social and does he enjoy the company of other dogs?

- Does he like to play?

- Does he avoid conflict and is non-reactive?

- If a dog mounts him, does he try to walk away and avoid or give a quick air snap?

- Can he read calming and cut-off signals and does he respect them?

- Does he have good training skills especially good recall, sit, attention/focus and the leave it commands?

- If over stimulated, can he calm down?

- Is your dog current on vaccinations and licensing? Is he healthy?

If the answer is yes to the following questions, your dog will probably not enjoy the dog park:

- If a dog mounts him, does he aggress and pin the dog?

- Does he exhibit bully play (body slamming, hard biting, stalking, or playing too rough?)

- Does he have resource guarding issues?

- Does he have space issues?

- When aroused, does he bark excessively, herd, or tip into bully play?

- Is your dog fearful of other dogs or people?

- Is your dog respectful of people? Does he jump and mouth? Is he demanding and obnoxious?

Following are some tips for experiencing pleasant and fun dog park visits:

Dog Park Do's
- Obey posted rules
- Make sure the dog has a clean bill of health and is current on vaccines
- Observe other dogs for potential health or behavioral problems
- Remove halters, choke chains and prong collars
- Reinforce good behavior and make sure your dog understands and listens to basic commands
- Be respectful of other humans in the park
- Check the entrance before entering to make sure dogs aren't congregating there.
- Supervise your dog at all times and be ready to interrupt play that gets rough, tense, or aggressive
- Give your dog an obedience break or leave the park if your dog is not exhibiting appropriate play
- Pay close attention to your dog's play style and interrupt rough play before it gets out of hand
- Learn dog body language so you understand tipping points that lead to aggression
- Be proactive not reactive
- Provide your dog frequent obedience breaks/reward for checking in
- Move around the park so that your dog needs to keep an eye on you
- Remove your dog if he appears afraid
- Remove your dog if he is bullying others
- Respect your dog's wish to leave
- Leave special toys at home to avoid resource guarding
- Bring treats for training, but be careful of resource guarding
- Clean up after the dog
- Interrupt rough play with a recall

Dog Park Don'ts

- Bring puppies under 4 months old

- Take sensitive dogs to crowded, enclosed parks

- Take dogs that are afraid of dogs or people

- Allow the dog to jump on people

- Allow dogs to form loose packs or gang up on others

- Allow the dog to bully

- Allow the dog to mount other dogs

- Allow the dog to hog the whole field

- Allow the dog to guard toys or treats from other dogs

- Bring intact males or females in estrus

- Bring small children

- Allow your dog to enter the park if there is a "gang" right next to the entrance

- Believe that dogs will "work it out" without intervention

- Congregate at a picnic table or other area and chat with dog owners, ignoring your dog

- Let your frightened dog remain in the park and simply hope things get better

- Listen to other park attendees' advice who may not understand your dog's needs

- Make excuses or blame others for your dog's bad behavior

- Assume a dog is aggressive when it is only trying to communicate his discomfort

- Give treats to other dogs without the owner's permission

What to do when things go wrong?

See *How to Break Up a Dog Fight* in the chapter *Aggressive Dogs* and know these key points:

- Remain calm

- Toss something over them like a coat to distract them

- Throw water on them

- If you must make physical contact, take hold of tails or hind legs (see info in the chapter *Aggressive Dogs* as this maneuver could injure dogs)

- Don't grab the collar as redirected aggression or accidental bites can occur and may intensify the situation

- Remove dogs that were in the fight*

*Stress hormones released can trigger another fight. Even the dog that was the victim can initiate aggression later due to stress. Keep the dogs out of the park for several days.

Etiquette

The bottom line of etiquette is to be aware of others' space and feelings, be they human or canine. Be alert to those using trails, parks, walkways, and eateries. Respect their right to enjoy these places without nuisance behaviors from unmannered dogs.

If your dog happens to make a mistake, even if it seems harmless, address it with an apology and take steps to prevent it from happening again in the future. Doing so sets an example of responsible ownership and ensures the "pets welcome" sign will stay posted. Furthermore, your good reputation and that of your dog will remain in tact.

And, always, always, always scoop the poop! Remember the poop bag rule: If you don't bring a bag, your dog will poop. If you bring one bag, your dog will poop twice. Bring plenty of bags so that you have extras to offer others if necessary.

Enjoy more of life in the real world with your well-mannered dog.

The End

At its best, the sensation of writing is that of any unmerited grace. It is handed to you, but only if you look for it. - **Annie Dillard**

Afterword

It is cliché to say that writing and illustrating this book was a labor of love, but that is the truth. I hope it has been an enjoyable and educational read. It's true what they say about the total emersion of inspiration. It was not difficult to rise early to write in the predawn hours. Admittedly, I had the assistance of Mr. Coffee to clear any first light cobwebs and Mr. MoJo to remind me of his breakfast time. But, mostly I had the muses guiding my fingers on the keyboard and my pen on the drawing pad. They are the true authors and artists.

I have learned so much by writing this book. I feel that the experience has made me a better trainer and put me on the path to being the trainer that I've always hoped I could be. Most importantly, I hope I have helped to enrich the lives of more than a few dogs and their people. Thank you for reading my labor of love.

About the Author

Pat Blocker, CPDT-KA, owner of Peaceful Paws Dog Training is a Certified Professional Dog Trainer with over 18 years experience. She has a passion for helping to enhance people's relationships with their dogs through education and training.

Pat was a full-time accredited trainer for 5 years before starting her private dog training business. Peaceful Paws specializes in solving canine behavior issues, offering group classes and in-home private training.

Pat Blocker became a Certified Professional Dog Trainer in 2003. She adheres to a code of ethics set forth by the Certification Council of Professional Dog Trainers and upholds her education and knowledge of current training methods.

Pat is a professional member of the Association of Professional Dog Trainers and an approved evaluator for the AKC's Canine Good Citizen program. She offers public speaking services and is a contributing feature writer for local dog magazines, business, and community newsletters.

Pat lives in Aurora, Colorado with two canine behavior experts…her dogs Mr. MoJo and Penny Lane.

Contact Pat:
Peaceful Paws Dog Training
www.peacefulpaws.net
pat@peacefulpaws.net

Resources and Recommended Reading

Books

Abrantes, Roger. *Dog Language: An Encyclopedia of Canine Behaviour* (Wakan Tanka Publishers 1997)

Abrantes, Roger. *The Evolution of Canine Social Behavior, 2nd edition* (Wakan Tanka Publishers 1997, 2005)

Aloff, Brenda. *Aggression Dogs: Practical Management, Prevention & Behaviour Modification* (Fundcraft, Inc. 2002)

Aloff, Brenda. *Canine Body Language: A Photographic Guide: Interpreting the Native Language of the Domestic Dog* (Dogwise Publishing 2005)

Booth, Sheila. *Purely Positive Training: Companion to Competition* (Podium Publications 1998)

Brown, Sue. *Juvenile Delinquent Dogs: The Complete Guide To Saving Your Sanity And Successfully Living With Your Adolescent Dog* (The Light Of Dog, LLC 2012)

Dodman, Dr. Nicholas H. *The Well-Adjusted Dog* (Houghton Mifflin Company 2008)

Donaldson, Jean. *Fight!* (Kinship Communications 2004)

Donaldson, Jean. *Mine!* (Kinship Communications 2002)

Donaldson, Jean. *Oh Behave! Dogs from Pavlov to Premack to Pinker* (Dogwise Publishing 2008)

Donaldson, Jean. *Dogs are from Neptune* (Lasar Multimedia Productions, Inc. 1998)

Dunbar, Dr. Ian. *Before You Get Your Puppy* (James & Kenneth Publishers 2001)

Dunbar, Dr. Ian. *After You Get Your Puppy* (James & Kenneth Publishers 2001)

Grandin, Temple & Catherine Johnson. *Animals Make Us Human: Creating the Best Life for Animals* (Houghton Mifflin Harcourt 2009)

Horowitz, Alexandra. *Inside of a Dog: What Dogs See, Smell, and Know.* (Scribner 2009)

King, Trish. *Parenting Your Dog* (T.F.H. Publications, Inc. 2004)

London, Karen B. & Patricia B. McConnell. *Feeling Outnumbered? How to Manage and Enjoy Your Multi-Dog Household* (Dog's Best Friend, Ltd. 2001)

McConnell, Patricia B. *The Other End Of The Leash: Why We Do What We Do Around Dogs* (The Ballantine Publishing Group 2002)

McConnell, Patricia B. *For The Love Of A Dog: Understanding Emotion in You and Your Best Friend* (The Ballantine Publishing Group 2005, 2006)

Maran Illustrated. *Maran Illustrated Dog Training* (maranGraphics 2004-2005)

Miller, Pat. *The Power of Positive Dog Training* (Howell Book House 2001)

O'Heare, James. *The Canine Aggression Workbook, 3rd edition* (DogPsych 2004)

O'Neil, Jacqueline. *Kids +Dogs = Fun: Great Activities Your Kids and Dogs Can Do Together* (Howell Book House 1996)

Pryor, Karen. *Don't Shoot The Dog: The New Art of Teaching and Training* (Bantam Books 1984)

Rogerson, John. *The Dog Vinci Code: Unlock the Secrets to Training Your Dog* (John Blake Publishing Ltd/Metro Publishing 2010)

Rugaas, Turid. *On Talking Terms With Dogs: Calming Signals* (Hanalei Training Center, Inc. 1997)

Sdao, Kathy. *Plenty in Life is Free: Reflections on Dogs, Training and Finding Grace* (Dogwise Publishing 2009)

Siegal, Mordecai. *Choosing the Perfect Dog for You and Your Family* (Contemporary Books, Inc. 1996)

Sternberg, Sue. *Successful Dog Adoption* (Howell Book House 2003)

Stilwell, Victoria. *It's Me or the Dog: How to Have the Perfect Pet* (HarperColling Publishers 2005, 2007)

Wilde, Nicole. *Help for your Fearful Dog* (Phantom Publishing 2006)

Wilde, Nicole. *Getting a Grip on Aggression Cases* (Phantom Publishing 2008)

Wilde, Nicole. *Don't Leave Me! Step-by-Step Help for Your Dog's Separation Anxiety* (Phantom Publishing 20010)

UC Davis Book of Dogs Edited by Mordecai Seigal (HarperCollins Books 1995)

Blogs and Websites:

ASPCA: http://www.aspca.org/

Association of Professional Dog Trainers: http://apdt.com/

American Veterinary Medical Association:
https://www.avma.org/Pages/home.aspx

Doggone Safe: http://www.doggonesafe.com/

Dogstar Daily: http://www.dogstardaily.com/

Dumb Friends League: http://www.ddfl.org/

Family Paws: http://familypaws.com/

Living With Kids and Dogs: http://www.livingwithkidsanddogs.com/

The Other End of the Leash, Patricia McConnell, Ph.D. (Blog):
http://www.patriciamcconnell.com/theotherendoftheleash/

The Whole Dog Journal: http://www.whole-dog-journal.com/

Dr. Sophia Yin http://drsophiayin.com

Made in the USA
San Bernardino, CA
31 January 2015